LIBRARY
Tel: 01244 375444   Ext: 3301

This book is to be returned on or before the
st date stamped below. Overdue charges
be incurred by the late return of items

Chester

A College of the

Quality and Access in
Higher Education

Quality and Access in Higher Education

Comparing Britain and the
United States

Edited by
Robert O. Berdahl,
Graeme C. Moodie,
and Irving J. Spitzberg, Jr

The Society for Research into Higher Education
& Open University Press

Published by SRHE and
Open University Press
Celtic Court
22 Ballmoor
Buckingham
MK18 1XW

and
1900 Frost Road, Suite 101
Bristol, PA 19007, USA

First Published 1991

British Library Cataloguing in Publication Data

Quality and access in higher education: comparing Britain
    and the United States.
    1. Great Britain. Higher education   2. United States.
    Higher education
    I. Berdahl, Robert O.   II. Moodie, Graeme C. (Graeme Cochrane) *1924–*
    III. Spitzberg, Irving, J.
    378.41

ISBN 0-335-09647-6

Library of Congress Cataloging-in-Publication Data

Quality and access in higher education: comparing Britain and the United
    States/edited by Robert O. Berdahl, Graeme C. Moodie, and Irving J. Spitzberg, Jr.
        p.   cm.
    'Outcome of the Second Anglo-American Seminar on Quality in Higher
    Education organized on behalf of the British Society for Research into Higher
    Education and the Council of Liberal Learning of the Association of American
    Colleges . . . held at Princeton, NJ, in September 1987'—Pref. Includes index.
    ISBN 0-335-09647-6 (hb)
        1. Education, Higher—Great Britain.   2. Education, Higher—United
    States.   3. Educational equalization—Great Britain.   4. Educational
    equalization—United States.   I. Berdahl, Robert Oliver.
    II. Moodie, Graeme C.   III. Spitzberg, Irving J.   IV. Anglo-American Seminar
    on Quality in Higher Education (2nd: 1987: Princeton, N.J.) V. Society for Research
    into Higher Education.
    VI. Association of American Colleges. Council for Liberal Learning.
    LA637.Q35   1991
    378.41—dc20
                                                                    90-14236
                                                                    CIP

Typeset by Rowland Phototypesetting Ltd, Bury St Edmunds, Suffolk
Printed in Great Britain by St Edmundsbury Press Ltd, Bury St Edmunds, Suffolk

Contents

Notes on Editors

Robert O. Berdahl is currently Professor of Higher Education and Director of the National Center for Postsecondary Governance and Finance at the University of Maryland, USA. He was joint author of the influential Duff-Berdahl Report on Canadian Universities. He has written on the British University Grants Committee as well as on coordinating systems of higher education in the American States. He has taught political science at various American universities, and served for a time as London administrator of the Commonwealth Fund (now Harkness) Fellowships programme.

Graeme C. Moodie was the first (and is now Emeritus) Professor of Politics at the University of York. He had previously taught and studied at the Universities of St. Andrews, Oxford, and Glasgow in the UK and Princeton University in the USA. He has written on British politics as well as, more recently, on higher education. He is a former chairman of the Political Studies Association of the UK and the Society for Research into Higher Education.

Irving J. Spitzberg, Jr is co-founder and President of The Knowledge Company, Maryland (in effect, Washington, DC). He has worked, previously, as a senior administrator with the Association of American Colleges and the Association of American University Professors. He has studied at the University of Oxford, UK, as well as in the USA.

Notes on Contributors

Tony Becher is Professor of Education at the University of Sussex, UK.

Robert E. Cuthbert is Head of Corporate Planning, Bristol Polytechnic, UK.

Michael J. Dooris is Senior Planning Analyst, Pennsylvania State University, USA.

Rowland B. Eustace was for many years Director of the Society for Research into Higher Education (UK) after a career in research and university administration in Africa and the UK.

Oliver Fulton is Director of the Institute for Research and Development in Post-Compulsory Education, University of Lancaster, UK.

W. Lee Hansen is Professor of Economics, University of Wisconsin-Madison, USA.

Richard M. Millard is Past President of the Council on Postsecondary Accreditation, USA.

Kenneth P. Mortimer is President of West Washington University, USA.

Sheldon Rothblatt is Professor of History, University of California, Berkeley, USA.

Michael L. Shattock, OBE, is Registrar of the University of Warwick, UK.

Jacob O. Stampen is Associate Professor of Educational Administration, University of Wisconsin-Madison, USA.

Martin Trow is Professor of Public Policy and former Director of the Center for Studies in Higher Education, University of California, Berkeley, USA.

Preface and Acknowledgements

This book is the outcome of the second Anglo-American Seminar on Quality in Higher Education organized on behalf of the British Society for Research into Higher Education and the Council for Liberal Learning of the Association of American Colleges. It was held at Princeton, New Jersey, in September 1987. The contributions are not, however, mere reprints of papers hurriedly prepared for the usual kind of academic conference. There were papers prepared before the Seminar – as background material for three days of intensive discussion among some fifty invited participants drawn from academics, researchers and decision-makers in Britain and the USA. But the chapters that follow are either very extensive revisions of some of those papers or, for the most part, specially written for this book in the light of the Seminar discussions. Only Chapter 2 has appeared in print previously; we are grateful to the Carfax Publishing Company for permission to include it here.

The Seminar was made possible only through the generosity of the Carnegie Foundation for the Advancement of Teaching, which covered all costs in the USA, and the British Council, which assisted in paying the fares of the British participants. To both these bodies we would here like to record our deep gratitude. We also wish to thank Dr Ernest Boyer, President of the Carnegie Foundation, and his colleague Dr Verne Stadtman for their personal involvement and support at every stage. On the organizational side we also wish particularly to thank Rowland Eustace and the other staff members of the SRHE in Guildford.

R.O.B., G.C.M. and I.J.S.

Note on British National Terminology

Formally (some would say, pedantically) speaking 'Britain' (more accurately 'Great Britain') refers only to England, Scotland and Wales, whereas 'the United Kingdom' refers to Great Britain *and* Northern Ireland. In everyday speech, however, few people distinguish between 'Britain' and 'the United Kingdom' – 'British' is the normal adjectival form for both – while many, especially in England and foreign countries (including the USA), often use 'England' to refer to Great Britain or the United Kingdom as well as in its proper and more restrictive sense.

In this book we have tried to avoid both pedantry and inaccuracy. This means that we talk mainly of 'Britain' – though frequently what is said applies also to Northern Ireland (with its two universities) and some of what is said does not fully apply even to all of Britain (e.g., we use the term 'polytechnic' to embrace both the English polytechnics and the not dissimilar Scottish Central Institutions and the one Welsh polytechnic. We also largely ignore the somewhat lower access rates in England compared with the rest of the United Kingdom). In most contexts these usages do not mislead – elsewhere we have tried to indicate the existence of exceptions and significant differences.

A potential problem arises from the fact that the British statistics sometimes refer to slightly different entities. The reason for this is that in some important areas there exist no fully reliable and comparable figures for the whole United Kingdom, for there is no single governmental authority with responsibility for education throughout the whole country (or, put differently, in all the countries within the United Kingdom). But England and Wales, with substantially the same kind of higher education, are together so much the largest unit, and all parts of the United Kingdom are subject to such similar pressures, that the slight incomparabilities do not significantly affect the analyses and generalizations made in this book.

Abbreviations

ABRC   Advisory Board for the Research Councils
CNAA   Council for National Academic Awards
CVCP   Committee of Vice-Chancellors and Principals
DES   Department of Education and Science
FTE   Full-time Equivalents (of student numbers)
GCE   General Certificate of Education
GCSE   General Certificate of Secondary Education
HMSO   Her Majesty's Stationery Office
PCFC   Polytechnics and Colleges Funding Council
UFC   Universities Funding Council
UGC   University Grants Committee

1

Setting the Scene

Graeme C. Moodie

Comparisons between American and British higher education are both perilous and potentially productive. In each country a certain amount of information about the other country is readily available, and the two countries share many ideals, traditions and concepts. For these very reasons we (the citizens of both countries) tend too easily to assume either that we know all that matters about each other or that the only things of value in the other are the ones we have in common. The result is that we do not always explore the differences with sufficient sympathy nor benefit sufficiently from the other's experience. Only if we do so, however, will we realize the potential value of serious comparison. The peril lies in the extent to which we live in very different societies and really are (as Bernard Shaw once put it) 'divided by a common language'; in the context of higher education, for example, even such everyday terms as 'university', 'college' and 'quality' have somewhat different connotations and associations on the two sides of the Atlantic. Without care, therefore, the comparisons mislead.

Both the risks and the potential were in the minds of those who organized the Anglo-American seminars on higher education held at Oxford in 1986, at Princeton in 1987 and at York in 1989. We believe that the seminars avoided the risks and illustrated the benefits of joint dialogue. Some of the papers prepared for the Oxford one have already been published (*Studies in Higher Education*, 13 (1), 1988), and the York one will also lead to publication. The chapters that follow in this book are based upon papers and discussions that formed part of the Princeton seminar. This introductory chapter, however, is designed primarily to set the scene for readers who know something, but not a lot, about one or other, and possibly both, of the two higher educational systems, and especially for those who (like so many of the participants before the seminars were held) know a little less than they need to if they are fully to understand the more specialized papers that follow.

The book focuses almost entirely on the institutions of higher education and on what happens to and within them. Some of the people who are working for degrees or other comparable qualifications are therefore excluded. Excluded are, for example, the minority of adult or continuing education students in the USA who are studying for a degree and the relatively small numbers of British students following degree courses in those technical and professional colleges that are mainly involved with sub-degree courses and qualifications. But it is worth noting in passing that some of the work and institutions which, in Britain, come under the broad label of 'non-advanced further education' would, in the United States, be included in the 'higher education' category, mostly under the subheadings of 'specialized institutions' and 'two-year colleges'. Much of the ground covered in a US freshman year of college, moreover, in Britain is included in the senior years of the secondary curriculum. Not even 'higher education', therefore, has precisely the same connotations in the two countries, any more than have the labels 'university' and 'college'.

In the USA there are two main systems by which institutions of higher education are customarily categorized. The older and simpler is the distinction between four-year and two-year institutions: the former award degrees and the latter, junior and community colleges, offer instruction for no more than the first two years of the bachelor's degree. The newer, Carnegie, classification lists specialized institutions (mainly offering a single field of study), two-year institutions, liberal arts colleges (four-year institutions teaching only to bacca-laureate level), comprehensive universities and colleges (which teach up to and including the master's degree), doctorate-granting universities, and research universities (which also grant doctorates, but which successfully place great emphasis on research as well). The last three of these categories are further subdivided into first and second rank.

Both classifications are fairly straightforward and comprehensible – but the terms are not translatable directly into British English. To take an obvious example: the American word 'university', meaning an institution that grants both first and higher degrees, would embrace not only the universities in Britain, but also the polytechnics and at least some of the colleges of higher education. To translate the last two into American as 'universities' would be, however, to overlook a major difference, namely that the British polytechnics and colleges do not award their own degrees. Instead, they design and teach their own courses and if, but only if, those courses are approved (or, in the case of the larger institutions, if the processes by which they are established and monitored are approved) by the central government-appointed Council for National Academic Awards (CNAA), then the students work for and on graduation will receive a CNAA degree. (Higher degrees obtained at these institutions are also awarded by the CNAA.) Many of the present Welsh and English (and here I mean specifically 'English' and not 'British') universities, it may be noted, began life as 'university colleges' that prepared their students for degrees that were not only awarded by an external body, as with today's polytechnics and colleges, but were also examined externally on the basis of an external syllabus. The University of London was for long the main external examining body, for outside institutions in England and Wales and the former Empire as for its own constituent colleges and institutes, just as Oxford and Cambridge Universities are for their constituent colleges.

Cutting across these American classifications is the further distinction between public and private institutions. The latter are autonomous, self-
governing, and heavily dependent for their funds on fees, research grants, and
gifts. The former are co-ordinated and ultimately regulated by state governments, funded in part from taxation, and thus are much less dependent on
(usually lower) fees, grants, and gifts. In every one of the Carnegie categories
both public and private institutions exist and thrive. Britain, too, has its private
and public institutions – but the distinction carries a different significance. For
one thing, the distinction tends to match rather than cut across the more usual
classification: the polytechnics and colleges constitute what (since the late
1960s) is commonly known as the 'public sector' of higher education and the
universities the 'private' one. Both parts of this 'binary system', however, draw
most of their resources from government, if by slightly different routes; both are
substantially self-governing in academic matters, subject to the validatory role
of the CNAA in the public sector; and both have little choice but to conform to
central government policy for higher education with respect to such things as
total expenditure, student numbers, and the balance of effort devoted to broad
areas of study (science, technology, medicine, architecture, arts, social sciences,
and so on). Legally, however, the universities owe their existence and authority
to, in the main, individual Royal Charters whereas the polytechnics and most of
the colleges owe theirs to a combination of legislation and government decree.
To slightly varying extents institutions in both sectors have significant, if not
unlimited, rights of ownership in their physical properties and private endowments. Only one British university, however, is fully private, as Americans
normally understand the term, and that is the University of Buckingham, which
opened as an 'independent university college' in 1976. It is small, restricted in
the range of courses it offers, and is relatively expensive for the students (to
whom a somewhat telescoped programme of study is given); it will not,
therefore, appear further in this account. The public/private distinction in
Britain today is thus less significant than in the United States. But in neither
country, perhaps, is formal control the most important characteristic distinguishing different institutions of higher education.

As has already been implied, 'college' also bears slightly different meanings in
the two countries. In Britain the label is attached, broadly speaking, to any
educational collectivity other than the highest academic levels of university and
polytechnic; examples range from the larger constituent colleges of the Universities of London and Wales (each comparable to many universities), through
the constituent academic and/or social units found in the 'collegiate' Universities of Oxford, Cambridge, Durham, Lancaster and York, to the numerous
colleges in the public sector of higher and further education and, though not
relevant to this discussion, many of the older private secondary schools. It is not,
as it is in the United States, used either precisely to mean a two- or four-year
institution of higher education or generally to mean the place to which
first-degree aspirants go when, after graduating from high school, they 'go to
college', become 'college students', and undergo 'the undergraduate experience' (to quote the subtitle of Ernest Boyer's 1987 book, *College*).

Later we will have something to say about the different usages of the term 'quality'. First we must look at some of the more substantive comparisons between the two systems of higher education, starting with one large general statement. It is that, *relative to one another*, the two systems are crucially distinguished by the facts that the American one is diverse and accessible and the British one homogeneous and selective.

That the American *system* is widely accessible is undeniable, at least by comparison with other countries: 60% of those who successfully complete secondary education go on to experience some form of higher education, even though fewer than two-thirds of these eventually graduate. One estimate is that the 12 million students enrolled, either full-time or part-time, amount to something over 40% of the relevant age-group. By comparison, the British system is highly selective, with only about 15% of the age-group admitted to what is there regarded as higher education: but one must remember that it is much more narrowly defined in Britain, and that almost all of the 15% are full-time students (whereas up to a third of America's 40% are part-timers). At least by this broad numerical test, however, the Americans may be said to enjoy mass higher education while the British sustain an élite system. On the other hand, measured by the numbers who obtain a degree or other equivalent qualification, the difference is very much smaller. (This issue is discussed further in Chapter 3.) This contrast between the systems is closely associated with the other distinctive characteristics of diversity and heterogeneity or uniformity to which we now turn.

It is widely accepted that the American bachelor's degree is a variable entity, not only with respect to the subjects that may be included but also in the level of achievement represented by success. Correspondingly, the levels of ability and attainment necessary for entry vary within a fairly wide range: in 1986, the mean combined Scholastic Aptitude Test scores ranged from 808 for those intending to take certain more narrowly vocational major subjects to 1124 for those planning to major in the physical sciences. Institutions also range widely in their requirements from those with virtually open access for anyone with a high school diploma to the highly selective (the University of California, for example, recruits only from the top 12% of high school graduates, and other institutions can be even more exclusive). Enrolment clearly depends upon the standards of those leaving the secondary system; a widely accessible system must therefore have entry requirements in some respects lower than or different from those imposed in more selective systems. What is notable about the American system is that it combines ready access (to some institutions and especially to the two-year colleges) with highly selective entry to other institutions (especially the top research universities and some of the four-year colleges). The great variety of entry standards is accommodated, this is to say, by the diversity of institutions within the system (there are more than 3000 of them) rather than of individuals within each institution.

It is not only with respect to entry that institutions vary, nor only in terms of the functions implied by the Carnegie classification. They vary also in terms of their aims or mission: they are denominational or not; they place more or less emphasis on participation in sports; they are more or less watchful over students' behaviour outside the classroom; they are more or less concerned to meet the demands (for courses, technical advice, research etc.) of the immediate community or other outside interests and they look for recruitment, support, and approval primarily to local, state, national, or even international constituencies. They vary greatly in cost, in expenditure-per-student, in the sums of money raised regularly from alumni, and in endowments. (With respect to the last of these: the wealthiest five institutions, all private, had endowments valued, in 1984, at over \$1 billion each, but two of the institutions within the public University of California each had endowment funds of over \$100 million; and, of course, the poorest had none.) They vary also in size – from over 50,000 students to under 200 – and in organizational structure, physical environment, the extent to which students are resident, and all the other ways in which the social and physical environment can be determined. Perhaps the most striking contrast with Britain, however, lies in their varying degree of permanency. It is only very recently in Britain that financial problems have resurrected the possibility of a university's death; and even in the public sector the many enforced closures and mergers of colleges in the 1980s came as a shock. But in the United States the *Federal Digest of Educational Statistics 1987* (to take but one example) devotes its Table 144 to 'Institutions of Higher Education that have closed their doors . . . 1960–61 to 1984–85'; there were 262 of them, split equally between two-year and four-year establishments. During the same period, 1960–85, the total number nevertheless increased from 2021 to 3146. For any sort of person, with any particular set of tastes and interests, there might seem to be a place, or the possibility of creating a place, in American higher education.

For many of their counterparts there most certainly is not a place in British higher education. It is not merely that fewer are admitted, but that those few are admitted to institutions which see themselves, and are seen by others, as offering substantially the same product. Some might be judged to be more successful or efficient, or in other respects to be more desirable places to be, but nevertheless and especially by comparison with the United States, they are all engaged in the provision of the same form of education. Throughout the British system the education provided is broadly academic in character (i.e. it inclines to be general, detached and abstract) and is distinctly at or near the highest level (i.e. in terms of difficulty and the levels of intellectual ability required). It is constrained, moreover, by the assumption that students will be full-time and resident, and will graduate (in most courses) three years after admission. The universities, moreover, and (in England and Wales) especially the two ancient ones at Oxford and Cambridge, traditionally have been regarded as forming the apex of a single scholarly hierarchy which reaches down through the rest of higher education to the 'brighter' and more academic streams that constitute the favoured minority of secondary schoolchildren. Even the nineteenth-century creations, which began with far more modest aims and attainments, have long since been assimilated into the system.

(A partial exception to many of the generalizations made in the previous paragraph and elsewhere in this book is provided by the Open University which received its Charter in 1969. It deals exclusively in distance learning, it is financed directly by the Department of Education and Science, it has very flexible courses and admission requirements, and in other ways too is a unique innovation within the system. Its degrees and students have achieved full 'respectability' within the world of learning, but its special features mean that it cannot be discussed in detail in this book. It has, however, provided access to higher education for large numbers of people and degrees for over 100,000 of them.)

The public sector has somewhat different roots, in adult and further educa- tion oganized by local government authorities to meet local needs and aspira- tions. The promotion of some of these local institutions into the realm of higher education, as colleges of advanced technology or, later, as polytechnics, was intended to balance the academic bias of the universities with a commitment to more practical service to more local communities. It was also intended to constitute a new sector that was cheaper to run and more responsive to society's needs (as articulated by economic interests and mediated by central govern- ment). To underline these expectations the decision (in 1965) to create the thirty polytechnics was accompanied by a public announcement that no new universities would be sanctioned by the government. This latter commitment was necessary because, in the previous fifteen years, nine new universities had been established, ten colleges had acquired full university status, and the government had also agreed to set up the Open University. The resulting total of almost fifty separate universities is not great by American standards, but it nevertheless seemed important to kill the idea that the process of creation would continue indefinitely.

The public sector has not been content to provide an obviously inferior product nor to consist of a lower class of institution (despite consistently lower levels of funding). The CNAA, moreover, was charged with the task of ensuring that the standards of its degrees were comparable to those obtaining in the universities. There ensued what has been called 'academic drift', by which is meant that the public sector, by intention and accident, became more like the private one the more securely it became established. There are still differences between the sectors – but they are lessening, and are likely still further to lessen as the provisions of the Education Reform Act, 1988, take full effect. This is because the Act moved the English polytechnics from the jurisdiction of local to that of central government and has introduced new mechanisms and organiza- tions for funding the university sector nationally and the public one in England and Wales that, if still separate, are virtually identical in their powers and organization. (The government has also urged us, with limited effect, to drop the labels 'public' and 'private' from discussions of higher education.)

In consequence, and despite the existence of a 'pecking order' among institutions, Britain still finds itself with a remarkably uniform system in which, for example, the *minimum* formal entrance requirements for students are the same (expressed as the number and level of passes in the secondary school examinations taken at and after the age of 16), people with similar qualifications apply for teaching posts in both sectors, and the salaries are comparable (as well as being nationally negotiated). Above all, however, there is the same general idea of what a degree is and of the level of academic attainment it should represent – and that is, among other things, a level which only a small minority of people are expected to achieve (or even aspire to) and which is generally believed to be represented, in the United States, only by the BA of the best and most selective institutions.

The comparability of British degrees is more than a matter of mere rhetoric. Through the system of external examiners – senior members of the academic staff of other institutions who are involved in the formal assessment of all degrees (except Oxford and Cambridge ones, where the federal structure is assumed to provide a sufficiently detached system of assessment) – an elaborate network of individuals (some of them from Oxford and Cambridge) plays a key role in setting and monitoring standards throughout the whole system, inluding the University of Buckingham. BA degrees with (say) second class honours in a modern language from different universities and polytechnics do not, of course, reflect the same programme of studies or identical teaching (and there is as yet no national system of transferable 'credits' for work done in other institutions). Nor will identical extra-curricular factors have the same influences upon learning and character in different places. Nevertheless, the degrees will not be worlds apart in their standards and an individual graduate would be expected to have obtained a degree of the same classification even if (s)he had attended a different institution.

By contrast with the period before the Second World War, almost all British students now take honours degrees (and not 'pass' ones) at the end of a three-year undergraduate course (with some exceptions, particularly in Scotland where the tradition has been for wider access). The change largely reflects the post-war expansion of secondary education and consequent increase in the number of qualified school-leavers. One result of this was, after a time-lag, a significant expansion of higher education too; but almost more significant, and certainly more rapid, was the concentration on admission for honours degree courses and the raising of entrance requirements through an insistence that applicants obtain more than the officially stipulated minimum grades. The emphasis placed by the system upon selectivity can hardly be more clearly illustrated. Most observers and participants therefore tend to conclude (or assume) that the main questions about British higher education relate to its accessibility and hardly at all to the quality of its degrees or instruction, just as many tend to assume that the questions about American higher education relate to quality and hardly at all to access. Even in this introductory discussion, both judgements must be qualified.

Public discussion and anxiety about the quality of American higher education might almost be labelled as an epidemic, and certainly as endemic, in the United States. Thus it is commonly alleged that too many courses (or instructors) make too few demands on their students and that too many institutions (if only a minority of the total) bear little more than a nominal resemblance to the traditional picture of a college. Much of this concern may, however, be seen as the corollary of even greater worry about secondary education and relates, in effect, to the low level of high school graduates and, for example, to the consequent and growing need for remedial work in college. But a second strand of critical analysis, which gives rise possibly to even greater anxiety, is directed not so much at the level of work expected from undergraduate students as at the kind of work. At the root of this anxiety is the swing to purely vocational subjects or to apparently incoherent packages of courses, both at the expense of the ideal liberal education (stressing development of the whole person through the systematic study of a balanced range of disciplines) and of the related ideal of education for citizenship. Both these strands, however, must be carefully distinguished from judgements about whole categories of institution.

Within the United States, if not sufficiently so outside it, there is general recognition that many of the smaller and two-year colleges, for example, are excellent in the sense that they do what they set out to do extremely well, while among the four-year colleges and comprehensive universities are some of doubtful quality, in that their standards are unduly low given the functions they claim to perform: in other words, they fall below the appropriate form of excellence. It is often said, nevertheless, that the quality of education offered even by some high-quality two-year colleges is lower than that offered even by some low-quality four-year institutions. In such a context, as in so many discussions of the topic, 'quality' is being used in more than one sense. We need to distinguish three of the senses in which the word is commonly used. It can be used to refer to a particular and reasonably high standard. It is also used to refer to a 'type' or 'characteristic' which might or might not be the right or most desirable one. And it is used in a more relative sense, as the equivalent of 'excellent (of a kind)'. It is primarily in the first two of these senses that America can plausibly be argued to have distinctive problems of quality. It is certainly not unique in having some institutions that fall below the level of performance set by the best of their kind but, as we have indicated, some critics do challenge both the level and the nature of much that counts as higher education. It is also these problems of quality that many see as being linked to, even as the price to be paid for, the accessibility of the system as a whole.

In terms of access most observers today would probably agree that American higher education provides a major example of comprehensiveness and openness, especially since the great efforts of the past twenty-five years to overcome the barriers to access by the major deprived groups – blacks, other ethnic minorities, women and the disabled. Despite the levels of student support made available by the Federal Government, however, it sometimes seems as though the needs of these readily identifiable and increasingly articulate groups have preoccupied writers and policy-makers to the exclusion of that other historic deprived group, the poor (or, at least, less well-to-do). Certainly less public attention is paid to them, and statistics about them are less readily available; in the 1987 *Digest of Educational Statistics*, for example, there is no table of figures about the family-income or social background of students. If this is a relatively neglected problem of access, a different and more subtle one was also raised at the Princeton seminar, and this is one directly linked with questions of quality. In at least some institutions, and particularly in some two-year colleges, it was suggested that it is not only entry standards that are kept low in the interests of accessibility, but also 'exit standards'. To the extent that this is so, then the education offered to the students affected will not be worthy of the individual and group struggles for educational opportunity that have been so important a part of American social history. Access, it was argued, must be access to quality if it is not to be, and be seen as, a deception and a new form of discrimination. If this fear is well founded, then indeed the United States still confronts a difficult problem about access.

That Britain faces its own major, and perhaps more basic, problem of access to higher education is clear, at least to the foreign observer. Such an observer, moreover, is often surprised at the relative lack of demand – from educationists, politicians, and even the 'excluded' themselves, for a significant widening of access – let alone organized pressure from disadvantaged minorities. It has seemed to be the case, however, that even the 15+% of the age-group in higher education represents a high proportion of those who wish it as well as of those with the minimum qualifications. A large part of the explanation – and here we find an echo of the quality problem in America – must lie in secondary education. There the normal practice is one of early specialization in a restricted range of subjects and the effective segregation of pupils into academic and non-academic streams. The schools, it seems, guide pupils in line with the teachers' expectations of their abilities, while the pupils' ambitions are influenced by the expectations prevalent within their own subcultures (both ethnic and class). To increase the effective demand for higher education may be at least as difficult to achieve as to increase its supply. The other side of the coin of selectivity is the high completion rate; some 80% of those who are admitted to higher education graduate. In the light of this record, British academics have been both puzzled and wounded that the 1980s should have witnessed complaints about the quality of British higher education. The government has been the principal and most vocal complainer, but it has been echoed by some employers if not, on the whole, by observers from overseas.

In Britain, as in America, people mean different things by 'quality'. Relatively speaking, and taken as a whole, British higher education does offer courses of high academic standard taught fairly intensively to a carefully selected intellectual élite – not that it is free from failures and shortcomings. Despite occasional assertions to the contrary, moreover, there is no firm evidence of a decline in the general standards of staff, students, or degrees over the past 35 years, and there can be little doubt that the general levels of competence and attainment have greatly increased over the past century. But this, one suspects, is not really the kind of issue that the critics have in mind when they raise questions about quality.

The quality that seems most commonly to be at issue in Britain is quality in the second of the three senses we distinguished earlier. It is the *kind* of higher education provided that is becoming the real matter of dispute. The government and some business spokesmen, for example, claim that higher education encourages a spirit hostile to economic enterprise and unsuited to the 'world of work'. More general, and usually supported by more evidence, is the suggestion from others that the tradition is too academic, too theoretical, and too exclusively directed to the cultivation of abstract thinking. This concentration, it is further argued, is at the expense of that culture 'which is concerned with doing, making and organizing', to quote from a statement issued in 1977 by a group of interested individuals under the title *Education for Capability*. Whatever might be thought of either line of criticism, the critics make their point that British higher education is remarkably homogeneous in its aims and content. The preoccupation with quality (high standards) has led (as we have already indicated) to something like a single academic hierarchy, with institutions seeking prestige through the provision of education of comparable quality (type or character) to the exclusion, until very recently, of much concern for excellence of different kinds. This third sense of 'quality', so widespread in the United States, is rarely encountered in Britain. In consequence the case for wider access has been blunted by arguments derived from cost (since the traditional university pattern is expensive) or the lack of suitable new potential applicants ('suitable', that is to say, for the single predominant type of higher education offered in Britain). Rare indeed have been serious arguments for providing different kinds of education to different kinds of student in, if need be, different kinds of institution – but they have begun to emerge (e.g. in Ball and Eggins, 1989).

What emerges from this book is that, in both Britain and the United States, the goals of quality and access are closely connected: they are both complementary and competing. The two countries have developed differently as they have chosen to emphasize the one rather than the other goal, but in each the overall quality is in part a function of the degree of access and vice versa. It is far from obvious that either has arrived at a stable and satisfactory trade-off between quality (in any sense) and access. Both systems face problems. The chapters which follow, like the papers and discussions on which they are based, elaborate on the tension between quality and access. They also help to cast light on the dynamics of the American and British systems of higher education and, in the process, on the interconnections, in any system, between these widely shared aspirations.

References

Ball, Sir Christopher, and Eggins, Heather (eds) (1989). *Higher Education into the 1990s*. Milton Keynes: Society for Research into Higher Education and Open University Press.
Boyer, Ernest L. (1987). *College. The Undergraduate Experience in America*. New York: Harper & Row.
Burgess, Tyrrell (ed.) (1986). *Education for Capability*. Windsor: NFER/Nelson.

2

Comparative Perspectives on Policy[1]

Martin Trow

I

Current dialogues between British and American academics differ in several respects from similar conversations that took place in the early and mid-1960s. [. . .] It is not merely that the mood among British academics today could hardly be in sharper contrast with the near euphoria that accompanied the Robbins Report. It is also that the trans-Atlantic conversations then had a kind of symmetry, the sharing of ideas and experiences between representatives of two great systems of higher education which despite their obvious differences had the strengths and virtues appropriate to the histories and characters of the very different societies that they served. Some of the ebullience on both sides was the reflection of a broader euphoria of an expanding economy, but much was a measure of the pride and confidence that comes from being part of important and respected institutions which were increasingly seen to be key institutions in both societies.

There have been changes in mood and attitude within the academic community on both sides of the Atlantic over the past several decades, but they have been immeasurably greater in England. In the United States attitudes in higher education are more sober – certainly less expansionist – and more self-critical, especially with respect to the quality of the undergraduate education offered in many of our 3300 institutions which offer credit toward degrees. Currently the United States is passing through a cyclical recurrence of its perennial concern for the quality and content of undergraduate education. This concern, as always, harks back to a golden age when there was presumably a consensus among people of learning about what knowledge is of most worth, when the undergraduate curriculum had, it is remembered or imagined, enough internal coherence to be thought of as a form of liberal education. The discussion has been, with some few exceptions, largely normative and hortatory (Trow, 1987b).

With respect to access, American have casually assimilated the otherwise extraordinary fact that enrolments in higher education have held almost perfectly steady over the past five years or so, at about 12.5 million, despite very sharp declines in the numbers of high school graduates, declines that reflect trends in the size of the relevant age groups. The predicted shortfall in college enrolments has been made up largely by part-time and older students; increasingly our system of higher education is providing continuing education to employed adults enrolled for credit, whether or not they take degrees (Trow, 1987c). Continuing education in the United States is no longer segregated in extension programmes or relegated to the community colleges, and even a public research university like the University of California is under pressure to admit more older part-time students (*Master Plan*, 1987, p. 26). This trend is bound to have effects on many American institutions which have traditionally served the 'college-age' population enrolled full-time for four, or perhaps five, years. But these traditional institutions are now finding ways to serve an adult employed population in ways and at times and places convenient to these mature students. (At the same time, more formal degree-credit higher education is being offered in college-level programmes provided directly by and in business firms (Eurich, 1985).) This trend is consistent with the enrolment-driven budgets and market sensitivities of American colleges and universities, public and private, and is the other side of the coin of the criticism of the undergraduate curriculum: a non-traditional student body cannot just be offered a traditional curriculum. I think that the incorporation of continuing education into the system of higher education, along with current efforts to reform and improve undergraduate education, are the most important trends in American higher education at the moment. Higher education's biggest *problem* in America remains the character and quality of the education its students receive *before* they get to college; and the colleges and universities have only modest leverage on that (Boyer, 1983).

But these are, one might say, the ordinary problems of a system of higher education in a 'post-industrial' society, increasingly living by its wits rather than on its labour or materials, a system in which the boundaries between institutions of higher education and the environing society are increasingly blurred, as are the familiar distinctions between life and learning. The great problem in our future may well be how to maintain the identity and integrity of American colleges and universities as they become increasingly enmeshed with other institutions in the society.

But matters in the UK are different, sufficiently different so that the old symmetries in our trans-Atlantic discussions have broken down. British higher education, after a remarkable burst of energy and expansion in the two and a half decades following the end of World War II, has entered a period of great stress, most markedly in the past decade. The problems, which taken together we can properly call a crisis, have developed largely in the public life of British higher education – in its finance, governance and organization – rather than in its private life, in the areas of teaching and learning. A crisis of this magnitude, however painful to those immediately affected, can be instructive and enlightening to the observer, as it wrenches old patterns and relationships awry, and makes suddenly problematic what has long been assumed. So much of this essay will be addressed to the crisis in *British* higher education rather than to developments in the United States.

II

Americans who have walked through the quads and gardens of Oxford and Cambridge, and who know that Harvard was modelled on a Cambridge college, often think of British universities as immeasurably older than our own. But in fact higher education as a system is much younger in the United Kingdom than in the United States. The US organizational revolution took place about 100 years ago, roughly between 1870 and 1910; the emergence of a British system of higher education is still underway. As Lawrence Veysey has put it, 'Looking back, it could be seen that the decade of the '90s witnessed the firm development of the American academic model in almost every crucial aspect' (Veysey, 1965, p. 339). By 1900, when only 4% of Americans of college age were attending college, we already had in place almost all of the central structural characteristics of American higher education: the lay board of trustees, the strong president and his administrative staff, the well-defined structure of faculty ranks, and in the selective institutions promotion through academic reputation linked to publication and a readiness to move from institution to institution in pursuit of a career. On the side of the curriculum the elective system, the modular course, credit accumulation and transfer based on the transcript of grades, all were in place by 1900, as were the academic departments covering all known spheres of knowledge, and some not so well known. Underpinning all was the spirit of competition, institutional diversity, responsiveness to markets and especially to the market for students, and institutional autonomy marked by strong leadership and a diversity of sources of support. The United States already had the organizational and structural framework for a system of mass higher education long before it had mass enrolments. All that was needed was growth.

What has happened since to American higher education? Of course, there was growth – an enormous expansion in the numbers of students, institutions, staff, research support, and everything else. But apart from expansion and growth, the most important structural change in this century has been the development of the community college system, and the way that has tied the four-year institutions and their degrees to the world of continuing and vocational education. Academic freedom is more firmly and broadly protected than at the turn of the century, thanks in part to the American Association of University Professors (AAUP). In addition, there is now broad federal support for student aid in the form of grants and loans, and this has supplemented rather than replaced other and earlier forms of student aid. Federal agencies support university-based research at a level that could hardly have been imagined 90, or even 40, years ago. The machinery of fund-raising, the organization of alumni and the associated development of big-time sports has gone further than one would have imagined, though the roots of all that were already in place at the turn of the century. And there are faculty unions in some hundreds of colleges and universities, though mostly of the second and third rank. But what is impressive about American higher education at the end of the '80s is not how much it differs from the system that existed at the turn of the century, but how similar it is in basic structure, diversity, mission, governance and finance. An interesting research question is how it came to be that a century ago the United States had already created a preternaturally precocious system of higher education with an enormous capacity for expansion without fundamental structural change.

Matters have been quite different in the UK. Of the existing 44 British universities, only five in England, four in Scotland and one in Wales had gained their charters by 1900; half have been created since 1945. In 1900 the total Treasury grant to all the English universities and university colleges came to only £25,000 a year (Robertson, 1976, p. 449).[2] In Britain a national system of higher education has been evolving slowly in this century; a landmark was the establishment of the University Grants Committee as the instrument for the distribution of the central government grant in 1919, with common admissions criteria, student grants, pay scales, honours degree standards and staff–student ratios all later developments.[3] The British system of higher education that exists today, and is the object of government policy, is a post-World War II creation.

British higher education appeared to have achieved a stable state, at least organizationally, by 1969, with the last of the plate-glass universities and the binary system in place. But serious and unsettling problems, both of finance and governance, lay just ahead, leading to its current deep crisis. It is only slightly ironic to suggest that some of these problems may in fact be the growing pains of a young and still evolving system of higher education, whose criteria for admission, structures of finance and governance, curricular patterns, and relationships between and among the different sectors, are all still in flux (Fulton, 1988).

III

Are the current problems of British higher education largely the product of an unsympathetic, indeed hostile, government, or of structural dilemmas within the system that are to some important extent independent of this government and would have shown themselves, although perhaps in less dramatic forms and with different solutions, under almost any British government in this decade?

The answer lies in how one sees the nature of the problems of British higher education. If the problems take the form of severe budget cuts, or direct government intervention and its contemptuous dismissal of university advice and sentiment, surely another government might have acted differently and the universities would not be suffering their current crisis of morale.

But if the 'problem' is seen differently, as the result of strains arising from Britain's efforts to create a system of higher education that can serve the varied requirements of an advanced or post-industrial society without at the same time surrendering the elite character and size of the existing system, then the roots of *that* problem do not lie in the present government's policies, but deep in British conceptions of the nature of the university, and in the relation of higher education to the larger society (Halsey and Trow, 1971). If the present crisis is a product of both: a crisis of structures and of government policy, then it may be that the first cannot even be addressed until the second is resolved.

My own judgment is that Britain, and not just the present government, has since World War II been trying to create a system of higher education which has some of the characteristics of mass higher education, especially its relevance to technological innovation and economic growth, without accepting the size and diversity of a mass system. Nearly a decade ago Britain achieved the level of 14 or 15% of the age grade in full-time degree granting courses. In the early '70s I suggested that that proportion of the age grade represented the limits to which a system could grow without becoming more diversified both in its student population and in the institutions which serve them, and pointed to:

> problems arising in the relations between institutions of higher education and the larger society and its economic and political institutions, as higher education moves from [the phase of elite to that of mass higher education]. An example here might be the greater concern for public 'accountability' of funds spent on higher education and the greater interference in the autonomy of higher educational institutions in the allocation and use of these funds, as costs rise and the higher educational system becomes more consequential and more significant to a wider range of social, political, and economic activities.
>
> (Trow, 1974, p. 73)

That describes, at least in part, the source of some of Britain's current problems and its relations with this government, though the attitudes and policies of the present government have converted the strains inherent in this thus far aborted transition to mass higher education into the present crisis of finance, autonomy, and morale.

It may be useful to review some of the steps that have led, if not inexorably at least decisively, toward the present crisis. Several authors place the top of this slippery slope in 1962, when for the first time Parliament rejected the UGC's recommendation for the quinquennium grant. An American might put the crucial events earlier: indeed World War II may have been the fateful watershed. In 1938–39 central government supplied less than one third of university income, though of course the proportion varied among the several universities. In 1951–52 central government already supplied nearly three-quarters of university income, and had taken on the bulk of student fees and student support grants (Heyck, 1987, p. 213).[4] This assumption by central government of virtually the whole of university support was welcomed by most academics at the time; it was in one sense the extension of the welfare state to a crucial area of cultural life not occupied by the sick, the unemployed, and the aged, and thus reduced the stigma of state support for all the others. In addition, it seemed a powerful democratizing force, consistent with other forces at work at the time, more significant than most in that it promised to make available to the whole society, at least its intellectually gifted, without regard for class or social origins, that part of the cultural heritage that heretofore had been reserved for the privileged. Indeed central state support had been the goal of the provincial universities almost since their beginnings – they saw in it (as many still do) a nobler and more dignified way of life than dependence on the fees of customers or payment for services to local business and local government.

So as the system expanded and became really expensive, more like the national health service than like a national theatre, governments began to exercise first greater interest in, and then greater influence over, the size and shape of British higher education. In 1964 the UGC's accountability was transferred from the Treasury to the newly created Department of Education and Science, that is, to a body which on one hand does not make the final decisions about funding, but on the other claims to possess educational competence and expertise (Maclure, 1987, p. 17).[5] The latter was the more ominous aspect of the shift: at last a Ministry of Education, not yet as *dirigiste* as its Continental counterparts, but looking over the UGC's shoulder and learning how to manage institutions of higher education through its relation with the new 'public sector' part of the binary system created in 1965 by Crosland and Weaver.

The creation of a 'public sector' of higher education, composed of polytechnics and 'colleges of education', could have provided an important institutional buffer for the universities, a sector of higher education serving the economy more directly and designed, so to speak, to take the brunt of governmental guidance and direction, while the 'autonomous' university sector preserved its autonomy. Alas, that hope was doomed by at least three events: First, the assurance by government at their founding that the new polys were to enjoy equality of esteem and academic standard with the universities, while pursuing a different mission. It turned out that the mission, through academic drift and student choice of subjects, was not so different, and over time the polys came to look more and more like universities, not quite so strong academically, but not much cheaper either. Indeed since government had promised them equality of esteem and standard, then it had to give their students the same support in fees and grants, the institutions applied comparably high entry standards, the Council for National Academic Awards assured the same standards for the degree, and that meant comparable staff–student ratios and opportunities for research, though in all these respects the polys were on the whole clearly second-class in relation to the universities. Secondly, central government allowed the universities to grow after the polys were established, so that the two sectors currently (1987) enrol roughly equal numbers of Britain's full-time degree students. The larger (and more expensive) the university sector became, the greater the motivation for central government to take a more active role in its affairs. And thirdly, the polys have been formally governed by local authorities, though most of their money comes from central government, and this arrangement has paradoxically given them more autonomy in some respects than the universities have enjoyed in recent years. And recent and projected changes in the governance and finance of both the polys and the universities will make for a further convergence between the two sectors (DES, 1987).

IV

During the past quarter century a number of events have marked the slow decline in university autonomy, while at the same time may have revealed the ineffectiveness of efforts – in universities or outside them – to slow or halt what has seemed increasingly to be an inexorable process. Each of these events pointed up the weakness of leadership in British higher education – in each university, but more importantly, of the 'system' as a whole. One of these events occurred in 1969, when the universities rejected then Secretary of State Shirley Williams' 'thirteen points' suggesting self-administered economies, on the grounds that they would threaten academic standards.

With the wisdom of hindsight, this relatively gentle intervention of government might have led to the creation of machinery by the universities to do the necessary planning and cutting. But who could have taken the initiative for such a radical innovation? What was needed was institutional leadership. The UGC and the Committee of Vice-Chancellors and Principals (CVCP) are the only bodies that speak for and to British universities as a whole. One might even imagine that they resemble the Boards of Trustees and the President's Office of big American state university systems (Caston, 1979). But neither the UGC nor the CVCP was or is able to function as the governing structure of the British university system. British universities are a system only as the *object* of policy; as the *source* of policy they are an aggregation of autonomous institutions. And into that policy vacuum central government has steadily moved, first through the UGC, and after 1988 through other instruments.

So Shirley Williams' 'thirteen points' were more a symptom of the weakness of university governance than an opportunity to reform and strengthen it. As a result, much worse was to come. The year 1973 saw the end of the quinquennium grant as a method of university financing – the loss of an important basis for predictability and planning as university budgets became subject almost immediately to substantial cuts in real terms. In 1979 a new government headed by Mrs Thatcher brought a different tone and policy to higher education. In 1981 the UGC found itself having to administer a cut in total resources to the universities of around 14 percent over three years. As we know, it chose to do this through a programme of 'selective' cuts – indeed the alternative, 'equal misery,' would have been a confession of institutional bankruptcy and irrelevance. That exercise, carried out in three months in great secrecy, distributed cuts markedly unequally as between such former colleges of advanced technology as Salford which took a cut of over a third in total resources, as compared with Cambridge which got off with a cut of some two percent over the whole period. As one observer comments, 'The 1981 cuts exercise undoubtedly was a landmark both in the history of the UGC and of the universities themselves . . . whilst the UGC had been *dirigiste* upwards before, e.g., over the capital grants in expansionist days, it now had to become *dirigiste* downwards, giving guidance on student numbers in much narrower subject groupings than heretofore' (Moore, 1987, p. 32). One might note in passing that the government of the day indicated clearly that it hoped that the process of selective cuts would result in shifts in resources towards science, engineering, technology, computer science and the rest. In fact, as we know, cuts fell more heavily on the former colleges of advanced technology, which, while offering work in those areas, presumably could not meet the UGC's criteria of academic distinction (largely measured by research grants and productivity) in competition with the older universities. This perverse demonstration of its independence by the UGC may have been a factor in the government's recent decision to kill it and replace it with a body that will not presume to thwart the government in such important matters of policy.

What was painfully apparent in 1981 was the inappropriateness of the UGC and its procedures for the tasks that it was assigned, and loyally tried to discharge. In a sense, the benign character of the UGC, its almost uninterrupted success for over 50 years in representing university needs and interests to government, prevented the emergence of a stronger agency which could both represent the universities, and force changes on them when needed. The UGC respected the autonomy of the universities so deeply and for so long, that when central government imposed heavy cuts on the system, the UGC had to attempt to change its character and its relationships with the universities and government fundamentally and quickly. And despite those efforts, in 1981 it had neither the authority nor the analytical and administrative capacity to resist the pressure from government and the DES, on the one hand, or work with the universities to develop coherent 'systemwide' plans for contraction, on the other. It could administer cuts to individual universities, but it could not force them to coordinate their cuts with one another, nor even effectively influence how any one would allocate its cuts internally.[6]

The history of the past few years, on the steeper end of the slippery slope, is perhaps too well known and too painful to need rehearsal here: the Green Paper of May 1985 – a grim technocratic document indeed; the UGC exercise of 1985–86 culminating in the allocation of grants for 1986–87; the Jarratt Report on rationalization and efficiency in the management of the universities; the Croham Report on the reform of the UGC; and the recent government White Paper, tolling its knell and describing – if as yet somewhat unclearly – the nature of the Universities Funding Council which is to replace it in 1988 (Shattock, 1987a; Moodie, 1987; Perkin, 1987).

V

If one looks at the recent erosion of the bases of university autonomy in Britain from a trans-Atlantic perspective, one might ask why governments which pay the piper – i.e. provide the bulk of support for a system of higher education – do not always call the academic tune? Or dropping the metaphor, how can any publicly-supported system retain a measure of institutional autonomy and self-direction? Wise governments in a number of countries, including both the US and the UK, have over time created arrangements through a series of self-denying ordinances for funding universities in ways that simulate private funds, such as unrestricted gifts or the interest from endowment, that come to a university without strings attached. Among the devices introduced specifically to insulate the universities that they fund from the direct impact of the preferences and policies of the government of the day we can note the following: multi-year budgets, such as quinquennium grants, which give assurances of continued support without political strings, symbolically denying the public and political sources of that support, and allowing autonomous planning by the institutions so funded; block grants which allow internal allocations; organizational buffers like the UGC; constitutional protections of autonomy; the provision of student support through loans and grants that go directly to students and come through them to the university in the form of fees independent of central governmental direction (Trow, 1983b). All of these and other protections have been in place in Britain in the recent past, and together they have allowed what since World War II have been largely publicly-supported universities to think of themselves, and indeed to act, as the 'autonomous' sector of British higher education. But almost every one of them has been lost or revoked in recent years. The quinquennium grant disappeared in 1973; the block grant has been eroded by the increasing earmarking of public funds and increasingly detailed conditions placed on their use. The UGC, even before its execution by the White Paper, was no longer serving as a buffer but more as a conduit of government policy and an agent of its implementation to the universities. Constitutional protection, which in the UK takes the form of the university charter, is under direct attack by government in relation to its provisions regarding academic tenure. And the important independence provided the universities by home student fees was lost when the government took them over and made them effectively part of the grant to the institutions. But this, along with central government's assumption of mandatory means-tested support grants to all students admitted to full-time higher education, was applauded by most academics as a further democratization of higher education, and its further insulation from the influence of the market. There was little thought of the cost to higher education in freedom and autonomy.

While the immediate threat to the autonomy of British universities flows from the attitudes and polices of a particular government and Prime Minister, the important steps that I have sketched and other more recent ones that I have not mentioned toward increasingly forceful and detailed intervention by the state in the life of the universities clearly continue trends apparent as far back as the 1960s. And this trend has been made possible by what, in a different context, Walter Metzger has called 'facilitating' events and factors (Metzger, 1987). In my view the two most important factors which facilitated this slide toward dependency and central government *dirigisme* were first, the increasing reliance of the universities on the state for the bulk of their support, and second, the assumption of high and uniform academic standards for entry and for the honours degree by all degree-granting institutions. This rejection of diversity by the academic community and government alike – indeed by almost everyone who had anything to do with British higher education – had precluded the emergence of a system parts of which might provide broader access, while permitting the survival of a smaller autonomous university sector maintaining its own high standards (Trow, 1987a). The concept of high and uniform academic standards is in British academic life something of a fetish or totem, the object of unquestioned and almost religious veneration and not of analytic scrutiny. Scarcely anyone raises the question of the cost of preserving such standards throughout the system of degree-granting institutions. In his report to the Committee of Vice-Chancellors and Principals on academic standards, and the reforms needed to maintain them (in the absence of any evidence that they are falling), Reynolds says firmly, 'It is of first importance . . . that degree classifications from different institutions approach as nearly as possible to common standards within the limits on comparability . . .' (Reynolds, 1986, p. 5). But Reynolds does not say *why* such uniformity of degree standard is of 'first importance'. It seems simply to be assumed that academic work at more modest standard offered to a broader student population must threaten the existing centres of excellence, as if Princeton were threatened by the standards of the state colleges or community colleges of New Jersey, or by Rutgers, its land grant university.[7]

The British commitment to high and *uniform* standards has also precluded a closer relationship between higher education and further education, a connection which surely is Britain's most feasible path to a system of mass higher education which combines access and excellence (Trow, 1987a).

The narrow financial base of British universities, their consequent vulnerability to state intervention, their lack of political friends and allies resulting from a narrow conception of their mission, and the conversion of academic standards into a fetish, all operate in a normative climate quite different from that with which Americans are familiar. All recent developments in British higher education are played out against a backcloth of cultural values marked still by an anti-industrial bias among the elite – remarked on in their different ways by such observers as Sheldon Rothblatt, Martin Weiner and Corelli Barnett, among others (Rothblatt, 1968; Weiner, 1981; Barnett, 1987). In addition, English men and women are simply not as interested in education as are Americans, and especially do not see higher education as the grand road to social mobility, financial success, and all other good things. Three-quarters of English youth still leave school at 16 years of age, and of the quarter who continue on to the upper secondary school, only about 15% earn the two A level passes that are required for entry to degree-granting institutions. (Only about 10% of those who enter higher education are currently admitted on other unorthodox criteria (Fulton, 1988)). So real expansion (if it were desired) would require major changes in secondary school credentialing and/or in higher education admissions criteria, as well as the establishment of a different basis for funding the whole operation. The nearly full funding of a high-cost system by central government operates not only to constrain growth but to justify its increasing intervention and direction of higher education.

So we see here in sketchy outline a network of attitudes, values and structures all working to constrain expansion, a system which would be very hard to change, and will change only by changes in government policy arising out of a perception of the failure of present policy. But from this perspective it is not at all clear what 'failure' must look like to be persuasive; and paradoxically the British university community must be dedicated to avoiding that very failure or to obscuring it where it occurs. Moreover, British higher education has such reserves of talent and creativity that it may cope with the present crisis more successfully than an American can imagine; some hints of how that might happen are offered by Graeme Moodie who suggests possible ways of handling and even profiting from the establishment of the new Universities Funding Council (Moodie, 1987). The British have a widely-remarked genius for not carrying things to their logical conclusions, nor allowing high principle to overwhelm common sense. The threatened shift of discretion and initiative out of the universities to other bodies cannot strengthen them, but much will depend on the actual terms of the relationship with the new funding body when it settles down and becomes routinized. And there the universities have the enormous advantage of possessing a monopoly on expertise in their several fields of study. That is nearly their last line of defence, but it is a strong one.

Incidentally, in reading the ongoing discussions among British academics about how to cope with the assaults on their budgets and autonomy, one hears the occasional lament that the universities have few friends outside their own walls, and especially few allies to plead their case at court. But there is in all this discussion almost no reference to the universities' own councils, which (Oxbridge aside) are the major groups of influential *laymen* actually inside and presumably attached to the interests of the university. Granted that British university councils are not nearly as powerful as are the boards of trustees of American universities; nevertheless, one wonders whether they have been mobilized, individually or collectively, in the fights for resources and the defence of autonomy. I suspect not, and I suspect also that their councils have been to the universities a source of mild embarrassment; reminders to institutions with national aspirations of their local ties and origins. But having arranged that they should not play any significant role in the life of the universities, the universities find them now impotent when they might be useful, unwilling or unable to help in a time of need. Whatever the value of these councils in defending their universities against pressures from central government, British universities need to cultivate friends more widely in the society – and chiefly by providing services to them. But that runs against the strongly held attitudes of some academics, for whom it is a betrayal of the mission of the university.

VI

As we see a British government taking a more clearly directive and intervention-ist role in higher education, trying to force changes of procedures, goals, relationships, and values against the will of most of the academic community, the question must arise of how it means to accomplish those ends, how a government imposes an unpopular policy on a resistant institution.

Some observers have already begun to reflect on whether and how universities might co-opt the new Universities Funding Council and use it to their own advantage. But alongside speculation on the character and attitudes of the Council, the topic of implementation raises the less exciting issues of the nature and size of bureaucratic staffs and information systems, both prerequisites to effective management of complex organizations. Where will such modern organizational weapons, needed to manage any large system of higher education, lie? Will the new Universities Funding Council, or perhaps a section of the Department of Education and Science, try to become a kind of ministry of higher education, against all British administrative tradition? Or will the government try to work through the administrative staff of the universities themselves? – in which case the instruments of implementation may also be instruments of resistance and sabotage. Universities everywhere, and in England not least of all, are skilful at subverting central government policy. Central governments and their creatures have of course the power of the purse, and can threaten financial punishment for recalcitrance or delay. But such atomic weapons are nearly useless against guerrilla warfare. It may be that the British university's most valuable asset in the years to come will be a strong and creative registrar.

I do not think that British governments – even this one – know or perhaps even want to know how to manage a university. And yet the present government wants to direct the system, if not to manage it. And this ambivalence about the exercise of power over the universities has led to such odd events as the 1985 exercise by the UGC involving the assessment of almost all university departments in Britain as an element in its preparation of the 1986–87 grant. That exercise revealed one aspect of the modern British dilemma in higher education – the reluctance by governments thus far to will the means when it has willed the ends. Indeed the present government may not be illogical in putting down the UGC and replacing it by another body charged to allocate sums to the universities through a system of contracts rather than grants, without giving unwanted advice or engaging in long-range planning. I do not think that the UGC with its character and traditions could in fact carry out such a mandate. It has not even been able to carry out recent softer mandates of central government very well. That is because, to its honour rather than its shame, the UGC is and remains a piece of liberal governmental machinery, part of an older tradition whereby central government in Britain governed in many areas through agencies which were not part of central government, but part of the network of institutions which were being governed.[8] (A familiar example has been the role of local government, the unions and the churches in primary and secondary education.) But central government since World War II, both Labour and Tory, has viewed these intermediate organizations with some suspicion, as undemocratic bodies likely to be captured by the special interests which they purport to govern, and in the service of practices and policies at odds with those of the democratically-elected government of the day. And the Thatcher government has been particularly unsympathetic to any agencies which intervene between its will and the objects of its will.

When the UGC, against its own strong advice to the government, found itself having to allocate very large cuts in 1981, it chose to make them, as we know, selectively, on the basis of assessments of whole universities, with the procedures held confidential. There was, of course, a storm of protest after the allocations were made, both about the fairness and validity of the assessments and the subsequent grant allocations. When the UGC was faced in 1985 with the allocation of further cuts, and indeed (as it appeared then) probably a succession of them indefinitely into the future, it found itself again having to devise procedures for allocating grants in some sort of selective way rather than on the basis of 'equal misery'.

The UGC's assessments of academic departments in every university, published in 1985, were based in part on the Committee's judgments of their research quality, in part on their success in getting research grants and contracts (Moore, 1987). Grants to the universities were based on the aggregate assessments of the research qualities of component departments, the *per capita* costs of instruction which varied by subject, and another factor to take into account special activities and circumstances of the several universities and the preferences of the committees. Again a cry went up that specific departments were assessed inaccurately or inappropriately. (There were good grounds for some of the complaints.) But a quite different set of questions about the Committee's procedures can be raised.

First, had the UGC looked at the long experience of the United States in assessing the research quality of university departments since the middle '20s? (Jones *et al.*, 1982; Trow, 1984). I believe it had not. Aside from American procedures, the UGC might have learned how effective quality rankings of departments can be even (perhaps especially) when totally separated from funding decisions; indeed the American exercise, sponsored by the Conference Board of Associated Research Councils, has little or no bearing on overall institutional support, but has quite a lot of influence on internal allocations by university presidents, provosts and deans who are interested in the objective indicators of the quality of departments for which they have responsibility. These assessments stimulate the spirit of competitive excellence, but equally important, they strengthen the hands of decision-makers close to the point where problems are indicated. That certainly was true in the case of biology at Berkeley (Trow, 1983a).[9]

But more importantly, the exercise in the UGC was designed primarily to cut funds as directed by central government in a way that seemed reasonable and fair, but not as a way to achieve any specific or intended changes in the universities. The UGC did not show any interest in how its allocations would have any particular outcomes in any particular institution. And this reflects the ambivalence of the UGC about its changing relationship with the universities. That ambivalence was reflected in its readiness to make broad assessments, and even narrow ones, but also in its continuing reluctance to tell the universities precisely how they should respond to that information – a survival of its traditional respect for the autonomy of the universities. And yet the exercise was based on certain unexamined assumptions in the UGC. For example, there was an assumption that weaker departments and units in the universities would somehow be punished financially for their weakness. But the UGC had not (I believe) considered the possibility that low ratings in crucial departments – for example mathematics or physics – might have to lead to *increased* investment rather than cuts, nor in such events how such funds could be drawn away from other more highly rated departments. Moreover – and here I think it reflected its own traditions – the UGC had not considered how universities actually distribute their grants, and whether any specific internal financial decisions would flow from the UGC's published quality assessments or its pattern of allocations. In other words, there is no evidence that the exercise included much analysis of what the consequences of that exercise would be – either intended or unintended.

What did the UGC want to do, apart from distributing a grant in a way that was broadly felt to be fair and legitimate? Did it have any purposes aside from being seen to be fair, and how did it see those purposes as being achieved? And specifically, did it anticipate how the universities would behave in the face of its assessments of quality? The UGC has provided no persuasive answers to any of these questions. To an outside observer, it seems as if the UGC were sending signals to a strong chief executive in each university to draw the appropriate inferences from the ratings of departments in his university and then to take actions consistent with those signals (and the political decisions behind them) appropriate to the special circumstances of his institution. That strong executive would be the necessary link between government policy (as expressed through the UGC) and the autonomous universities (as defended by the UGC). But that strong executive does not exist in most British universities, which are still largely governed by their academic guilds, organized in Senate and union.[10]

And yet under present conditions in the UK strong institutional leadership may be necessary for the survival of institutional autonomy, however incompatible that may be with other aspects of the 'English ideal of university governance' (Eustace, 1987). Indeed, strong leadership is so important to university autonomy that the UGC has to pretend it is there even when it is not.[11] But without that strong leadership in each institution, a government which has, as it sees it, the legitimate right to determine the size, shape and general direction of higher education for which it provides the bulk of the support, finds itself frustrated by the autonomy of the universities, and by the inability or reluctance of senates to translate signals (or 'guidance') from the UGC into decisions that affect parts of the university differentially. It is frustrated also by the reluctance of its own instruments, the UGC and the DES, to violate university autonomy too openly and brutally. So slowly and on the whole clumsily, central government, reshaping or discarding its instruments as it goes, starts to make decisions not just about the broad character of the system, but about the internal academic and research life of individual institutions, decisions better made by vice-chancellors and senates. And that is a very bad habit, though an easy one for central governments to acquire. Governments, including Britain's current government, tend to suffer from the illusion that they know better than academics what should be taught, how, and to whom. Even the clumsy and largely ineffective efforts to force the 'switch' to science and technology away from social science and the humanities has not seemed to teach any lessons – especially the lesson that there are too many variables, and government does not control them all (Maclure, 1987).[12] And as government's role in the direction and management of higher education grows, so, I suspect, will the magnitude of its mistakes.

The chief check on damaging interventions by government into the private life of the universities before World War II was the diversity of funding sources coupled with the tradition of university autonomy as institutionalized after 1919 in the UGC. After World War II the concentration of financial support in central government increased the importance of the instruments of governmental self-restraint – the quinquennium grant, the block grant, above all the UGC as it was before 1981. But as these lines of defence have been lost or eroded, the main protection for university autonomy may come to lie chiefly in government's reluctance or inability to administer the universities closely. Even continental countries with long traditions of bureaucratic centralism are having difficulty managing their increasingly large and diverse systems. In France, for example, some universities openly flout laws and directives which forbid selective admissions to holders of the 'bac'. And everywhere the call is for more 'decentralization' of university governance.

It seems unlikely that the current (or any future) British government will be prepared to develop the large administrtive and bureaucratic machinery necessary for direct management of the universities, or to install a governmental civil servant – a 'curator' – inside the university administration, as in Germany and Italy. One would imagine that Britain's administrative traditions and its government's disinclination to expand the ministerial bureaucracies would both preclude that.[13] Graeme Moodie's rather gloomy optimism about the possibilities of co-opting the new funding Council, and Maurice Kogan's cool scepticism that the Council will apply its performance indicators to University College, London, or do a cost–benefit analysis of Trinity College, Cambridge, may suggest the limits of *dirigisme* without a big bureaucracy (Moodie, 1987; Kogan, 1987b).[14]

But that is cold comfort to those who know and respect British universities. Sad to say, it seems likely that British higher education in the foreseeable future will be the object of central governmental policies based on suspicion and a lack of trust, and it faces that grim prospect without many friends, in government or outside it. This climate of mutual hostility between higher education and the state must change before Britain can get on with the much larger challenge of creating a system of higher education, marked by high quality and broad access both, that is worthy of the society, its people and its future.

Acknowledgements

My thanks to A. H. Halsey and Rowland Eustace for their comments on an early draft of this paper.

Notes

1. [This chapter first appeared in print in the *Oxford Review of Education*, **14** (1) 84–96 (1988). It is based on the opening address to the Princeton Seminar.]
2. By contrast 30 years earlier the American government had endowed American colleges and universities with public lands equal in area to the whole of the Netherlands or Switzerland, and had followed that up in the '90s with a system of regular subventions to these land-grant colleges and universities (Ross, 1942).
3. The rationalization and nationalization of student admissions standards and student grants both followed the Anderson Report (1960) (Maclure, 1987, p. 8).
4. 'From the late 1940s until around 1980 the UGC recurrent grant allocations represented about 90% of the average university's budget' (Shattock, 1987b), though in recent years under central government pressure that proportion has been falling.
5. A further weakening of the UGC–universities relationship occurred in 1968, when a committee of Parliament assumed the audit of university accounts – an extension of accountability to political authorities and away from the UGC.
6. See, for example, Austin (1982) on the process by which the 1981–82 cuts were allocated in the University of Manchester.
7. The cult of 'standards' is nearly universal among British academics. One of the founders of the only chartered private university in Great Britain, Lord Beloff, argued the case for university autonomy on the ground that State control must involve an attack on standards. His defence of the private university in Britain is made not in terms of broader access, nor the freedom to innovate, nor stronger ties to other social institutions, but the defence of academic standards, against a state which *also* sees itself as the bulwark of academic standards. Rowland Eustace, after quoting Lord Beloff, shrewdly observes that 'half the problem today is that the State supposes itself to be attacking on behalf of standards, even if it thinks they need not be so expensive' (Eustace, 1987, p. 12).
8. Maurice Kogan (1987a) shows that the DES was also partly captured by the values and assumptions of the institutions for which it had responsibility, in part because of the limits of its power over them. In this sense, it was, like the UGC, part of the older liberal pluralist world. But as the system grew in size and cost, 'the incorporation of higher education policy into the mainstream of Whitehall became inevitable' (p. 232). That trend has been accelerated under the present government, which has undertaken to resocialize the DES, while abolishing the UGC.
9. Such rankings (1) carry early warning signals calling for action; (2) they justify action to local interested parties; and (3) they can be ignored if the institution decides they are dated or are erroneous for some other reason.
10. On this, see Eustace (1987) and his sources.
11. But that class of strong 'presidential' vice-chancellors is beginning to emerge – at Salford, Warwick, Bristol, among others – in response to the needs and pressures I am discussing.
12. 'As early as January 1965, shortages of good [science] applicants started to become

apparent. In schools the rise in the number of science students was well below the proportionate rises in other subjects' (Moore, 1987, p. 27). Over two decades later, despite heroic efforts, '. . . the sciences and engineering suffer from a growing shortfall of good undergraduate applicants so that entry levels are showing a decline in quality, and departments are failing to fill student places' (Shattock, 1987b, p. 4).

13. Yet Stuart Maclure suggests that 'an increase in bureaucracy could well turn out to be the main outcome' of current trends (Maclure, 1987, p. 28). And a consultative document on university finances and auditing being prepared by the DES 'is expected to argue that auditors of universities should have a responsibility to government as well as to clients' (*The Times Educational Supplement*, 2 October 1987).

14. And Kogan, citing Carswell, reminds us of internal divisions within the DES, for example, between '[those] believing in autonomy and [those] believing in state intervention in higher education' (Kogan, 1987a).

References

Austin, D. (1982). A memoir, *Government and Opposition*, **17**, 469–98.

Barnett, Correlli (1987). *The Audit of War: the illusion and reality of Britain as a great nation.* Basingstoke: Macmillan.

Boyer, Ernest (1983). *High School: a report on secondary education.* Princeton, NJ: The Carnegie Foundation for the Advancement of Teaching; New York: Harper & Row.

Caston, Geoffrey (1979). Planning, government, and administration in two university systems: California and the United Kingdom, *Oxford Review of Education*, **5**, 183–94.

Department of Education and Science (1987). *Higher Education: meeting the challenge*, 114. London: HMSO.

Eurich, Nell, P. (1985). *Corporate Classrooms.* Princeton, NJ: The Carnegie Foundation for the Advancement of Teaching.

Eustace, Rowland (1987). The English ideal of university governance: a missing rationale and some implications, *Studies in Higher Education*, **12**, 7–22.

Fulton, Oliver (1988). Elite survivals? entry standards and procedures for higher education admissions, *Studies in Higher Education*, **13**, 15–25.

Halsey, A. H. and Martin Trow (1971). *The British Academics.* London: Faber.

Heyck, Thomas William (1987). The idea of a university in Britain, 1870–1970, *History of European Ideas*, **8**, 205–19.

Jones, Lyle V., Gardner Lindzey and Porter E. Coggeshall (eds) (1982). *An Assessment of Research-Doctorate Programs in the United States.* Committee on an Assessment of Quality-Related Characteristics of Research–Doctorate Programs in the United States, 5 vols. Washington, DC: National Academy Press.

Kogan, Maurice (1987a). The DES and Whitehall, *Higher Education Quarterly*, **41**, 225–40.

Kogan, Maurice (1987b). Review of the Report of a Committee under the Chairmanship of Lord Croham, GCB, *Studies in Higher Education*, **12**, 349–51.

Maclure, Stuart (1987). The political culture of higher education. In Tony Becher, *British Higher Education*, pp. 10–28. London: Allen & Unwin.

The Master Plan Renewed: unity, equity, quality, and efficiency in California postsecondary education (1987). Sacramento, California: Commission for the Review of the Master Plan for Higher Education.

Metzger, Walter P. (1987). The academic profession in the United States. In Burton R.

Clark (ed.), *The Academic Profession, National Disciplinary and Institutional Settings*, pp. 123–208. Berkeley: University of California Press.

Moodie, Graeme C. (1987). Le roi est mort; vive le quoi? Croham and the death of the UGC, *Higher Education Quarterly*, **41**, 329–43.

Moore, Peter G. (1987). University financing 1979–86, *Higher Education Quarterly*, **41**, 25–41.

Perkin, Harold J. (1987). The academic profession in the United Kingdom. In Burton R. Clark (ed.), *The Academic Profession, National Disciplinary and Institutional Settings*, pp. 13–59. Berkeley: University of California Press.

Reynolds, P. A. (1986). *Academic Standards in Universities*. London: CVCP.

Robertson, Paul L. (1976). The finances of the university of Glasgow before 1914, *History of Education Quarterly*, **16**, 449–78.

Ross, Earle D. (1942). *Democracy's College*. Ames, Iowa: Iowa State College Press.

Rothblatt, Sheldon (1968). *The Revolution of the Dons*. London: Cambridge University Press.

Shattock, Michael (1987a). The last days of the UGC? *Minerva*, **25**, 471–85.

Shattock, Michael (1987b). Financial pressures: a threat to quality in the British university system, Paper prepared for the Anglo-American Conference on Access and Quality in Higher Education, Princeton, New Jersey, and reprinted in a revised form as Chapter 8 of this book.

The Times Higher Education Supplement, no. 778, 2 October 1987.

Trow, Martin (1974). Problems in the transition from elite to mass higher education. In *Policies for Higher Education*, from the General Report on the Conference of Future Structures for Post-Secondary Education, pp. 55–101. Paris: Organisation for Economic Co-operation and Development.

Trow, Martin (1983a). Reorganizing the biological sciences at Berkeley, *Change* (Washington, DC), **15**(8), 28, 44–53.

Trow, Martin (1983b). Defining the issues in university–government relations: an international perspective, *Studies in Higher Education*, **8**, 115–28.

Trow, Martin (1984). The analysis of status. In Burton R. Clark (ed.), *Perspectives In Higher Education: Eight Disciplinary and Comparative Views*, pp. 132–64. Berkeley: University of California Press.

Trow, Martin (1987a). Academic standards and mass higher education, *Higher Education Quarterly*, **41**, 268–92.

Trow, Martin (1987b). The national reports on higher education: a skeptical view, *Educational Policy*, **1**(4), 411–27.

Trow, Martin (1987c). American higher education: past, present and future. In G. W. Lapidus and G. E. Swanson (eds), *Social Welfare and the Social Service: USA/USSR*. Berkeley, California: University of California Press.

Veysey, Lawrence R. (1965). *The Emergence of the American University*. Chicago: University of Chicago Press.

Weiner, Martin J. (1981). *English Culture and the Decline of the Industrial Spirit, 1850–1980*. London: Cambridge University Press.

3

Gold, Silver, Copper:
Standards of First Degrees

Rowland B. Eustace

Standards, quality, excellence: they have always been essential to higher education. From the start, there was no point in giving public recognition to a university except to validate the *ius ubique docenti* for its graduates; if they could not make a claim to the 'right to teach anywhere' there was no university.

Comparison of any standards, and certainly of international ones, is frustrating and perhaps impossible. But by looking at the processes of two systems, rather than at the standards themselves, and by doing so from a historical and more than usually distant standpoint, it may be possible, at the risk of over-simplification, to show up patterns not otherwise often discussed.

This chapter examines, mainly from an English point of view and with the primary emphasis upon England, part of the process by which one of the standards found in higher education, that of the bachelor's degree, has been determined over a long period. This relatively narrow focus offers two advantages. First, it happens that in common parlance, in Britain at least, 'academic standards' has very generally referred to a level of achievement at the first degree. Second, it allows us largely to ignore the history of the master's degree. We should note, however, that in fact it was the master's and not the bachelor's degree which conferred the *ius ubique docenti*.

Before tackling the subject directly, however, we must examine one of the myths that sometimes fog Anglo-American comparisons, that of the antiquity of the British system. In Britain we have always had a deep respect for age and a gut-belief in the power of tradition to deliver excellence. This is not foolish: education can indeed 'seep out of walls' and more readily than out of a unit of resource. From this belief flows a tendency, rather touchingly shared by many Americans, to suppose that the British have an inbuilt advantage deriving from the mists of time, especially as to standards. But it is possible to argue that in important aspects the American system is not the more recent.

The American pedagogic tradition, to take an important initial example, has developed from the seventeenth century without suffering the atrophy which afflicted England in the eighteenth and has done so in a remarkably straight line. The aims of clerical moral humanism echo down in Bok's (1986), in

Boyer's (1987), and indeed in Bloom's (1987) calls for 'coherence', 'integrity', 'integration', 'community', 'understanding' and 'enduring values' – and they echo with a confidence denied to English traditionalists like Moberley (1949) or Oakeshott (Fuller, 1989), and even indeed to the Scots (Davie, 1961 and 1986). As another example we can cite the extent to which, as we shall see, the standard-setting mechanisms of the present British system originated in 1836, a date that falls six years later than the end of the period that Metzger allots to his 'second generation' of American foundations. The American (and Scottish) mode of degree validation by the teaching institution itself was not established in England, it might also be noted, until the twentieth century. More remarkable, if less important, is the reflection that the governance of the American system as a whole today has more in common with that of Dunster's Harvard than has modern Oxford's with its own governance under Laud. (Dunster was President of Harvard in 1636, the year in which Laud, as its Chancellor, gave Oxford its new Statutes.) And in which country are university buildings of before say 1875 (Oxbridge colleges apart) more abundant?

Thus, when we wish to compare provision at the first degree level in the light of traditions, it is more illuminating to think of our present two systems as having pretty equal claims to academic antiquity (and lesser claims to academic continuity than the Scottish, but greater than any continental European system). What is more, neither developed the criterion now essential to the idea of the university – research – until the last third of the last century. The important differences relevant here relate to the standards themselves, the mechanisms by which they are set and maintained, and the numbers to which they apply.

The history of English first degree standards has throughout the modern period been that of the 'golden sovereign': that is, of a national minimum standard perceived by contemporaries as the best possible academically, and as warranted by an impartial assayer. The history may be taken as starting at Cambridge with the introduction of the Tripos (degree structure) in 1798. That reform was based upon what Rothblatt (1987, p. 156) calls the 'Cambridge Principle': the separation of teaching (by the colleges) from the examining or assessing process (conducted by the university).

This principle gained great national importance in 1836 when the national government, in order to control an almost American-style proliferation of institutions, recommended a Charter for a new institution to King William IV. The government proposed that 'a Board of Examiners [should] perform all the functions of the Examiners in the Senate House of Cambridge . . . this body to be termed "the University of London"' (University of London, 1912, p. 8). This board was to examine students taught by the new colleges in London, to which the government denied the right to self-validation. The Chancellor of the Exchequer, in delivering this recommendation, promulgated a policy that has since marked an important difference between the British and American systems. He said 'what is sought is an *equality in all respects* with the ancient Universities' (University of London, 1912, p. 9, italics added). From this it is clear that the new degrees were intended to be of the same metal as those of the

Tripos. And the practical result of this logical extension of the Cambridge Principle (to the point where the teacher was totally excluded from validation) was to ensure that the British method of degree validation would differ from the American.

For the rest of the nineteenth century the State insisted on the Cambridge Principle, setting up examining boards in India, Ireland, Wales and Manchester and preparing to strip the Scottish universities of their long-standing degree-granting powers (though in the event the 'National University of Scotland' never came into being). In 1900, however, the 'London system' of 1836 was unexpectedly breached by a politician (Joseph Chamberlain) who arranged that his home-town college should receive a Royal Charter as the University of Birmingham. The State thereafter hesitantly let the rest of the Victorian university colleges validate their own degrees in the Scottish and American manner, as universities, but subject to certain restrictions (to which we will return) and then only over a fifty-year period. It did not, however, go so far with the great London colleges, which instead found themselves as constituent parts of a new federal University of London, founded by an Act of 1900, whose chief function has been to validate them. (Confusingly, the State at that time preserved the old 1836 Examining Board as a separate function operating in double harness within the University, catering for 'External Students'.)

State policy continued to stress comparability of standards. Its instrument, the UGC, ensured that these new universities 'had to be at least as good as London' (Flexner, 1930, p. 148). Thus the standard at the 'Redbrick' (or provincial) universities was the national gold standard of London. The same standard was selected, after the Second World War, for higher education in the Colonies – London examined at these new university colleges too (Carr-Saunders, 1961, p. 36). In the same period, but at home, the debates about the foundation of new universities at Keele in 1949 and, in the 1960s, at Sussex and elsewhere were intently fixed on methods of achieving *equivalence* with the other (indeed with the ancient) universities (Scott, 1971, pp. 317–22). Lord Ashby was thus able to say of the system that

> there is in Britain an approximate parity between degrees, and *even between their gradations* into 'Firsts' [etc.]. This adherance to an *academic gold standard* is jealously guarded. Hull [etc.] do not want their degrees to be more easily gained or to have a lower currency in the market than degrees in Cambridge or London
>
> (1964, p. 8, italics added).

Two decades later the Committee of Vice-Chancellors and Principals (CVCP) went a little further. Its *Academic Standards in Universities* is succinct on the point. 'It is of the first importance . . . that degree classifications from different institutions approach as nearly as possible to common standards' (July 1986, p. 5). Meanwhile, in 1964 the State had created a new validating body on the 1836 model in the form of the Council for National Academic Awards (CNAA) about which we will have more to say shortly.

A standard may of course remain aspirational, and a policy objective be qualified by street-wisdom. There is thus truth in Becher's reference to the claim of equivalence as a 'polite fiction' (1987, p. 144). But the pursuit of equivalence has been backed by finance: academic salaries were equalized across the system in 1948 and by the 1960s the teaching unit of resource (the notional cost of teaching a student that formed the base of government funding) had in effect been nationalized. And the fact remains that no innovation, no extension, can be mooted (or attacked) without a phrase claiming that standards will be guaranteed (or endangered). The gold standard in British higher education must today be described as a national intention and as State policy. Few other State policies have survived since 1836.

In the United States things are different. America started from a point not dissimilar from England's – from colleges each as independent as Oxbridge colleges managerially and in not so much more tenuous academic relations (sometimes formal) with the validation authorities on Isis and Cam. But with the failure of the plan for a University of Washington at about the time when the Tripos and the 1836 University of London were putting externality – the Cambridge Principle – into the English system, the American rejected a national standard on the English or continental European model, while the Supreme Court, in the Dartmouth College case, removed the possibility of government interference (on the lines of British Royal Commissions) with the private colleges which dominated the American scene until the Second World War.

Today, provision may be infinitely varied in infinitely varied contexts, and the overall intent may have a less sharp outline than in Britain, but the American first degree still has a distinctive national character. The variety of provision by no means excludes first degrees comparable to the 'gold sovereign'. The good student who wishes to extract gold may do so – the pressures put on British students on exchange schemes with good schools are sufficient evidence of that. The provision also by no means excludes a 'copper currency'. But despite this wide range, there none the less exists, in general, a standard at first degree perfectly understood by the natives that is as American as the silver dollar.

With this background in mind we may now look at some of the main mechanisms used to establish and maintain standards in the two countries. We will look, in particular, at the more important thresholds (see Chapter 6) that have to be crossed on the road to a first degree, the first of which is the formal recognition of the institution that is to grant it.

In Britain the right to grant degrees is conferred by the State, through Royal Charter (or Act of Parliament). In 1836, as we have seen, it was concerned to check what threatened to become an American-style proliferation. A hundred and thirty years later the founders of the private University of Buckingham faced an opposition to their new type of institution much as had the founders of London. In neither case was the real issue academic (that, as Buckingham later found, can be side-stepped); it was public reluctance to accept degrees not licensed by the State (Pemberton, 1979, pp. 67–8 and 73). Most recently, the State has agonized about the status of the polytechnics (Eustace, 1987a, p. 9), coming down at the last with an almost inexplicable formula by which they are franchised to grant the degrees of a non-university (the CNAA).

In the United States, by contrast, there is no single threshold for institutions of higher education, but rather a series of them, all much lower than in Britain. England's polytechnics, in America, would long since have been authorized by individual states, or even municipalities. It is almost, to paraphrase Ezra Cornell, a matter of 'any person . . . any college'.

The next thresholds are those faced by prospective students, of which the first are the minimum requirements for entry. In America, the normal minimum is represented by graduation from (in English: 'successful completion of') high school. In England it is the passage of a State-ordered test, until very recently almost wholly an externally set and marked examination (the 'GCE A – for Advanced – level'). This has been, to all intents, set on a national basis, and by the universities. It is now being modified, and other routes to entry widened, but this national test has still set the basic level on which first degree courses can be built. The secondary school that hopes to present candidates must therefore meet what are in effect higher education's terms. No American Accrediting Agency has that power, even within its own area, and the high schools are more in control of their own graduation. They 'are not to be a handmaiden of higher education'; it is the university which must adapt (Clark, 1987, p. 7).

In England no student, however qualified in terms of the entry threshold, has a right of entry in the continental European or American state college style. Every institution operates a *numerus clausus*; and the severity of this has been determined physically and financially by State action. Academics, honourably enough, are anxious to raise the level at which they need begin to teach. As it was succinctly put by the vice-chancellor of a small university: 'we like working with good students, and we intend to keep it that way' (Saul, 1988). ('Good' in such contexts means, in practice, 'academically advanced before entry'.)

There have been two ways in which this has been brought about, one of which can be traced far back. It affected both the length and content of the English degree course. In 1900 the standard of entry to English universities was the 'London Matriculation' (or local equivalent). It admitted to the 'Intermediate', a two-year ('freshman and sophomore') course. That course was followed by a two-year ('junior and senior') degree course leading to the Final Examination. The new 'sixth forms' in the secondary schools set up by the State after the major Education Act of 1902 gradually, however, delivered entrants who already held exemption from the Intermediate. There thus ensued a period when a degree could be won (but not obtained) in two years (being followed by a fallow 'suspense year' before graduation). The dilemma was resolved by formally adding a year to the English degree curriculum, with the effect that where the university course had, in England, America and Scotland been of four years, in England it became of three years. This new course, however, started from a point at least a year beyond normal 'high school graduation'. From this 'shortening' of the degree course stems much of the English system's claim to economy of operation.

We are not talking only of the distant past. Robbins faced down calls for yet further lengthening of the degree course by asserting, most significantly for us, that such lengthening 'must have low priority in relation to the general claims of expansion' (*Report*, 1963, §282). Had Robbins not preferred access to standards no doubt the then Conservative government, urged on by *The Times*, would have added a four-year course to the present definition of gold. The last Chairman of the UGC dealt more cuttingly than Robbins with the latest calls for further lengthening by State manipulation: he encapsulated much of the argument of this chapter by saying of the calls that 'they assume that the level of knowledge you should achieve for your BA is a standard established by God' (Swinnerton-Dyer, 1988, p. 39). Except that it is the State.

But it is the second form of levering up the point of entry that has been more perceptible to the public. As well as raising the basic qualification, the price of entry in terms of the grade-point score achieved in the A-level examinations has also been raised. This price has come to be charged on a directly market basis (marginally modified by the claim of some universities that some other factors are taken into account) as a rationing device for entry to the most sought-after institutions and courses which have operated most of the time in a sellers' market.

Already, by the time of the Robbins Committee demand had driven up entry standards to a height that the Committee found to be both unnecessary and deplorable in its effects on the secondary schools, such as the premature specialization carried to such lengths in England (*Report*, 1963, §196ff.) Even the greatest and most academic of the public (i.e. private) schools had been forced to adjust drastically, while the state schools that did not do so often made little attempt to offer candidates for higher education, with important effects on popular access. Expansion of higher education provided no lasting alleviation and the results spilled wide; in 1987 we find that even the vice-chancellors regarded the normal A-level course as 'unacceptably narrow' and, because of 'inflation of syllabus content', 'unacceptably demanding'. They go on, moreover, to praise 'the experience of our European *and American* competitors' (CVCP, 1988a, p. 2, italics added).

The A-level 'price', having begun as a rationing device, has now been given a new function, and one that well illustrates how non-academic forces enter into the equation. The price charged for entry has been adopted by the State's grant-giving bodies as an indicator not of student, but of institutional performance. When Aston University's government grant was hard hit in 1981, the University raised its entry price in order to lay a claim to lost grant (Walford, 1987, fig. 4.51). Today, the price has become a formal indicator of grant-worthiness for all universities. Thus what started as a defence of academic standards has become, in effect, a safeguard of academic income.

In the United States too, of course, there is a correlation between income and the test-scores of students entering particular institutions; but it is less pervasive. It probably has too little, rather than too much, effect on the mass of high schools whose offerings can be, in Clark's term, 'pathetic'. But there is still no question either of the test-scores being used as performance indicators by grant-giving bodies or of their being the simple consequence of institutional aspirations in a quasi-monopolistic market. And there remains the basic difference that in the United States there does not exist either so single a national market or so uniform a national entry standard.

Let us return, however, to the main theme and consider the next threshold: that of the mechanisms for validating the degree. In Britain, as we have already implied, there are two modes: institutional self-validation and validation by an outside examining board. The second of these, stemming from the Cambridge Principle and the 1836 London degree, covers over half of all British degrees. London, in its 1836 guise, still awards degrees to external students from anywhere and, as the federal University of London, still awards degrees to the internal students taught by its constituent colleges and institutes as does the non-teaching University of Wales to students of its five colleges. Oxbridge, of course, retains much of the Cambridge Principle. But the majority of degrees validated in this mode have another fount: the CNAA. An offspring of the Robbins Report, it is a radical invention to the extent that a council, and not a university, was given a Royal Charter to award degrees; but essentially it is a vigorous extension of the Cambridge Principle and a means of furthering the 1836 objective while permitting a vast extension of the academic gold standard beyond the university sector of higher education. Its commitment to the gold standard is made explicit in its 1964 Charter. It must award degrees 'comparable in standards to awards granted and conferred by Universities' (later changed to 'other institutions of higher education') (Statute 8(5)(a)). This it has done largely by itself appointing the examiners who audit the results. By the 1988 Education Act the polytechnics were given greater autonomy, and even before then the stronger of them were given greater leeway by CNAA, but even so they still must use the CNAA's mint-mark for their degrees. About the long-term future of the CNAA, with its reduced role, there seems to be some question, but whatever now happens it will be many years before English higher education can be understood without understanding the Cambridge Principle.

The other mode, that of validation by the teaching institution, even if first introduced into English higher education only in 1900, has come to be regarded by British academics as the norm – indeed as the natural method. It is at first sight also the method prevalent in America; but there are important differences. In America, scholars are generally perceived as being little trusted to manage their own institutions; certainly this is so by contrast with their British colleagues (Eustace, 1987a). The American scholar, distrusted in the counting-house, has none the less been remarkably trusted in the classroom. The institution has of course powers over the curriculum, but the mechanisms for monitoring adherence is not found a major constraint in class. The scholar is assumed to be able, personally and directly, to validate what he or she reckons to have taught – and that is not the case in Britain. When Alison Lurie's character Chuck asks his colleagues the question that the CNAA is there to answer, he is met with blank incomprehension. He asks 'how can we really know what some kid has learned on our course?' and his colleagues' faces 'harden at these words. They silently give Chuck's speech a B-minus' (1974, p. 142).

In Britain it is radically otherwise. The validation is, first, *collective*. The key

element in this collectivity is the Board of Examiners. Its roots go back to the
Tripos and the 1836 London board, even although most of the members today
will be the teachers in the relevant subject(s) within the institution. Most, but
not all of the members, however: for the second distinguishing feature of
university validation is that it too relies on *externality*. Each Board of Examiners
must include at least one External Examiner and no degree is awarded without
the agreement of the External Examiners. In sharp contrast to the American
system, no British teaching institution when granting first degrees is allowed to
trust its own teachers alone. This externality is regarded by the State as
fundamental. It appeared in the 1900 Charter of the path-breaking University
of Birmingham (Statute 18:1). It is retained in the Privy Council's 'Model
Charter' of 1963 (Clause 3(B)), issued as a guide to all British universities. The
State has never been happy without it, whether we look at 1834 or 1990. Many
Americans find the system so strange that they have difficulty distinguishing
between 'external examin-*er*' and 'external examin-*ation*'. It is remarkable that
no American critic of the American first degree ever contemplates any invasion
of the classroom. Not even Gardner does so when noting that 'American higher
education has striven to . . . maintain respectable academic standards . . .
sometimes succeeding and sometimes not' (1988, p. 231). Why do Americans
concerned either about the lack of 'coherence' or about standards not consider
the relevance of external mechanisms?

Government concern for standards throughout higher education, reinforced
by the polytechnics' pressures for equal treatment and status, has put the
universities' modes of validation on the defensive. External examiners (who are
commonly academics from other institutions within the system) have been seen
as too well socialized to be much use in policing what British politicians believe
are standards. In an attempt to combat government scepticism the CVCP had
already set up a committee on standards; one of its first Codes of Practice
(1987b) related to the role and use of external examiners. Under continuing
government pressure the CVCP in 1988 set up a continuing Academic
Standards Unit. It is unlikely to reintroduce the Cambridge Principle but its
mere appearance testifies to the pervasive persistence of State distrust of tertiary
teachers.

This entire apparatus for the control and monitoring of first degree standards
is, in England, designed to produce gold. Of course there is silver, and even
copper, to be found. But since copper is unintended it is regarded, reasonably
enough, as improper – as the product of mean funding, or of poor organization,
or of incompetence and idleness. Americans agonize a bit about copper and the
literature abounds with breast-beating and unadopted prescriptions. But there
can also be, and conspicuously is, great pride in the production of copper when
copper is what is intended. It thus acquires the status of specie: it ministers
to excellence of provision for the population, it enlists commitment and
enthusiasm, and it generates the first ingredient of good education – respect. It
is Fit for Purpose.

This comparison of the processes and mechanisms which establish and
maintain standards at the bachelor's level in Britain and the United States

suggests two broad generalizations: American concern is primarily about delivery, British about control; and, where there is control of standards in America it is more academic, but in Britain it is more entwined with the civil power. To adapt the old saw that purported to describe the difference between the British and Imperial German exercise of authority, it is the American signs that start 'Please' and the British that end '*streng verboten!*'.

No comparative discussion of these two countries' first degrees can end, however, without a brief look at two vital contextual characteristics: numbers and graduate education.

It is a commonplace in the comparative literature that America, but not Britain, has a 'mass' system of higher education. In numerical terms this is often expressed as the contrast between 12 million American students and 15 per cent of the British age-group. But this can be misleading. Hansen and Stampen convert the 12 million to just under 9 million full-time equivalents, which they express as 43 per cent of the 18–24 age-group (1987, table 11; and see Chapter 4 below). Of these the great majority are on four-year courses. Since the comparison is with the British three-year degree, the freshman year may reasonably be set aside: except to note that since the retention rate is at its lowest in that year (Tinto, 1987, p. 21) that first year accounts for more than a quarter of the undergraduate enrolment. Nevertheless, even if we add on to the British figure adults, foreigners, and much of what the British describe as non-degree work, it remains reasonable to say that a higher proportion of the American population enjoy something of Boyer's *Undergraduate Experience in America* (1987) than enjoy the British offering. It is also clear that this is likely to remain so, whatever party is in power in Britain.

The picture changes, however, if we reintroduce the distinction between gold and silver. The British 15 per cent is made up of persons on course for gold, and nearly all taught by institutions which expect to prepare for the doctorate. We have seen that some American students achieve gold. Without attempting any close comparison, it is possible to suggest an upper limit to the proportion who might do so. If we take the Carnegie *Classification of Institutions of Higher Education* (1987), and if we can accept as approximate the equivalence of its 'Research Universities I and II', 'Doctorate-granting Universities I and II', and 'Liberal Arts Colleges I and II' with the range of institutions covered by British higher education (see Chapter 1, above), then we can be reasonably sure that the enrolment in these groups represents the upper limit of Americans likely to achieve gold (for, as we have seen, the majority of undergraduates at most American schools aims for silver). Between them, these Carnegie groups enrol 4 million students, a third of the total 12 million. This figure includes graduates and freshmen, suggesting an undergraduate enrolment comparable to the British of under 3 million. The British expect to enrol a million students in higher education in 1990, of whom perhaps 750,000 are on gold degree courses. If the population of the USA is 4.3 times that of Britain, then the British enrolment may be proportionately more than that of the top six Carnegie groups, the equivalent of over 3 million.

Further direct comparison would probably be unrealistic, but it must be remembered that the American figures used refer to the maximum numbers taking gold; in fact, even at the institutions included here most students are probably aiming at silver, and it may be that no more than one-third aim at gold. If so, then it might be as little as 5 per cent of American youth that is provided with the sort of expensive bachelor's education that the British have come to regard as academically minimal and that they seek to provide – with some success – for 15 per cent of British youth.

In comparing their first degrees with American ones, British academics and politicians have long felt that the balance of standards and numbers was much as we have just argued it is. They have tended to conclude that they have therefore little to learn from the comparison unless it be that 'more means worse', and that there is no benefit to be gained from imitation. Leaving aside the many arguments that can be adduced in favour of different standards, of lessening the pressures on the secondary schools towards absurdly premature specialization, or merely of social equity, this typical British conclusion is another reflection of British preoccupation with the first degree. That pre-occupation is deep-rooted. The current history of Oxford University remarks of the eighteenth century: 'at this point . . . one of the most serious weaknesses of the educational system appeared . . . Colleges placed all their undergraduates under tutors [but] no such arrangements were made for bachelors' (Greaves, 1986, p. 405). Efforts to prepare for the *ius ubique docenti* were 'feeble' and 'ineffective' and indeed remained so throughout the nineteenth century. Even today there is a deep corporate reluctance to enter on the heart of learning that must owe much to the pastoralist and cultural concerns associated with Newman's Idea of the University (as distinct from his 'Academy'). A few instances will illustrate it. In 1882, a former Provost of King's College, Cambridge, accused that university of having since the Second World War 'neglected and disgracefully short-changed' graduate students (Annan, 1982, p. 16). Major reports of that year expressed similar sentiments, but three years later the government's Green Paper complained of the slow pace of reform (DES, 1985b, §5:18). These and other indicators led the present writer to surmise that a proportion of our scholars must be 'functionally illiterate and can hardly be better than incompetent' (Eustace, 1988, pp. 81–4). By 1989 Annan's old university had lost its national accreditation for important postgraduate awards (those of the Economic and Social Research Council). Not surprisingly, therefore, appraisal of the American system does not always take sufficient account of American master's and doctor's degrees. It is in the American graduate school that gold abounds, it is there that people achieve the highest levels of academic work. The value added at graduate level is in general much greater in America than in Britain. But the production of gold at this stage imposes a much lesser burden on the population at large. Perhaps it is not necessary, in order to achieve scholarly eminence, to provide as large and expensive a 'golden' undergraduate base as the British have chosen.

At the end of this survey a number of reflections and questions may be articulated. The first reflection is upon the role of the British State in influenc-ing, even when it does not actually determine, crucial aspects of the standards

ruling first degrees, among them: the recognition of institutions, entry requirements, academic salaries, the length of course, the knowledge to be acquired
and the proof thereof. The gold standard has been almost as much an
administrative policy as an academic principle. Even so, there has never been
much discussion of the purposes behind the policies. One result has been, in
contrast to the United States, to push the ancient degree downwards into the
schools. The contrast between the two countries is at its sharpest, however, in
terms of the effort devoted to the mechanisms used to achieve 'academic'
(meaning 'undergraduate') standards. The curious aspect is that the street-wise
in either country – British politicians apart – worry little about all the
mechanisms. To the citizen of either country the value of a first degree is almost
wholly calculable in terms of the 'halo effect' from the institution granting it.
Even more curious is that the alarm about the deep-rooted British aversion from
educating graduates touched on above has not excited the politicians at all –
instead, they have reduced funding for it. Perhaps they have been led by the
international success of British scholars to think that libraries, laboratories and
research training can easily be run down; or perhaps they simply do not see that
academic standards are the standards of academics.

The key question for Britain is 'at what points should resources be concentrated if standards are to be protected?' To answer that involves raising further
questions related to: whether governmental obsession with objective guarantees
for standards delivers educational value commensurate with the effort involved;
whether an academic system that was suitable for 3 or less per cent of the
age-group is likely to be suitable for 20 or more per cent; whether, and to what
end, the gold standard can be stretched much further; and whether there really
is so little to learn from abroad.

The comparison between Britain and America, and especially the gap
between the mechanisms used by the two systems – especially the difference in
elaboration – and between their allocation of resources suggests a more
immediate question: 'in what way and through what mechanisms does emphasis on the first degree achieve higher academic standards than emphasis on
other academic objectives, such as degrees conferring the *ius ubique docenti*?' This
question could be phrased differently, as: 'would bachelors be less well educated
if taught less by better scholars?' To this one might add: 'what advantages are
there in achieving a lower level of value-added at graduate level than do the
Americans?'

Perhaps the reflection of greatest importance for British politicians and
academics alike, as they appraise the British system, is that the thresholds are as
much constructs of social as of academic policy. They are, in much part, images
of prestige and outcomes of markets. Much of the territory defended by
academics in speeches and letters today was thus delimited, over a long period
of social development, by non-academics and for non-academic reasons. The
gold standard, after all, was never engraved on tablets of stone.

References

Books and papers

Annan, Noel, (Lord) (1982). A personal retrospect, *Minerva*, **XX**, 2–24.

Ashby, Eric, (Lord), (1964). *African Universities and Western Tradition*. Cambridge, Mass.: Harvard University Press.

Ball, Christopher J. (1985). *Fitness for Purpose*. Windsor: SRHE.

Barnett, Ronald (1988). The maintenace of quality in the public sector of UK higher education, *Higher Education*, **16**, 279–301.

Becher, R. A. (ed.) (1987). *British Higher Education*. London: Allen & Unwin.

Bloom, Allan (1987). *The Closing of the American Mind*. London: Simon & Schuster, and (1988) London: Penguin.

Bok, Derek (1986). *Higher Learning*. Cambridge, Mass.: Harvard University Press.

Boyer, Ernest L. (1987). *College, The Undergraduate Experience in America*, New York: Harper & Row.

Carr-Saunders, Sir Alexander (1961). *New Universities Overseas*. London: Allen & Unwin.

Church, Clive (1988). The qualities of validation, *Studies in Higher Education*, **13**(1), 27–43.

Clark, Burton R. (1987). *The Academic Profession*. University of California.

Cobban, Alan B. (1988). *The Medieval English Universities*. Scolar Press.

Corbett, J. P. (1964). Opening the mind. In Daiches, David (Ed.), *The Idea of a New University*. London: Deutsch.

Davié, George (1961). *The Democratic Intellect*. Edinburgh: University Press.

Davie, George (1986). *The Crisis of the Democratic Intellect*. Edinburgh: Polygon.

Dundonald, James (pseud.) (1962). *Letters to a Vice-Chancellor*. London: Arnold.

Eggins, Heather (ed.) (1988). *Restructuring Higher Education*. Milton Keynes: SRHE and Open University Press.

Engel, A. J. (1983). *From Clergyman to Don*. Oxford: Oxford University Press.

Eustace, Rowland, (1987a) The English ideal of university governance: a missing rationale and some implications, *Studies in Higher Education*, **12**(1).

Eustace, Rowland (1987b) The audit of teaching: a British historical accident? Center for Studies in Higher Education, Occasional Paper No 57, Berkeley: University of California.

Eustace, Rowland (1988). The criteria of staff selection, *Studies in Higher Education*, **13**(1), 88

Flexner, Abraham (1930). *Universities American, English, German*. New York.

Fuller, Timothy (ed.) (1989). *The Voice of Liberal Learning: Michael Oakeshott on Education*. London: Yale University Press.

Gardner, David P. (1988). Issues confronting American higher education, *Higher Education Quarterly*, **42**(3), pp. 230–7.

Greaves, Robert (1986) Religion in the university. In Sutherland and Mitchell (1986).

Hansen, W. Lee and Stampen, Jacob O. (1987). *Balancing quality and access* (Paper given to Anglo-US seminar, Princeton, September 1987).

Lurie, Alison (1974). *The War between the Tates*. London: Heineman.

Metzger, Walter P. (1987). The academic Profession in America. In Clark (1987).

Moberley, Sir Walter (1949). *The Crisis in the University*. London: SCM Press.

Moodie, Graeme C. (ed.) (1986). *Standards and Criteria in Higher Education*. Windsor: SRHE.

Mountford, Sir James (1972). *Keele*. London: Routledge & Kegan Paul.

Oldham, Geoffrey (ed.) (1982). *The Future of Research*. Guildford: SRHE.

Pemberton, J. and Pemberton, J. (1979). *The University College at Buckingham.* Buckingham: Buckingham Press.
Perkin, Harold J. (1987). The academic profession in the United Kingdom. In Clark (1987).
Richmond, Sir Mark (1988). Speech to Nuffield Conference; Inner Temple. CVCP.
Rothblatt, Sheldon (1987). Historical and comparative remarks on the federal principle in Higher Education, *History of Education,* **16**(3), 151–80.
Rudd, Ernest (1985). *A New look at Postgraduate Failure.* Guildford: SRHE.
Saul, Berrick (1988). Struck by market forces, Guardian, 4 October, p. 25.
Scott, Drusilla (1971). *A. D. Lindsay: a biography.* Oxford: Basil Blackwell.
Shils, Edward *et al.* (1982). The academic ethic. *Minerva,* **20**, 105–208.
Simpson, Renate (1983). *How the PhD Came to Britain.* Guildford: SRHE.
Squires, Geoffrey (1987). The curriculum. In Becher (1987).
Sutherland, Dame Lucy and Mitchell, L. G. (1986). *History of the University of Oxford Vol. V The Eighteenth Century.* Oxford: Oxford University Press.
Swinnerton-Dyer, Sir Peter (1988). Keynote speech in Eggins (1988).
Symonds, Richard (1986). *Oxford and Empire.* Oxford: Oxford University Press.
Tinto, Vincent (1987). *Leaving College.* Chicago: University of Chicago Press.
Trow, Martin (1988). Comparative perspectives on higher education policy in the UK and the US, *Oxford Review of Education,* **14**(1), 81–96; and Chapter 2 of this book.
University of London (1912). *The Historical Record, 1836–1912.* London: University of London Press.
Walford, Geoffrey (1987). *Restructuring Universities: politics and power in the management of change.* London: Croom Helm.
Warnock, Mary (1988). *A Common Policy for Education.* Oxford: Oxford University Press.
Williams, Gareth *et al.* (1974). *The Academic Labour Market.* Amsterdam: Elsevier.
Williams Gareth and Blackstone, Tessa (1983). *Response to Adversity.* Guildford: SRHE.

Documents

Carnegie Foundation for the Advancement of Teaching (1987). *A Classification of Institutions of Higher Education,* 1987 Edition. Princeton, NJ: Princeton University Press.
Committee of Vice-Chancellors and Principals (CVCP) (1987a). *Summary of Joint Submission from the CVCP and the Secondary Schools Heads to the Higginson Committee, 29/1/87.*
Committee of Vice-Chancellors and Principals (CVCP) (1987b). *Code of Practice* (Foreword by Prof. Philip Reynolds).
Committee on Higher Education (1963). *Report* ('Robbins Report'), London: HMSO, Cmnd 2154.
Council for National Academic Awards (CNAA), (1964; amended 1986). *Charter.*
Department of Education and Science (DES) (1985a) *Academic Validation in Public Sector Higher Education* ('Lindop Report'). HMSO, Cmnd 9501.
Department of Education and Science (DES) (1985b) *Development of Higher Education into the 1990s* (Green Paper'). HMSO, Cmnd 9524.
Enquiry into the Social Science Research Council, *Report* (1982) ['Rothschild Report']. HMSO, Cmnd 8554.
Joint ABRC/UGC Working Party on support of University Scientific Research, *Report* (1982) ['Merrison Report'], HMSO, Cmnd 8567.
Working Party on Postgraduate Education, *Report* (1982) ['Swinnerton-Dyer Report']. HMSO, Cmnd 8537.

4

Quality, Access and Financial Pressures on Higher Education Institutions and Students

W. Lee Hansen and Jacob O. Stampen

Introduction

This chapter attempts to illuminate recent discussions about the increased financial pressures experienced by students, their parents, and colleges and universities in paying for the costs of higher education in the United States.[1] It does this by placing these developments in the context of long-run pendulum-like swings in society's interest in promoting greater access to and enhancing the quality of higher education. These swings are made apparent by a new approach to organizing and analysing the data on higher education finance.[2] The conclusion that emerges is that, after a long period that emphasized equity and access, the emphasis has shifted to improving quality. This emphasis on quality is accompanied, however, by an intense struggle over how the costs of quality improvements are to be shared among students, their parents, state and local taxpayers, voluntary contributors, and in the case of student financial aid, the federal government.

We start with the assumption that goal setting in higher education is influenced by a wide variety of internal and external forces. That is, goals do not emerge exclusively or even principally from internal analysis and deliberation. Rather they grow out of external forces and events. This pattern is reflected in the common practice among educators of moving toward new goals and pushing for increased levels of funding in the wake of external political events (e.g. increased institutional support after Sputnik and new student financial aid programmes after the beginning of the War on Poverty). These developments are followed by some new event that sets off a reaction in another direction. And so the process repeats itself.

Precedent for this view emerges from the research of historians as well as other scholars who have tried to capture these alternating patterns of change, using terms such as tensions, cycles, pendulums, spirals and dialectics.[3] Observers generally agree about the nature and identity of these cycles whose lifespans average between twelve and seventeen years.[4] They also agree that political cycles alternate between emphasizing public action and private interest, described by Hirschman as the 'frustrations of public life', and by others as 'liberal versus conservative' traditions. Whatever the term, the meaning is generally the same. The most active exponent of the cycles view is Arthur M. Schlesinger Jr who notes that each cycle 'must flow out of the conditions and contradictions of the phase before and then itself prepare the way for the next recurrence'.[5]

Schlesinger's analysis provides a useful framework for sharpening our research questions in analysing recent changes in higher education goals and financing. The principal questions that guide this analysis are:

1. Have the goals of higher education and levels of investment in it changed over the past forty years? What were the key turning points during this period?
2. Do the turning points in higher education reflect cyclical mandates for change in higher education? If so, what were these mandates?
3. Did changes in the goals of higher education affect the level of investment in instructional programmes, the sharing of costs between students and society, and the ability of students and their families to finance college attendance? How did these effects show themselves?
4. Can these cycles and patterns in the financing of higher education help us assess past progress and better understand issues affecting the future of higher education?

The data available for identifying finance-related changes are not ideal. Routinely gathered federal statistics are not highly detailed, and the definitions of key variables change over time, thereby making it difficult to document consistently both the financial trends and the changes they produce. Thus, the variables selected for observation are necessarily broad and, of course, reflect to a considerable degree our own judgements. None the less, the general patterns that emerge offer explanations of changes in higher education that are directly pertinent to the current policy debate on quality and access in higher education.

Cross-currents in higher education

American higher education has been buffeted by numerous forces over the past half-century. Perhaps the most dramatic force was demographic. With the depression of the 1930s college enrolments grew more slowly than they had in the past, and with the beginning of World War II they plummeted dramatically. This was followed by an enrolment surge after World War II resulting from the GI Bill; some observers viewed this surge as 'making up' for the slower enrolment growth of the 1930s and early 1940s.[6] After the bulge of veterans enrolment levels remained relatively stable until the late 1950s. After a gradual increase into the early 1960s, an explosion of enrolments occurred by the mid-1960s as the post-World War II 'baby-boom' population reached maturity. Enrolments rose even more as efforts were made to increase the enrolment of previously under-represented ethnic minorities and also women. Enrolment growth slowed considerably in the 1970s and has remained relatively unchanged since then. Since the mid-1970s college participation rates declined for most minority groups and also for males generally; meanwhile, significant gains occurred for females.

Political forces also exerted a powerful influence on the growth of higher education. These forces are revealed most immediately in governmental actions; ultimately, however, these actions reflect an even more powerful force, namely, the changing priorities of the citizenry who determine the focus of political action and the availability of resources for higher education. For example, the rhetoric of having to compete with the Soviets after Sputnik and of broadening access to minorities in the late 1960s and early 1970s proved effective in galvanizing public opinion and increasing the allocation of resources to higher education. The impact of student unrest in the early 1970s had an opposite effect. It remains unclear, however, whether higher education can be an effective instrument for enhancing our international competitive situations and actually produce some shift in resource allocation.

Another factor is higher education's effort to chart its own course, as reflected by numerous recent reports that articulate the goals and aspirations of academic institutions. Closely related are the efforts of economists, historians and other social scientists periodically to offer ideas that stir the air and stimulate thinking about the course of higher education.

Periods of analysis

To facilitate this analysis we define four distinct periods. The first from 1947–8 to 1957–8 represents a period of readjustment following World War II and the playing out of the GI Bill's effect. The second from 1957–8 to 1967–8 captures the enormous expansion of higher education and the emphasis on that elusive dimension of quality, spurred by concern that American technology was falling behind the Soviet and resting on widely publicized studies establishing the link between investment in education and economic growth.

The third period from 1967–8 to 1980–81 reflects the search for ways to expand opportunities for students to attend college. It began with initiation of federal student aid programmes in 1965 and culminated with the federal decision in 1972 to establish a national need-based student aid system, called Basic Educational Opportunity Grants (BEOG) and later renamed Pell Grants. The fourth period from 1980–81 onward reflects a sharp swing in the opposite direction, with concerns about the quality of instruction, the efficient use of resources, and economic growth rising to the forefront once again.

These periods and their alternating swings between quality and equity (or access) closely correspond with the pendulum-like political cycles mentioned earlier. When society promotes public action on equity issues, higher education is asked to expand access; when it promotes private interests, higher education is mandated to improve quality.[7]

Analytical framework

Having established the time periods for this analysis, we go on to describe the changing dimensions of the nation's investment in higher education institutions. We then examine the higher education expenditures data to highlight major trends and reveal the interplay between the external and internal forces affecting resource allocation within higher education. This information opens the way for measuring the burden of higher education costs and describing how these costs are shared among students/parents, state and local taxpayers/private donors, and also federal taxpayers through federal student financial aid programmes.

We rely largely on official data from the Department of Education and its predecessor, the US office of Education. Because of changes in the data collection systems as well as periodic alterations in the definitions of expenditures and revenues, the detailed data are not completely comparable over the 40-year period under study. None the less, the broad categories employed here are generally consistent. The analysis begins with 1947–8 because data from 1946–7 are incomplete.[8]

Enrolment growth

Enrolment growth is described by two different sets of data. One is total head count enrolment, for which the data are readily available. The other is full-time

Table 4.1 Enrolment in higher education institutions

Year	Total head count enrolled (000)	Total FTE count enrolled (000)	Percentage civilian non-institutional population age 16+		Current fund exp. as % GNP	Instr.-related exp. as % of GNP
			Head count	FTE count		
	(1)	*(2)*	*(3)*	*(4)*	*(5)*	*(6)*
1947–48	2616	2222	2.6	2.2	0.8	0.5
1957–58	3068	2395	2.7	2.1	1.0	0.6
1967–68	6912	4591	5.3	3.5	2.0	1.3
1972–73	9298	6973	6.5	4.8	2.3	1.5
1980–81	12097	8819	7.2	5.3	2.3	1.5
1985–86	12247	8943	6.9	5.0	2.4	1.5

Source: Derived from Hansen and Stampen (1987) and updated to 1985–6.

equivalent (FTE) enrolment which often must be estimated. Both of these series are shown in Table 4.1 (columns 1 and 2).

Total enrolment edged up only slightly from the late 1940s (to 2.6 million) to the late 1950s (to 3.0 million), almost doubled by the late 1960s (to 6.9 million), almost doubled again by 1980–81 (to 12.0 million), and then edged upward only slightly in the early 1980s (to 12.2 million). The enrolment increases in the 1980s are at odds with many projections from the 1970s that anticipated decreased enrolment by the early 1980s because of declining numbers of high school graduates.

An appreciation of the implications of enrolment growth is provided by data on total enrolments as a percentage of the adult population. The total percentage enrolled from the civilian non-institutional population aged 16 and above increased from 2.7% in 1947–8 to 6.9% in 1985–6. In short, a substantial expansion in demand for higher education occurred, but its uneven rate of growth was heavily influenced by demographic forces.[9]

Total resources for higher education

Providing for the ever-growing numbers of students required raising substantial amounts of new revenue from taxpayers, private donors, students, supporters of research, and others who purchase services from higher education institutions. Current revenues and expenditures grew rapidly and at identical average annual rates from 9 to 14%.[10] This pattern of growth is not surprising because the level of expenditures is conditioned by the amount of revenues available. As Howard R. Bowen[11] explains, higher education institutions are essentially non-profit organizations which must live within their available resources. However, in contrast with most European nations, governmental authority is decentralized and custom permits colleges independently to advocate increases in public investment the better to serve their students and society.

Higher education revenues

More interesting for our purposes is the relationship between higher education's revenue growth and the economy's capacity to support higher education. As shown in column 5 of Table 4.1, total current fund revenues averaged about 1% of GNP in the 1940s and 1950s, rose to slightly over 2% in the late 1960s and into the early 1970s, and then stabilized at about 2½% of GNP in the 1980s.[12] These results demonstrate the close connection between enrolment levels and the proportion of the nation's total resources allocated to support higher education. This connection exists in considerable part because funding formulas in the public sector give considerable weight to enrolments. The revenue component of particular interest here is tuition and fee payments by students. These payments represent an important component of student costs, in fact, the only one captured in the institutional revenue data.

Higher education expenditures

The increase in total current-fund expenditures parallels that of revenues inasmuch as higher education institutions typically cannot operate for any length of time with deficits. In any case, the overall expenditure data are not particularly helpful in understanding the impact of changes on the quality of higher education. The reason is that total expenditures include funds allocated to carry out many other activities not central to the instruction-related activities of colleges and universities; among these activities are public service, research and auxiliary enterprises.

How do we construct estimates of instruction-related expenditures? Several categories of expenditures need to be excluded from total current-fund expenditures to arrive at instruction-related expenditures. The first category includes self-financed activities, such as hospitals, dormitories and related activities. A second category includes research expenditures, which are heavily financed by outside sources, and also public service expenditures. Research expenditures prove to be a substantial component of total expenditures and grew rapidly in the 1950s and 1960s; since then their growth has slowed appreciably. While research is an integral element in the mission of universities and many colleges, it is not directly related to instruction, especially at the undergraduate level, and hence it is excluded.

A third category, institution-awarded student financial aid expenditures, is also not central to the instructional activity of institutions even though it may be highly important in promoting access. By way of illustration, student financial aid expenditures from institutional sources may affect not only the mix of students at individual institutions but also overall enrolment levels; this does not imply that such expenditures are in any way related to instruction.

If these three categories of expenditures are excluded, we arrive at something that can be identified as instruction-related costs. These costs represent approximately sixty per cent of total current fund expenditures. If some part of research activities were viewed as an essential component of instruction, the percentage figures would be higher, of course.

Student aid

As noted above, a small portion of student aid is provided directly by higher education institutions in the from of what are called 'scholarships and fellowships'. This leaves out student aid provided under various federal programmes, such as Pell Grants and Guaranteed Student Loans. The remaining student aid funds – those provided through federal programmes – do not flow to institutions but are distributed directly to students through federal and stage grant and loan programmes. To capture fully the impact of student financial aid, we must also take into account federal student aid funds. This financial aid, as well as that provided by institutions, is allocated primarily on the basis of student financial need; hence, not all students receive student financial aid.

Instruction-related costs, tuition and fees, and student aid

Having now assembled the data, we explore the relationship between the costs of instruction, the charges students pay in the form of tuition and fees, and the amounts of financial aid students receive.

For our purposes here instruction-related costs are viewed as an indicator of efforts to promote quality. Tuition and fees less student financial aid funds are viewed as indicators of efforts to improve access. We recognize that these magnitudes are at best crude proxies for what we want to measure. Rather than total student aid, we would prefer to focus on the portion of aid that enables young people from lower income families to attend and persist in higher education; in the absence of such aid, they would not be able to attend or persist. And similarly, rather than all instruction-related expenditures, we would prefer to focus on the portion of those expenditures that 'make a difference' in quality (i.e. that which produces greater and more lasting increments of student learning).

Even more important is how changes in these categories of expenditure affect quality and access. Spending more or less would change the dollar totals, but whether, for example, additional expenditures would enhance quality or improve access is more difficult to say. None the less, we shall for purposes of this analysis take the dollar totals and changes in these totals as crude indicators of the relative priority given to quality and access in higher education.

Sharing the costs of higher education

The institutional costs of higher education as well as the costs of student financial aid are shared by students (and their parents) through the tuition and fees they pay, by those who provide the underlying support to higher education institutions which comes through taxes and voluntary contributions, and by federal taxpayers who fund student financial aid programmes. The student share reflected by tuition payments can be described as the *gross student share* because it is not offset by student financial aid. When these offsets – institution-awarded student financial aid (which we describe as the student share net of institution-awarded aid) and federal student financial aid – are subtracted from tuition and fees, we have the *net student share*. This net student share reflects the impact of society's commitment to offset the costs of instruction through what are commonly described as 'tuition subsidies' (the non-student share) plus student financial aid.

How are instruction-related costs shared between students through their tuition and fee payments (their gross share) and non-students, namely state and local taxpayers as well as those who make voluntary contributions to institutions of higher education. As shown in Table 4.2, except for 1947–8 and 1985–6, the shares paid by these two groups are relatively constant. The 1947–8 data reflect in part the special financing arrangements of the GI Bill. By 1985–6,

Table 4.2 Sharing the costs of higher education: percentage shares of total instruction-related expenditures

Year	Total instruction-related costs (1)	Non-student: State-local Taxpayers and private donors (2)	Gross student share: Tuition and fees (3)	Student share net of institutional-awarded aid (4)	Net student share: net of all financial aid (5)
1947–48	100.0	72.8	27.2	23.6	−36.3
1957–58	100.0	65.4	34.6	29.8	13.1
1967–68	100.0	67.0	33.0	26.1	16.9
1972–73	100.0	66.7	33.3	25.9	−1.0
1980–81	100.0	65.4	34.6	28.3	−8.2
1985–86	100.0	61.7	38.3	31.4	4.0

Sources: Derived from Hansen and Stampen (1987) and updated to 1985–6.

however, the gross student share rose to more than 38%, a change that can be given at least two interpretations. One is that colleges and universities found it relatively easy, in light of the strong demand for higher education, to increase their total revenue by raising tuition and fees. An alternative explanation is that the student share of costs was forced up by the slow growth of support from the non-student sector. We return to this point below.

When institution-awarded student financial aid and federal student aid are subtracted from the gross student share, a significant drop in the net student share of the costs occurs. (We recognize that student aid funds can help pay for more than tuition and fees; they can also help pay for other costs of attendance such as room, board, books and incidental expenses.) The net student share becomes negative in 1947–8 because of the large infusion of educational benefits arising from the GI Bill. Despite the diminishing effects of the GI Bill by 1957–8, the magnitude of this aid was still sufficient to keep the net student share well below the gross student share.

By 1967–8 the net student share rose to roughly one-half the gross share, largely because of the phasing out of the GI Bill. However, by 1972–3 the dramtic effects of rapidly expanded federal need-based student aid programmes are evident. In fact, total student financial aid funds grew so rapidly that by 1972–3 they exceeded the total amount of tuition and fees paid by students. This situation continued through the 1970s so that by 1980–81 student aid exceeded tuition and fees by an even larger relative margin. This pattern reversed itself in the early 1980s as a result of efforts to control federal spending. By 1985–6 the net student share rose, but remained far below the 1967–8 level.

This change in the net student share hides two noteworthy shifts. One is the sharp rise in tuition and fees as a percentage of total instruction-related costs.

The other is an almost equally large percentage point increase in the student share net of institution-awarded financial aid; this change indicates that only a small part of the added tuition and fee income was redistributed in the form of student aid.

How burdensome were these costs?

Nothing has been said yet about the burden of college attendance costs on the ability of students and their families to pay for higher education; nor has anything been said about the adequacy of the resources available to higher education institutions to carry out their mission.

One straightforward approach calls for comparing instruction-related costs with some comprehensive measure of the nation's capacity to finance higher education costs. Such a comparison enables us to avoid having to convert any of the data from nominal to real values to correct for price level changes. Thus, rather than working with total dollar values, we show how over the period of our analysis instruction-related costs per student compare with a similar measure of the public's capacity to support higher education, but expressed on an individual or personal basis. Because gross national product (GNP) provides such a convenient and well-understood measure of aggregate output and hence aggregate capacity to pay, we use GNP per member of the labour force as an indicator of individual capacity to pay. GNP is preferable to other widely used measures because it reflects the value of all goods and services produced in the economy; it can also be related more directly to frequently made comparisons of higher education expenditures with GNP (i.e. higher education expenditures as a percentage of GNP). Moreover, using GNP per member of the labour force gives us a measure of the output produced by the average person, including those people who want jobs but are unable to find them. It can therefore be viewed as reflecting the capacity of the average member of the labour force to provide tax and non-tax support for higher education.

The patterns representing the two measures selected, instruction-related costs per student and GNP per member of the civilian labour force (CLF), are shown as Table 4.3, based on 1985–6 data.

The GNP-oriented measure (GNP/CLF) highlights the relationships between the level of instruction-related costs, who pays for them, and how financial aid affects the student share of these costs. Most immediately apparent is the small variation in the gross student share (tuition and fees), the much more pronounced variation in instruction-related costs and net student share, and the remarkably parallel movement in instruction-related costs and net student share. Thus, our measures of quality and access move in opposite directions.

We observe in Table 4.4 that instruction-related costs per student as a percentage of our GNP measure rose sharply through 1967–8, hitting a peak of 21.1% in 1967–8. It then declined sharply by 1972–3 and remained virtually unchanged through 1980–81. After that it rose again to 19.3% in 1985–6. The

Table 4.3 Instruction-related cost per FTE student as percentage of GNP output per member of the CLF

$$\frac{\text{Instruction-related cost per FTE student}}{\text{GNP output per member CLF}} = \frac{\$6,755 \text{ each for } 8.9 \text{ m. FTE students}}{\$34,733 \text{ each for } 115 \text{ m. members CLF}} \text{ or } 19.4\%$$

Based on

Instruction-related cost (expenditure for instruction less expenditures for research, public service, scholarships and fellowships, and auxiliary enterprises)	= 1.5% GNP
Instruction-related and scholarships and fellowship (what we call institution-awarded aid)	= 2.1% GNP
Total institution current fund expenditures	= 2.6% GNP
Total institution current fund expenditures and all other student financial aid	= 3.2% GNP

non-student share of costs as a percentage of the GNP measure showed less variation, increasing through 1967–8, declining through 1980–81, and increasing only modestly since then. Meanwhile, the gross student share, reflected by tuition and fees, after remaining constant from 1972–3 to 1980–81, increased by 1.3 percentage points to its 1985–6 near-high level of 7.4%.

What many students actually pay differs from the gross student share, as already noted, because institution-awarded aid reduces the student share as a percentage of the GNP measure. This share has remained approximately constant since 1957–8, varying within a narrow range. After dropping from 1967–8 to 1972–3, it began increasing again, and jumped substantially from 1980–81 to 1985–6.

The net share paid by students was on average strongly affected by the greatly increased amounts of student financial aid that became available during the past two decades. The net student share starts out negative in 1947–8 because of the GI Bill. By 1957–8 the percentage turns positive but remains lower than the gross student share because considerable numbers of veterans were still receiving GI Bill benefits. By 1967–8 the net share rose even more because of declines in federal support, despite accelerating increases in funding for new federal student aid programmes; this increase would have been even greater were it not for the rapid expansion of institution-awarded financial aid.

The substantial growth in student aid from 1967–8 to 1972–3, the year before funding for the BEOG programme (now called the Pell programme) took effect, is illustrated by the drop in the net student share from 3.8% to −0.2%. Put another way, total student aid in 1972–3 for the first time since 1947–8 exceeded total tuition and fees. With the expansion of the Pell programme, and as a result of the relaxed standards applying to federal grant and loan programmes as a

Table 4.4 The burden of the costs of higher education

Year	Instruction-related costs per FTE student (1)	GNP per member of the civilian labour force (2)	Instruction-related costs per FTE student as a percentage of GNP per member of the civilian labour force				
			Instruction-related costs (3)	Non-student share (total instruction-related less tuition & fees) (4)	Gross student share: tuition & fees (5)	Student share net of institutional-awarded aid (6)	Net student share: net of all student aid (7)
1947–48	505	3963	12.7	9.2	3.5	3.0	−4.6
1957–58	1128	6738	16.7	10.9	5.8	5.0	2.2
1967–68	2229	10555	21.1	13.3	7.8	5.5	3.8
1972–73	2483	13935	17.8	11.9	5.9	4.6	−0.2
1980–81	4519	25547	17.7	11.6	6.1	5.0	−1.1
1985–86	6755	34733	19.4	12.0	7.4	6.1	0.8

Source: Derived from Hansen and Stampen and updated to 1985–6.

consequence of the 1978 Middle Income Student Assistance Act, student aid resources expanded greatly. The net student share in 1980–81 exceeded total tuition and fees by an even greater margin, −1.1%. But, by 1985–6 the net student share had become positive once again, at 0.8%.

What explains this reversal since 1980–81 of efforts to promote greater access through low tuition and abundant financial aid? One may be a belated realization that declines in instruction-related costs since 1967–8 brought with them some erosion in quality, an erosion that could be halted only with increased spending for instruction. Another explanation emerges from dis-aggregating the components of the change. Recall that instruction-related costs increased by 1.7 percentage points from 1980–81 to 1985–6. However, the share of these costs financed by traditional sources of support – state and local taxes as well as voluntary contributions – rose by only 0.4 percentage points. This means the gross student share had to make up the gap of 1.3 percentage points. The only source of revenue was increased tuition and fee charges.

Put another way, increases in instruction-related costs had to be met largely by higher student charges because no other support was available. At the same time the gross student share after adjusting for institution-awarded aid rose 1.3 percentage points, meaning that increases in institution-awarded aid were not large enough to offset increases in tuition and fees. But the bottom line, the net student share, rose by 1.9 percentage points, from −1.1 to +0.8. The fact that the net student share increased by more than either the gross student share or the student share net of institution-awarded aid indicates that federal aid grew more slowly than either instruction-related costs or tuition and fees. What remains most striking is that the net student share of 0.8% in 1985–6 still constitutes little more than one-tenth of the gross share. This indicates that the commitment to access continues to be strong despite some erosion of effort in the 1980s.

Understanding what happened requires knowing what caused instruction-related expenditures to rise so sharply (by 1.7 percentage points) from 1980–81 to 1985–6. A key factor was the need to raise faculty salaries which had lagged seriously throughout the 1970s. Early in the 1980s it became evident that higher salaries were required to attract young people into the academic profession and to retain faculty members who were becoming increasingly receptive to outside offers, particularly for non-academic jobs. At the same time the costs of goods and services had escalated because of the largely unanticipated price increases in the late 1970s. In addition, maintenance expenditures deferred because of the tight budgets of the 1970s needed to be financed. Finally, changes in technology, perhaps best represented by the expanded use of computers, required extensive expenditures.

For these reasons, institutions found it necessary to augment their revenues to meet these cost increases. They presumably concluded that it would be easier to pass on these costs to students via increased tuition and fee charges than to win substantial additional support from traditional sources, namely, state and local taxpayers and private donors. This is not to suggest any lack of effort to raise additional public revenues. Rather, the depressed state of the economy, indicated by the relative stability of real GNP through the early 1980s, combined with pressures on tax revenues from other programmes, made it difficult to generate additional revenues. Student demand, however, continued to be strong as a result of growing concern among the youngest cohorts of the baby-boomers about getting good jobs.

Another important explanation deserves mention. Higher education institutions, often in response to state mandates to improve the quality of education, argued that tuition increases were required to improve the quality of the education they were providing. By paying higher faculty salaries, increasing expenditures to update equipment and facilities, and introducing new technology to the classroom, institutions believed they were improving quality. Most institutions would have preferred to find other ways of meeting these increased costs; they would have liked to receive more state and local revenue as well as larger voluntary contributions. Despite the much-publicized fact that tuition and fees increased so sharply, public reaction against these increases has not been noticeably strong. It has certainly not been strong enough to elicit additional support from other sources.

Summary and conclusions

In examining the goals and the financing of higher education over the past four decades, we find systematic patterns of change. These changes reflect political cycles similar to those noted by Schlesinger – cycles that no doubt exist for a variety of public policy issues. For higher education, however, these cycles translate into essentially two alternating mandates, one to improve quality and the other to improve access.

What we find particularly interesting is how changes in the goals of higher education affected quality, access and the sharing of costs between students and society. The relative constancy of the gross student share, represented by tuition and fees, in contrast to fluctuations in instruction-related costs and the net student share, is remarkable. That these other two measures exhibit such variation is an interesting commentary on changing priorities in higher education finance. Equally surprising is the fact that total student financial aid exceeded total tuition and fee revenues in two quite different time periods – through most of the 1970s and much earlier, just after World War II.

At the moment, a shift in public and institutional priorities appears to be under way, away from access and toward quality. This shift is being financed largely by students through tuition increases rather than by traditional sources of support such as state and local taxpayers and private donors, or federal taxpayers. In a sense, by trying to respond to growing concern about quality, institutions sought whatever financial support they could; in the absence of other support, tuition and fees had to be raised.[13]

We need to know more about how the emphasis on access in the 1970s contributed to the nation's goal of enhancing equal educational opportunity. The net cost of college attendance did decline sharply for young people with incomes low enough to qualify for student aid; this proved to be a major accomplishment. While college participation rates for low-income students did not by itself an important determinant of dropping out of college; the availability of financial aid largely offset the effects of low family income.[15] Increasingly, it appears that academic ability, as reflected by academic performance in high school and by performance on standardized tests, constitutes the most important remaining barrier to expanding access to college.[16] This finding suggests that access will be difficult to increase without improving quality.[17]

The moral of this analysis is that while pursuing the current and much-needed mandate to improve quality, adequate amounts of targeted student financial aid support must be maintained. Concurrently, efforts are needed to enhance the academic performance of students, particularly minority students, in their pre-college years. Only then will these students have a reasonable chance of performing satisfactorily in college. The need for improved college preparation will be even greater as higher education institutions accentuate their emphasis on quality. In the meantime increased reliance on tuition to finance improvements in quality, along with reductions in need-based student aid, will raise financial barriers. Perhaps even more important, they will undercut incentives for young people, especially those from low-income families, to adequately prepare for college by taking full advantage of learning opportunities in the elementary and secondary schools.

Acknowledgements

This research was supported by the National Center for Postsecondary Governance and Finance and by the Wisconsin Center for Education Research, under a grant from the US Office of Educational Research and Improvement (OERI-G-86-0009) and also by the Graduate Research Committee of the University of Wisconsin-Madison. The authors acknowledge the intellectual stimulus of Marshall S. Smith, the research assistance of Marilyn Rhodes, the editorial assistance of Deborah M. Stewart, and the typing of Karen Donnelly. In addition, constructive comments have been received from numerous readers of earlier versions of this paper; among those deserving special mention are Howard R. Bowen, Ernest L. Boyer, David Breneman, Eileen Collins, Robert H. Fenske, Art Hauptman, Joseph F. Kauffman, Michael McPherson, Donald K. Smith, and Pat Smith.

Notes

1. This paper draws on a longer but now obsolete paper by the authors: 'Balancing quality and access in financing higher education', December 1987.
2. For other recent discussions of higher education finance, see the papers from a recent conference on College and University Adjustment to a Changing Financial Environment, sponsored by the National Science Foundation in the summer of 1986: Paul T. Brinkman and Dennis P. Jones, 'College and university adjustment to changing financial and enrollment conditions', (Boulder, CO: National Center for Higher

Education Management Systems, 1986); Joseph Froomkin, 'The impact of changing levels of financial resources on the structure of colleges and universities' (Washington, DC: Joseph Froomkin, Inc. 1986). Also, see Durward Long, 'Financing public universities and colleges in the year 2000' in Leslie W. Koepplin and David A. Wilson (eds), *The Future of State Universities: Issues in Teaching, Research, and Public Service* (New Brunswick, NJ: Rutgers University Press, 1985).

3. The importance of cycles has been emphasized primarily by the Schlesingers: see Arthur M. Schlesinger, Jr, *The Cycles of American History* (Boston, MA: Houghton Mifflin, 1986), and Arthur M. Schlesinger, *Paths to the Present* (New York: 1949). Also see, Herbert McClosky and John Zaller, *The American Ethos: Public Attitudes toward Capitalism and Democracy* (Cambridge, MA: Harvard University Press, 1984); Carl Kaestle, 'Social reform and urban schools', in *History of Education Quarterly*, **2**, Summer 1972, 211–28; A. O. Hirschman, *Shifting Involvements: Private Interest and Public Action* (Princeton, NJ: Princeton University Press, 1982); George Hegel, *Encyclopedia of the Philosophical Sciences in Outline* (Heidelberg, 1817).

4. Arthur M. Schlesinger, Jr, op. cit., p. 24.

5. Schlesinger goes on to say that such cycles 'cannot be determined, short of catastrophe by external events. Wars, depressions, inflations may heighten and complicate moods, but the cycle itself rolls on, self-contained and self sufficient' (pp. 27–9). Hegel might have characterized each cycle as part of a dialectical process wherein each asserts a thesis which as time passes draws opposition resulting in the formation of an anti-thesis, causing a new cycle to begin. However, surviving elements of a previous cycle's thesis become permanent parts of a presumably richer and higher array of public policies.

6. John F. Folger and Charles Nam, *Education of the American People* (Washington, DC: Bureau of the Census, 1960).

7. These shifts do not emerge full-blown. Rather, they reflect the aggregation of not only changes in individual attitudes and behaviour but also perceptions of change emerging within higher education institutions and the actions these perceptions generate. We do not dwell on these micro-level developments even though they constitute an important part of the story.

8. We caution readers that this analysis for all of higher education obscures differences between public and private-independent institutions; these differences will be examined in a subsequent paper.

9. Full-time equivalent enrolment grew progressively more slowly because of the steadily increasing proportion of part-time students where numbers increased from 22% of all students in 1947–8 to 41% in 1985–6. Relative to the civilian non-institutional population age 16 and over, the FTE enrolment percentage rose from 2.1% to 5.0%. The large rise in part-timers is attributable to several developments, the most important being the substantial increase of older students, those age 25 and over, who for occupational or family reasons typically cannot attend full-time.

10. Note that this analysis excludes capital expenditures and revenues.

11. Howard R. Bowen, *The Costs of Higher Education* (San Francisco: Jossey-Bass, 1980).

12. Since current fund expenditures are approximately equal to current fund revenues, the percentages shown here can be applied to either measure.

13. W. Lee Hansen, 'Cost containment in higher education', forthcoming in John Lee (ed.), *The High and Rising Costs of College: Is There a Problem?* (College Park, Md.: National Center for Postsecondary Governance and Finance, 1988).

14. W. Lee Hansen, 'Economic growth and equal educational opportunity: conflicting or complementary goals in higher education', in Edward Dean (ed.), *Education and Economic Growth* (Boston, MA: Ballinger, 1984).

15. Jacob O. Stampen and Alberto F. Cabrera, 'Exploring the effects of student aid on attrition', *Journal of Student Financial Aid*, **16** (Spring 1986).

16. Stampen and Cabrera, op. cit., and Stampen and Cabrera, 'The targeting and packaging of student aid and its effects on attrition', *Economics of Education Review*, **7**(1988).

17. This means that current efforts to improve the quality of instruction can be effective also if academic performance improves among low-income and ethnic minority students. As larger proportions of these students enter college with better preparation and are able to perform well in college, student financial aid will become even more effective for ensuring greater equality of opportunity in higher education.

5

Governance, Quality and Equity in the United States

Richard M. Millard

Some historical background is critical to the understanding of the continuing tension between quality and equity in higher education in the United States and the relevance of governance to this tension. The term 'governance' for the purposes of this paper is being used in a broad sense to include internal institutional governance, system governance (where it applies), communal self-regulatory activities that directly affect governance such as accreditation, and in particular the impact of state and federal governments on higher or post-secondary institutions.

Early history: 1636–1860

According to the reserve clause of the United States Constitution, the primary responsibility for education at all levels rests with the states. Soon after the United States became a nation the Congress, through the Northwest Ordinance, provided public lands to the states for the support of education in the new territories and enjoined the states to support forever education for the sake of the happiness of mankind and as essential to good government (Article III). The states have developed complex systems of post-secondary and higher education with roots that go back to the beginning of the nation. The University of North Carolina was established in 1795 and the University of Georgia in 1801. Currently more than three-quarters of the students in higher education are in public state-supported institutions.

It should be kept in mind that the first higher education institutions in America were private even though the distinction between public and private was not sharply drawn until the middle of the nineteenth century. Harvard, founded in 1636, though private, received public funds from the colony and then the Commonwealth of Massachusetts through the first quarter of the nineteenth century. Until World War II students at private institutions outnumbered those in public institutions. Until well into the nineteenth century American higher educational institutions operated on the British curricular model and were primarily designed for persons preparing for the clergy and law. The curriculum was classical. As late as 1828 the Yale faculty closed the curriculum for 'all time' against such insidious intrusions as modern languages and the natural sciences. The primary emphasis among the more prestigious private institutions was on a conservative and élitist conception of quality, not on access or equity.

1860 to World War II

Many of the 'reforms' in higher education have come about as the result of external pressures rather than from within the academy. The first major thrust in the direction of access came from the federal government. This major turning point was the passage in 1862 of the Morrill Land Grand Act which provided land to the states to establish colleges for the children of mechanics, farmers and other citizens of the states. The 1862 Act, followed by a second Morrill Land Grant Act of 1890, not only opened the door to persons who previously were not considered college material but opened the curriculum to include the natural sciences and modern languages, the mechanical arts and agriculture. Until relatively recently most land-grant institutions accepted any high school graduates from their states.

The latter part of the nineteenth century saw the development of graduate education based on the German rather than the English model and with it a renewed emphasis on quality in contrast to access. The 1870s and 1880s saw a migration of American students to German universities for advanced education. The development of doctoral work was largely based on the experience of the returning American scholars and scientists. Development of graduate programmes led to questions about adequacy of undergraduate programmes as preparation for graduate work and, by extension, to the adequacy of secondary school programmes as preparation for college.

One important result of this concern with adequacy or quality of programmes was the coming together in various parts of the country of representatives of schools and colleges to deal with such issues as articulation with secondary schools, definition of college-level work, and preparation of students for graduate education. Out of such meetings in New England (1885), the middle Atlantic states (1887) and the Southern states (1895), plus the review of high schools by the University of Michigan in co-operation with other colleges in the Middle West, there developed the regional associations that were to become the institutional accrediting bodies. The initial concern of these accrediting bodies was identifying quality institutions defined in terms of those whose programmes and graduates measured up to those of the 'best' institutions in each region. 'Best' was largely determined by success of students in graduate school. This original 'outcomes' approach was rather quickly translated into terms of quantitative characteristics of the 'best' institutions.

It was not until the 1930s that this quantitative approach was challenged by a report of a task force of the North Central Association of Colleges and Schools

which called for qualitative assessment of institutions based upon the specifica-
tions of their educational objectives, the appropriateness of those objectives,
and their effectiveness in achieving them. This approach has since been adopted
by most of the institutional and specialized or professional (e.g. medicine, law,
etc.) accrediting bodies in the United States.

While the Land Grant Acts had major impact on higher education in
broadening the curriculum and while the state colleges and universities provided low tuition and places for all interested and capable high school graduates
in their states, access and equity were not major concerns of the nineteenth
century or of the first half of the twentieth century. The number of persons going
to college constituted a relatively small percentage of the total population and
the amount of funds provided to the public institutions by the states was not
excessive.

Increased tempo of change: The pendulum effect

Since World War II, the situation has changed radically. We have gone through
a series of periods in which not only institutions but the public, state governments and the federal government have become highly conscious of and
concerned about matters of equity including access and quality in higher
education. There has been something of a pendulum effect in which during
certain periods concern with equity has tended to be predominant and others in
which concern with quality has tended to be predominant. This has been
illustrated in a paper by W. Lee Hansen and Jacob O. Stampen of the
University of Wisconsin-Madison entitled 'Balancing quality and access in
financing higher education' (1987)[1] and in Chapter 4 above. The presence of
this tension and pendulum effect does not mean that the concepts of equity and
quality are necessarily antithetical nor that they are obverse and reverse sides of
a coin as is sometimes assumed. It means that there have been periods in which
one or the other has tended to be in the ascendancy in public and academic
awareness and commitment.

1946–7 to 1957–8: Veterans and the post-war decade

Hansen and Stampen identify five periods since 1947. The first, from 1946–7 to
1957–8, was a period of readjustment after World War II. On the whole it was
also a period in which concern with equity and access predominated, but access
primarily for returning veterans. Congress in the Servicemen Readjustment Act
(GI Bill) of 1944 provided that any returning veteran who desired or thought he
could benefit from post-high-school education would receive tuition and support for such education. The period began with a rapid increase in enrolments of

returning veterans who started or continued their education with the help of the GI Bill. In spite of a decline in the latter part of this period of the college-age population, enrolments held up as a result of extension of the GI Bill to veterans of the Korean War. There was concern in some academic quarters that the influx of veterans would lead to a lowering of academic standards. Exactly the opposite turned out to be the case. The veterans came with a seriousness and commitment that tended to offset what they may have lacked in pre-war motivation, background and/or continuity of educational experience.

Experience with the veterans demonstrated (1) the feasibility of providing financial support for large numbers of students, (2) extending access does not necessarily lead to a diminution in quality, and (3) a far larger portion of the population can benefit from post-high-school education than most people had assumed. It was during this period that the groundwork for later expansion of the student aid concept was laid. As early as 1947 the Truman Commission on Higher Education suggested that as veterans completed their education a larger portion of the general population should be educated. It argued that at least half of all high school graduates could benefit from higher education if financial barriers could be removed by providing grants, loans and work-study to students based on financial need.[2]

Although need-based student support programmes were delayed until the 1960s, higher education emerged during this period a much more important part of the American scene due both to its involvement in veterans transition and to increased confidence (in part growing out of the war experience) in its relevance to resolving national problems.

1957–8 to 1967–8: Sputnik, quality and expansion

The period from 1957–8 to 1967–8 began with a primary emphasis on quality but became the period of the most rapid expansion in the history of higher education. In the process of this expansion, while quality remained a major concern, access was provided to a far wider range of students than ever before. In 1957 Sputnik shocked the nation into recognizing the need for increasing the human resource base and for reinforcing the quality of education particularly in the sciences, engineering and technology. The result was the National Defense Education Act of 1958 which provided limited loans and scholarships, re-inforced science graduate programmes, provided for establishing centres of scientific excellence at additional universities around the country. The primary emphasis of the Act was on strengthening higher educational quality and research in the natural sciences to meet the challenges of the cold war and the beginning space age.

Meantime the impact of the war and post-war baby boom began to be felt. There were 2.3 million 18-year-olds in 1957. By 1965 this number had increased to 3.8 million.[3] Between 1960 and 1970 college enrolments increased 126% – from 3,789,000 to 8,580,000. Although expansion occurred in both public and private institutions, the public institutions expanded at a far more rapid rate. Over 400 new public institutions were created by the states in this decade.[4]

The most phenomenal growth during the decade and one that extended access to higher education to an increasingly wide range of individuals occurred among two-year community and junior colleges. These colleges are closely related to their communities, within commuting distance of their students, and offer occupational as well as transfer programmes. While a few junior colleges go back to the early part of the century most community colleges have developed since World War II and of these over half were started in the period from 1960 to 1970.[4] Currently, two-year colleges account for more than a third of all higher education enrolments.[5]

Four other developments call for special note. First, on the state level, with the increasing number of students, size of institutions, number of institutions and programmes, and the inevitable jockeying for state funds among the public institutions, most of the states that did not already have state higher education agencies established them. The primary state concern was that in the process of expansion, priorities should be established and quality should not be sacrificed. Between 1960 and 1970 some 23 co-ordinating or governing boards were created bringing the total number to 47. While these varied from state-wide governing boards to advisory commissions the majority of the boards established during this period were co-ordinating boards with some responsibility for planning, programme review and budget review.

Second, the late 1950s and the 1960s saw more federal higher education legislation enacted than in all the previous history of the country. Some 17 Acts affecting higher education were passed including the National Defense Education Act which was followed by the Health Professions Educational Assistance Act of 1963, the Vocational Education Act of 1963, the Higher Education Facilities Act of 1963, the Civil Rights Act of 1964 and the Higher Education Act of 1965 with Amendments in 1968. The latter incorporated some of the earlier legislation, expanded student grants (Educational Opportunity Grants), loans and work-study, and, with subsequent amendments from then until now, has served as the basic higher education legislation.

Third, in 1954 the Supreme Court in *Brown* v. *Topeka Board of Education* ruled separate but equal schools for black students unconstitutional and thus laid the groundwork for the civil rights movement which during the 1960s became progressively more important. It refocused attention on access to higher education for minorities and underprivileged groups.

Finally, 1964 saw the beginning at Berkeley of a period of student unrest that deeply shook and shocked the academic community, the political community and the public at large. It developed in part out of the civil rights movement, in part out of resistance to the conflict in Vietnam, but it was focused on higher education institutions generically and challenged the curriculum, the structure, the relevance, the social commitment and the objectives of higher education. While it did not reach its zenith until 1970 it had become a major political concern in the election of 1968 and contributed to the renewed emphasis on equity.

1967–8 to 1972–3: Accent on access and equity

The period from 1967–8 to 1972–3 deserves special attention because it was during these five years that the various functions and trends related to equity tended to coalesce. The period culminated with the Higher Education Amendments of 1972 which firmly established the federal policy of support for higher education primarily through and to needy students rather than directly to institutions. In addition to the civil rights movement and student unrest a series of influential reports helped shape national policy. Two reports by Clark Kerr who was then organizing his Carnegie Commission on Higher Education call for mention. One was a chapter in the 1968 Brookings Institution volume, *Agenda for a Nation*,[6] in which he listed greater equality of educational opportunity and the problems of financing higher education in view of rising costs as two of the six major issues facing higher education. He proposed that the solution to both problems should be federal. The second report was that of the Carnegie Commission, *Quality and Equity: New Levels of Federal Responsibility for Higher Education* (1968).[7]

These were followed in 1969 by a report of an advisory task force created by the Department of Health, Education and Welfare under the direction of Alice Rivlin, *Toward a Long Range Plan for Federal Financial Support for Higher Education*.[8] Both the Carnegie and Rivlin reports called for an expanded federally financed system of need-based student financial aid grants and direct institutional grants tied to the number of students receiving support. All three reports involved 'an integrated set of proposals whose goal was to promote greater educational opportunity'.[9]

President Nixon in his first major higher education message to Congress (19 March 1970) stated: 'No qualified student who wants to go to college should be barred by lack of money. That has long been a great American goal; I propose that we achieve it now.'

The 1972 amendments to the Higher Education Act of 1965 established a range of student assistance programmes with the Basic Educational Opportunity Grants (later called Pell Grants) as the foundation. Added to these were Supplemental Opportunity Grants, National Defense Student Loans and the work-study programme, all of which were primarily administered through institutions, plus the Guaranteed Student Loan Program administered at that point through the states and the federal government. The primary factor in providing aid of whatever kind was to be student need. The act also provided incentive funds to the states to develop their own need-based grant programmes. Finally, as indication of the emphasis on equity and the range of educational opportunities involved, the focus of the Act was not just on 'higher education' in the traditional sense but on post-secondary education – that is, all forms of education beyond high school: public, private and proprietary institutions, and certificate and diploma short-term programmes as well as degree programmes.

1972–3 to 1980: Consolidating equity gains

From 1972–3 to 1980–81 attention was focused on consolidating and extending equity gains. As a partial answer to the period of student unrest colleges and universities experimented with non-traditional approaches to education including increased emphasis upon lifelong learning and adult continuing education, thus extending the concept of equity to include adult and part-time students. The first recommendation of a prestigious Commission on Non-Traditional Study in 1973 was: 'Full educational opportunity should be realistically available for all who may benefit from it, whatever their condition of life'.[10] The emphasis on diversity and non-traditional modes of educational delivery raised questions of quality control and comparability. The newly formed (1975) Council on Postsecondary Accreditation with the support of the W. K. Kellogg Foundation undertook a major study directed by Grover J. Andrews on *Assessing Non-Traditional Education*.[11] Its report, published in 1978, stressed the critical importance of the assessment of education accomplishments or outcomes (p. 127) as crucial to quality control particularly in non-traditional education but in traditional education as well.

In the meantime, slowed-down economic growth and increasing inflation with increasing college cost led middle-income families to pressure Congress to provide greater access to student aid, particularly of loans, to their children. The result was the Middle Income Student Assistance Act of 1978 which removed from the Guaranteed Student Loan Program the requirement of demonstrating financial need for eligibility.

The concern for equity reached its height with re-authorization of student aid programmes in 1980 calling for major increases in both grants and loans.

1980–81 to 1987–8: Re-emphasis on quality

The period from 1980 to the present has seen the pendulum swing progressively in the direction of concern about quality. This has resulted from a number of factors. The first was the election in 1980 of Ronald Reagan as President with a Republican majority in the Senate. From the outset the Reagan Administration emphasized reduction in federal support of social programmes and of the federal role in education. One of his election promises was to dismantle the newly formed Department of Education – a promise he was not able to keep. In 1981 student assistance came under sharp attack in the Senate. Two important changes were made. The income requirement was reinstated for guaranteed student loans (thus nullifying the Middle Income Student Assistance Act) and educational benefits in the Social Security Program were eliminated.

The Reagan Administration and the Department of Education, while cutting back or holding even on funds for education, played a major role in shifting the discussion from access to quality. A National Commission on Excellence in Education was set up under the National Institute for Education chaired by David Gardner. Its primary focus was on elementary and secondary education.

It was concerned with such items as declining Scholastic Aptitude Test scores, drug problems in the schools, and what seemed to be increasing functional illiteracy of high school graduates. The Commission issued a report in 1983 called *A Nation At Risk*. It argued that 'the educational foundations of our society are being eroded by a rising tide of mediocrity that threatens our very future as a Nation and as a people'.[12] This report was preceded and followed by a series of other reports focusing on elementary and secondary education, all of which were highly critical. The result was a series of elementary–secondary educational reforms led primarily by the states rather than the federal government.

It is not surprising that the criticism, concern, and call for reform began to spill over into higher education. To follow up on the National Commission a Study Group on the Conditions of Excellence in American Higher Education was set up under the National Institute of Education. The Study Group published its report, *Involvement in Learning: Realizing The Potential of American Higher Education*, in 1984.[13] The report concentrated primarily on undergraduate education. While not as devastating as *A Nation At Risk* it lamented the shift of undergraduates away from the arts and sciences and into narrow specialties, professional programmes, and primarily occupational interests. It called for greater student involvement in the learning process and for a major focus on the results or outcomes of that process. This was followed a month later by a report from the National Endowment for the Humanities authored by the soon-to-be Secretary of Education, William Bennett, called *To Reclaim a Legacy*,[14] and in the following spring by a report published by the Association of American Colleges called *Integrity in the College Curriculum*.[15] All three reports at least by implication gave the impression that in our concern for equity we had been less than alert to the importance of preserving and enhancing quality.

Among the many reports that followed, two that call for special note were primarily state based rather than from the federal government or the academic community. The one issued by the Education Commission of the States was entitled *Transforming the State Role in Undergraduate Education*.[16] The second was a report of a Task Force on College Qaulity made up of state governors and chaired by Governor John Ashcroft of Missouri and was published in a series of task-force reports on education under the auspices of the National Governors' Association called *Time for Results: The Governors' 1991 Report on Education*.[17] Both stressed the state role in educational improvement and reform, noted that the initiative had passed from the federal government to the states, and accepted the initiative for the states. Both warned against prescriptive or hasty legislative actions but called upon the states to provide incentives to qualitative improvement of undergraduate education.

Both reports called for clarification of the role and mission of institutions individually and as part of state systems of higher education. They called for assessment of the academic needs of students entering higher educational institutions. They particularly emphasized the importance of continuous assessment of outcomes, results, or effectiveness of undergraduate education and the evaluation of institutional programme quality in the light of such assessment. While both reports stressed the use of multiple means of assessing undergraduate programmes and their effectiveness and enlisted the support of the accrediting community, the Governors' task force particularly called for the accrediting community not only to require institutions to collect and use information about student outcomes but to require demonstrated levels of performance in granting institutional accreditation. On the whole, however, both reports placed the primary responsibility for assessment and use of outcomes in improving undergraduate education with the institutions themselves but reinforced by accrediting bodies and state incentives and oversight.

State actions or initiatives in relation to assessment of outcomes have already taken a number of forms. These include in a few states mandated state-wide testing programmes. Some of these (Florida, Georgia and South Dakota) require examinations in order to advance to the junior year in college. Others assess basic skills of entering freshmen. These may be used diagnostically or in some instances as screening tests for admission. Some states have raised admission requirements at public institutions. Others have provided for informing prospective students of what will be expected of them in collegiate institutions. Some states have developed early intervention programmes at high-school or middle-school levels to encourage more adequate preparation and articulation. By far the majority of states, however, have primarily acted to encourage institutions to develop their own assessment plans.[18]

This emphasis on institutional and programme specification of goals and objectives, on assessment in the light of these, on outcomes and results as related to educational quality, and on quality enhancement in higher education was neither new nor unique to the 1980s. Beginning with the mid-1930s the accrediting community progressively had moved toward a conception of quality assessment based on institutional and programme effectiveness in utilizing resources to achieve appropriate educational objectives. Achieving objectives clearly involves consideration of results or outcomes. Under the auspices first of the Federation of Regional Accrediting Commissions for Higher Education and then the Council on Postsecondary Accreditation a major study of outcomes including an extended inventory of evaluation instruments was carried out and published in 1975. The Council on Postsecondary Accreditation study of evaluation of non-traditional education with its emphasis on outcomes (1979) has already been noted.

What is new is state interest in assessment and outcomes specifically in relation to undergraduate programmes. This is somewhat surprising although not necessarily contradictory to the high interest of governors and legislators in the early 1980s in graduate education and research as keys to economic development and competitiveness. States and state higher education agencies have been concerned with accountability, with planned development to meet the wider state higher and post-secondary education needs, and with programme review to avoid needless duplication, to provide for reasonable fund allocation and to assure that public institutions are operating within their scopes. Within these parameters the issues of quality and accountability in undergraduate education have been included as part of the total picture but not singled out as 'the' primary concerns of state interest. Seen as an extension of concern with upgrading elementary and secondary education related to in-creased levels of literacy of the population as a whole such a thrust makes sense. However, seen as a general state focus on increasing the impact of higher education on state economic development, interstate and international com-petitiveness, and service to the total state community, primary focus on undergraduate education appers to be a somewhat truncated emphasis. Re-search and public service, particularly in complex institutions, for example, are also of major importance. That an institution should be judged in terms of accomplishing its mission and objectives is clear but its effectiveness and thus its quality is a function of how well it accomplishes its mission as a whole, and not just one part, important as that part may be. A more recent report from the National Governors' Association, by a completely different task force, returns to the theme of higher education's role in promoting economic growth and stresses research and graduate and professional education much more fully.[19]

Concern with equity and quality

As one looks back historically the tension between equity and quality seems to have been present almost from the beginning. There have been periods in which concern with equity has tended to predominate and periods in which concern with quality has been predominant. However, in no period since 1862 has concern with either equity or with quality been wholly absent. What is striking is that at least up until 1980, while there are exceptions, the primary impetus to 'equity' has tended to come from external sources, from the federal government and the states representing popular concerns including the perception of higher education as the key to social mobility, from the impact of the courts, and from social movements such as the civil rights movement and student unrest. The primary impetus to 'quality' has until recently tended to come from the academic community itself and organizations indigenous to the academic community such as accrediting bodies although frequently reinforced by the states. To some extent at least the concern with quality has been a concern with preserving or conserving what are perceived as particular academic values. Where 'quality' has been identified with a particular curriculum, specific governance structures, or a single or limited range of academic traditions it has tended to be exclusionary and élitist. Where 'quality' has been more closely identified with programme or institutional effectiveness seen as effective utiliza-tion of resources to achieve appropriate educational mission or objectives, and the missions or objectives are developed in terms of educational needs of society, quality and equity have tended to reinforce each other.

The period from 1980–81 to the present seems in some respects to reverse the trend with both the federal government and the states expressing increased concern about quality. However, unlike earlier periods, the changed federal position has not been accompanied by increases in tax revenues available to higher education to implement changes. Whether there will be a reversal in federal policy under President Bush is still in 1990 unclear.

Concern with equity and quality in the academic community

Regardless of general historical precedents what does seem clear is that the tension and/or complementation of equity and quality in higher education is present not just at federal and state levels but at every level within the academic community itself. Decisions that affect access and quality may be made in departments, by college and university administrators and faculty, and by trustees either of institutions or systems including state-wide systems. Such decisions are also made by accrediting bodies whose members are the institutions accredited or the programmes, educators and professionals in specialized fields which are external to individual institutions but integral to the academic community. In addition, the positions taken by the national organizations such as the American Council on Education representing the various segments of higher education through their federal relations operations do have impact on both federal legislation and the regulations developed to implement such legislation.

Determining the policy framework

The federal government and the states play a major role in determining the policy framework and context in which discussions and actions in relation to equity and quality take place within the academic community. The primary instrument of the federal government is legislation which at least theoretically reflects the public interest. Thus, for example, federal concern wth equity is reflected in the Morrill Land Grant Acts, the GI Bill, the extension and development of student aid in its various forms as related to student need, and in the relevance for higher education of the civil rights and affirmative action legislation.

While historically the primary federal thrust has tended to be in the direction of access and equity, the concurrent federal concern for quality has been reflected in the National Defense Education Act with its emphasis on increased quality in the natural sciences; in provisions in the Higher Education Act and its amendments for libraries, improved and new facilities, support of graduate education; in targeted programmes not just to ensure the number but the quality of health and health-related programmes; and in the reliance on accreditation to help establish institutional and programme eligibility for federal funds. It should also be noted that through the National Science Foundation, the National Institute for Health, and other federal agencies the government has provided major resources for support of research at academic institutions, and such support is continuing. Since 1980 the administration has sought to cut back radically on student aid and other higher education programmes. While Congress has prevented such cuts, there have been no appreciable increases. The administration, through the Department of Education, has attempted to shift the responsibility for quality improvement to the states, the accrediting community and the institutions.

The states have made major contributions to equity through supporting the radical expansion of higher education in the 1960s and 1970s; development usually in co-operation with local governments of community college systems; creating their own need-based student assistance programmes; and maintaining in most states low tuition in public institutions. A number of states have supported, even mandated, remedial programmes for students from educationally disadvantaged backgrounds. One of the most important roles that states play in providing both for access and quality is through the state-wide planning process. On the access side, a major aspect of the planning process is to ensure an appropriate diversity of higher education institutions and programmes to meet the variety of needs of citizens of the states and nation.

On the quality side in state planning clear definition of role and scope is crucial. Such definition not only indicates range of opportunities available but also serves as a basis for determining institutional effectiveness.

Most states with either co-ordinating or state-wide governing boards also carry out some form of programme review. Such programme review clearly relates to quality although the primary purpose may be more closely tied to planning and fund allocation. How, and the extent to which, programme review is carried out differs considerably from state to state. In most states such review is limited to public institutions; however, there are exceptions such as New York and Louisiana where private institutions are also involved. The power to review new and existing programmes clearly rests with state-wide governing boards whether they exercise it or not. In addition, some state co-ordinating agencies have the power to review and approve all programmes. Other states review and approve only new programmes. In some states the agency may review and recommend programmes but it does not have approval power.

While quality is or should be a factor in state-wide programme view it is seldom, if ever, the only factor. In the case of new programmes the issues are likely to be whether the programme involves unnecessary duplication, whether the resources are available, and whether it fits within the institutional mission. Review of existing programmes is normally related to state-wide planning and priority judgements as to how funds are spent. In a number of states the boards are charged with comparative programme review among public institutions to decide when programmes will be added, reinforced, curtailed, or eliminated. Quality should indeed be one of the factors involved. Current state concern with assessment of outcomes will probably play an increasing role in such state-wide programme review.

Other areas in which state agency actions have a direct impact on quality include, where applicable, setting more rigorous admission requirements or encouraging institutions to do so. This can have a major negative impact on equity if through so doing potential students who would benefit from post-secondary education are disqualified. To avoid increasing the group of 'at risk' young people a number of states have recognized the importance of working more closely with the secondary schools to improve college preparatory programmes and of providing remedial or developmental education both at secondary-school and at college levels to enable students to prepare for college-level work. Some states in addition to need-based grants offer state merit scholarships to help recruit and retain superior students.

Finally a number of states provide special incentives to institutions for improvement. These incentives range from financial inducements to establish endowed chairs for outstanding faculty to special competitive grants for projects designed to improve and strengthen curriculum and institutional practices.

Crucial role of institutions in equity and quality determination

In one sense the federal government and the states have more control over whether or not equity exists in higher education than over quality. Legislation can mandate affirmative action; can impose penalties for discrimination in admission, hiring, and promotion; and, most important, can provide assistance for students who need it. However, whether or not equity exists in practice, the way in which students are treated in classrooms, are counselled, are encouraged to persist, and are made to feel an integral part of the programme and institution cannot be legislated. These are functions of the institution itself and its decisions. Quality is somewhat more elusive and more directly under the control of the institution or programme. States in particular and the federal government to some extent through appropriate funding can help create conditions conducive to quality, can provide incentives to quality attainment, can even require outcomes assessments by the institution or programme, but quality cannot be externally imposed. It is a function of the institution or programme itself and how it utilizes its resources to achieve its appropriate educational objectives.

Accrediting bodies as part of the post-secondary education self-regulating structure can bring the communal impact of academic and professional peers to bear on quality assessment and enhancement. But they, like the states, cannot impose quality on an institution or programme. To the extent that the institution or programme internalizes the self-study process and welcomes site visitors as consultative peers, the more likely the procedure is to enhance institutional and/or programme quality.

The crucial role both in assuring equity internally and in sustaining and enhancing quality rests with trustees, administrators, faculty, students and to some extent alumni. It is at the institutional level that the tension between equity and quality primarily exists and where if the tension is to be resolved it must take place. Trustees, whether of individual institutions or of systems, constitute the corporate bodies of control and at least in theory either determine or approve institutional policy. It is they who must formally approve and adopt the institutional mission and objectives in the case of private institutions. Where in the case of some public institutions mission is determined by the state legislature or co-ordinating board, it is the trustees who must translate the mission into specific institutional objectives. Among these objectives are the institution's position in relation to equity such as policy on utilization of scholarship funds, general admission, affirmative action in recruitment of students, faculty and staff, and the role of remediation. In relation to quality the responsibility of the trustees again involves institutional objectives and assurance that they are being effectively translated into action. The trustees can require internal self-evaluation, assessment and programme review. It is their responsibility to ensure that the programmes are commensurate with the institutional objectives, to help ensure that funds are adequate to meet the objectives and that these funds are effectively utilized in achieving them.

The administration has the responsibility for translating policy into practice as well as assuring that the appropriate policy issues are transmitted to the trustees for consideration. In public institutions it is the administration which usually must deal with the state higher education agency, the legislature, the governor and the state executive offices to request appropriations adequate to meet equity and quality needs. In private institutions the administration usually has a primary responsibility for fund raising from outside sources. It is the administration with the help of faculty committees, department chairmen and others that must determine fund allocation internally and thus play a large role in how policy in regard to both equity and quality is implemented. Admissions, counselling, student financial aid, housing and placement all fall under the aegis of administration. All of these have direct bearing on equity and quality in institutional practice.

The faculty role is crucial both in developing and carrying out academic policy and in assuring or in some cases negating conformity of practice to institutional objectives. It is the faculty directly through teaching and research and in constant contact with students that determines teaching and research effectiveness, receptivity and encouragement to students, and quality of instruction. Through committees the faculty largely determines curriculum, graduation requirements, academic standards, and, in co-operation with administration, operational policy in such areas as admission and academic standing.

Questions of the tensions between or complementation of equity and quality in some form are basic for any institution and every level of governance relevant to each institution. Equity, however, is not to be confused with open or unlimited access. It clearly is not equitable to admit students with no chance of success or students with inadequate backgrounds, and thus to perpetuate what has sometimes been called the revolving door. What constitutes equity in a particular institution relates to institutional mission, degree of selectivity, presence of remedial programmes, and availability of student assistance.

In a public institution questions of access and equity may also involve the institution's relation to other institutions in the system. One of the functions of state-wide planning is to help ensure an appropriate diversity of institutions and programmes to meet the educational needs of the state. Thus the state system may provide access for all who believe they can benefit from post-secondary education but it may do so through differentiated admissions to different types of institutions as, for example, in California where the University of California system accepts California students only in the top eighth of their high school graduating class, the California State University system accepts students in the top third, and the community colleges have open admissions. However, given the differential, if equity is to be assured, (1) each type of institution must be expected to achieve excellence in kind (e.g. as a community college), (2) within its given mission each institution can be expected to seek a diversity of students including minorities commensurate with its mission, and (3) there should be effective transfer agreements within the system so that there are no 'dead ends' for capable students.

Demography and future directions

The changing demography of the country as it relates to higher education will undoubtedly call for further change in emphasis. While emphasis on quality should persist, concern with equity is likely to increase. At the present time, of the 12.5 million students in higher education only about 2 million are traditional 18- to 22-year-old resident full-time students.[20] The number of part-time and older students has increased considerably during the 1980s and promises to continue to do so. What this may call for in many institutions is a refocusing of mission, a greater concern with the relevance, quality and outcomes of continuing education in the total college structure, and an increased concern with meeting the needs of older students.

Of equal if not greater concern is the situation in relation to minorities – particularly blacks and Hispanics. While the number of 18- to 24-year-olds continues to decline, this decline is primarily in the white population. The black and Hispanic populations are increasing and will constitute a progressively larger portion of the population in general and the college-age population in particular. If present trends continue the Population Reference Bureau predicts that by 2080 more than half of all Americans will be black, Hispanic, or Asian. By the turn of the century or soon thereafter the present minorities in California are expected to be the majority – and Texas is not far behind California. As far as college population is concerned the proportion of minorities is expected to increase from approximately 25% in 1987 to some 30.6% by the year 2000.[21]

In spite of these trends and projections, while minority representation in colleges and universities increased in the 1960s and 1970s, a Task Force report of the State Higher Education Executive Officers on minorities in higher education summarizes the situation as follows:

> Despite two decades, and more, of effort to improve minority educational attainment, minority students remain seriously underrepresented in our nation's colleges. Enrolment gains achieved in the mid-to-late 1970s have plateaued and, in some cases, slipped. Equally troubling is the fact that achievement levels (in terms of both academic performance and persistence to the baccalaureate degree) of minority college students tend to lag behind those of their majority peers.

(p. iv)

Further, the distribution of minority students by type of institution leaves much to be desired with far more minority students in two-year colleges and predominantly black institutions than in four-year baccalaureate institutions and research universities.

What all of this seems to call for is a renewed concern with access and equity at all levels of governance. The fact that the State Higher Education Executive Officers have addressed the issue through a special task force indicates renewed and growing concern at the state level. That task force developed a series of ten recommendations to institutions, states and the federal government which range from further removal of economic barriers to increased support of institutional programmes to 'better equip minority students to function well in the institutional environment, to adapt that environment to better accommodate the needs and interests of minority students' (p. v).

As and if, however, there is a renewed focus on equity, the probability is high that the more recent emphasis on quality, assessment and outcomes will not be lost or essentially diminished. The concept of equity that is likely to inform the renewed concern is that of ensuring not only access but access to and retention in quality education institutions and programmes. From this standpoint the current emphasis on assessment, outcomes and educational effectiveness is likely to continue, to be strengthened, and to be seen as integral to any adequate concept of equity. If this is to be the case all levels of governance in and related to institutions will of necessity have to be involved.

Notes

1. W. Lee Hansen and Jacob O. Stampen,. 'Balancing quality and access in financing higher education'. Unpublished paper prepared for the National Center for Postsecondary Governance and Finance, University of Maryland, College Park, Maryland, September 1987.
2. President's Commission on Higher Education, *Higher Education for American Democracy*. Washington, DC: US Government Printing Office, 1947.
3. Hansen and Stampen, p. 6.
4. Richard M. Millard, *State Boards of Higher Education*. ERIC/Higher Education Research Report No. 4, 1976. Washington, DC: The American Association for Higher Education, 1976, p. 11.
5. Debra E. Gerald, *Projections of Educational Statistics to 1992–93*. Washington, DC: National Center for Educational Statistics, 1985, pp. 51–2.
6. Clark Kerr, *Agenda for a Nation*, ed. Kermit Gordon. Washington, DC: Brookings Institution, 1968.
7. Carnegie Commission on Higher Education, *Quality and Equity: New Levels of Federal Responsibility for Higher Education*. New York: McGraw-Hill, 1968.
8. Alice Rivlin, *Toward a Long Range Plan for Federal Financial Support for Higher Education*. Washington, DC: Department of Health Education and Welfare, January 1969.
9. Hansen and Stampen, p. 8.
10. Samuel B. Gould, *Diversity by Design*. San Francisco: Jossey-Bass, 1973, p. 7.
11. Grover J. Andrews, *Assessing Nontraditional Education*. (Washington, DC: Council on Postsecondary Accreditation, 1978, p. 127.

12. National Commission on Excellence in Education, *A Nation at Risk*. Washington, DC: US Department of Education, 1983, p. 5.
13. Study Group on the Conditions of Excellence in American Higher Education, *Involvement in Learning: Realizing the Potential of American Higher Education*. Washington, DC: National Institute for Education, 1984.
14. William J. Bennett, *To Reclaim a Legacy*. Washington, DC: National Endowment for the Humanities, 1984.
15. Association of American Colleges, *Integrity in the College Curriculum*. Washington, DC: Association of American Colleges, 1985.
16. Education Commission of the States, *Transforming the State Role in Undergraduate Education*. No. PS-86-3. Denver, Colorado: Education Commission of the States, 1986.
17. National Governors' Association, 'Task force on college quality'. In *Time for Results: The Governors' 1991 Report on Education*. Washington, DC: National Governors' Association, 1986, pp. 153–71.
18. Carol Boyer *et al.*, 'Assessment and outcomes measurement: A view from the states'. In *AAHE Bulletin*, **39**(7), 1987.
19. National Governors' Association, *Jobs, Growth, and Competitiveness*. Washington, DC: National Governors' Association, 1987.
20. Harold L. Hodgkinson, *Higher Education: Diversity is our Name*. Washington, DC: National Institute of Independent Colleges and Universities, 1986, p. 6.
21. State Higher Education Executive Officers Task Force on Minority Student Achievement, *A Difference of Degrees: State Initiatives to Improve Minority Student Achievement*. Denver, Colorado: State Higher Education Executive Officers, 1987, pp. 7–8.

6

Institutional Government, Quality and Access in the United Kingdom

Graeme C. Moodie

In Britain, universities (and, in England, polytechnics since 1989) are legally autonomous bodies. There are increasing external pressures, and even direction, which might in the next few years yet further and substantially modify the political reality of autonomy. But at the moment and quite possibly for the foreseeable future, within the contracting limits of their resources and of government policy as implemented by the relevant intermediaries, universities are governed primarily by their academic staff and polytechnics increasingly so. This is true as a matter of political fact, if not of their 'constitutional law'. In this respect the differences between 'Oxbridge' and the other British universities are unimportant and those between the university and polytechnic sectors, though important, are only relative and in any case shrinking. This is not to say that academics are the only important actors on the internal stage. It is to say only that they have tended to be the most important ones at institutional level and, at least in the eyes of British academics, they are significantly more so than their counterparts in most American colleges and universities, whether public or private, and much more so than on the European continent; but things are changing.

We cannot here attempt a full description of the British system of internal management nor offer a comprehensive comparison with the American one; nevertheless, a few comparative generalizations, initially about the university sector, may help to establish an appropriate context (see, e.g. Moodie and Eustace, 1974; van de Graaff *et al.*, 1978). The first is that the general pattern of decision-making reflects that found in the governmental organization of the two countries. If one excludes the houses of Congress and Parliament from consideration (on the ground that they argue and authorize rather than run things) then it is notable that the USA has a leaning towards rule by the one-person executive (president, governor, mayor, city manager, agency head and the like), whereas in Britain there is a greater preference for the committee (cabinet, local authority committees, and numerous public boards), even if the traditional British committee commonly functions under firm guidance from a strong 'chair'. Somewhat similarly, the president of an American college or university is *the* executive, aided, assisted, and hindered by other individuals (administrative vice-presidents and deans in particular) and by various faculty bodies (senates, assemblies, departments, unions, and the many standing or ad hoc committees), but undoubtedly (s)he is at the head of an administrative and policy-making hierarchy and exercises certain powers and prerogatives vested in the office. British vice-chancellors are also central figures within their institutions who exercise considerable influence, but they exercise remarkably few formal powers and derive their influence (personal charisma apart) almost entirely from their focal position within the internal network of communications and from their occupancy of the chair of most major decision-making bodies (usually including the academic 'legislative' bodies, appointment committees, and the major planning and resource-allocating committees). Most of the bodies they chair, moreover, are decision-making organs of internal government which, if formally advisory (as many are), give advice not to the vice-chancellor, but to other committees. Notably, too, such positions as deputy vice-chancellor and dean (of faculties) are normally part-time, of limited term, and filled by election by and from members of the academic staff who continue (with few exceptions) to teach and be employed as academics. (In matters of detail the position at Oxbridge is different – for example, the vice-chancellor, partly because (s)he is a head of college on secondment for a limited period only, but partly also because (s)he does not chair the analogue of senate, is in many respects less important than elsewhere in British higher education, but this of course makes the predominance of the committee even more marked.) Moreover the vice-chancellor still generally comes from an academic career, perhaps at one remove. Indeed, the number of vice-chancellors called in from outside the profession seems to be diminishing and recent recruits have been conspicuously academic. Interestingly, too, as they are forced by government and material necessity into a more managerial stance, and possibly for that reason, noticeably more vice-chancellors are retaining (or reclaiming) the title 'Professor'.

Typically, therefore, the internal government of universities has been collective and to a large degree consensual (if not always among the same people). Its essential style, moreover, has been one in which those closer to the centre or at the 'higher' levels of the decision-making system dispose of initiatives from the more peripheral parts. This diffuse system has accommodated the need for more centralized management in recent years by the use of more professional administrative officials and techniques to brief vice-chancellors and planning committees and to assist them in the preparation of initiatives about the allocation of resources. Since 1989, moreover, institutions have been pressed by the State to prepare, often hastily, detailed financial and academic plans that can be initiated only by centralized 'management teams'. But still the characteristic style is that of proposing action to academic-dominated bodies that dispose of the proposal. Less characteristic are those styles associated more with, for example, investigation (unless by ad hoc committees), or close supervision of the work of others (unless they are students), or the disciplined, centrally directed, pursuit of a single purpose.

It is possible to push this line of thought too far and to exaggerate the contrast between the British and American systems – and I may have already done so to the extent that I have not mentioned the key governing bodies in either country: the board and council. Presidents in America and vice-chancellors in Britain have a crucial role in common – that of mediating between the academics and others working within the institution on the one hand and, on the other, the boards (of trustees or regents) and the university councils or equivalents (largely consisting of 'outsiders', except in Oxbridge) that are responsible for the management of the financial and general affairs of their institution.

In both countries, this is to say, committees play key parts at the summit of authority, but important differences remain: in Britain there is substantial academic representation on these committees, reinforcing the convention that these governing bodies take academic decisions (if at all) only on the advice and the recommendation of the other, academic, boards and committees; and, as a general rule, vice-chancellors must base their long-term influence and hence their effectiveness on their academic constituency (regardless of the formal powers of appointment to the post), whereas presidents (however scholarly and however considerate of academic wishes and interests) must above all retain the confidence of the boards to which they are formally accountable and to which they owe their office. The fact remains, therefore, that British universities constitute an area of academic self-government, of rule by the professional guild, to an extent found in America only in a few small colleges and rarely exceeded (Black Mountain comes to mind as at least a one-time example). The difference between the two systems is most marked, one should add, at the level of institution-wide decision-making, and least noticeable at the basic level of the subject or department, the level at which academic autonomy (as distinct from the authority to decide for others) is greatest. Given that American institutions tend to be much larger and more diverse than British, this may explain why American academics are sometimes surprised to find that the British believe themselves to be more autonomous.

In certain respects the pattern of internal government prevalent in the polytechnics and colleges is closer to that found in America. Their directors (principals in the case of colleges) are expected to be strong executive figures and are assisted in this role by full-time administrative assistant directors comparable to American college vice-presidents. The academic boards, which have evolved from the purely advisory bodies that existed in some of the institutions from which the polytechnics were created, are confined to decision-making about academic issues defined strictly in a way more familiar to American faculty boards than the British university senates. And the budget has tended to be a matter for negotiation with non-academic bodies rather than another sphere for substantial academic influence. For the polytechnic director, those bodies have been Courts of Governors and, beyond them, the appropriate local authorities, all of them operating within the resources allocated by the Department of Education and Science on advice from the National Advisory Board (NAB) and Committee for Public Sector Higher Education. (By the terms of the 1988 Education Reform Act, however, the English polytechnics –

and some colleges – have been emancipated from local authority control and the NAB and Committee are to be replaced by the Polytechnic and College Funding Council; there is therefore no point in saying more about directors' relations with local authorities or NAB and as yet no reliable basis on which to speculate about their new relations with governors and central government.) Because the polytechnics and colleges, unlike both American and the rest of British higher education, teach and assess their students for awards by an external national body, the Council of National Academic Awards (CNAA), which is also extensively involved in evaluating and validating the academic performance of the institutions, their academic staff, in this respect too, are less self-governing than, traditionally, their colleagues in universities.

On the two sides of the binary line, therefore, one also finds significant differences (as well as important similarities and some reciprocal influences) in the manner in which academic quality is monitored and sustained. We will begin with the universities because they are older, because their degrees have established the standards for all of higher education, and because many in the polytechnic world have aspired to close the perceived gaps (in character and prestige as well as funding) between the universities and themselves. Given the role of academics in universities their attitudes towards access and quality have assumed all the more importance. The key point here is that, broadly speaking, academics have been and are more enthusiastic about the latter than the former; British academics are not, on the whole, zealots for very much wider access to higher education and certainly not for anything approaching a system of mass higher education. This conclusion is unaffected by the occasions when individual institutions have actively sought to increase student enrolment, for these have usually arisen when their own survival or status was at issue. Examples include: the university colleges anxious, between the wars, to consolidate their positions on the list of bodies eligible for support from the University Grants Committee; the earliest years of the new universities founded in the early 1960s; and, since the early 1970s, the newly created polytechnics. Today, similarly, both universities and polytechnics may indeed seek 'overseas' students to raise income, and they may favour a wider access (especially of women and mature' students) than seems to be envisaged by government spokesmen. But the welcome is conditional on a supply of resources at a 'proper' rate, and it does not extend much beyond the numbers needed to avoid contraction.

These academic attitudes cannot be dismissed or censured as being perverse, anti-social, or even simply self-serving, though a case could be made at least for the last of these labels. Those of us who taught the ex-service students (veterans) demobilized after the end of World War II still recall that as a golden age of mature, dedicated and industrious learners among whom only the very brightest of the usual school-leavers made much impression. Not surprisingly, perhaps, the greater pressures for access in the 1950s were met, initially, by raising the threshold for admission, and the later plans for expansion were regarded with some reservation – allegedly on grounds of quality, but also, as Halsey and Trow (1971) argued, from a less articulate reluctance to change. But whether 'more' is believed to herald 'worse' or merely 'different', most teachers see expansion as threatening standards either via a heavier teaching load for them (and also less research and possibly less intensive teaching) or an enlargement of the profession that might (and some now say 'did') dilute the profession with less committed, less scholarly, or simply less competent entrants. Similarly, expansion was feared as threatening the standards of students at entry. The attitude becomes clearer if we note that, once it is known that resources (crucially, the staff–student ratio) will be maintained, teachers may favour expansion as a route to larger departments, more specialized teaching (and research), and promotion. From the point of view of the researcher also, wider access is of limited benefit, being desirable only up to the point needed to assure an adequate supply of future graduate students and research assistants – a point inescapably circumscribed by quality. Nor do these arguments derive their weight merely from the large say given to academics. Another form of internal government might, perhaps properly, give them less weight, but it would still have to take them seriously into account.

Not even academic attitudes exist independently of circumstances, as has already been suggested. If this were ever doubted, the response of British higher education to government insistence that students from overseas (excluding fellow-citizens from the European Community) be charged something like the full cost of their courses would suffice to lay the doubts to rest. After a considerable initial drop in income as overseas fees were more than doubled, intensive recruitment drives, streamlined admission procedures, and (it has been suggested) more generous entrance conditions to some institutions, not to mention the design of new courses aimed especially at overseas targets, have in fact led to a significant increase in both numbers and income over the last few years. But attitudes are not responsive only to financial incentives. More importantly, they have been nourished by established methods of maintaining standards that are themselves deeply consonant with the universities' style of government (and its diffused initiatives). These methods may briefly be described as 'threshold control', and exemplified by looking at four areas crucial to quality.

The principle of threshold control is perhaps most clearly illustrated by the process of acquiring university status. Whether one looks at the way in which institutions have been accepted on to the UGC list of grant-aided universities and university colleges, or even the setting up of new universities in the 1950s and 1960s, the same processes are evident. From among several claimants or petitioners the UGC selected by reference to a number of 'entry' criteria (e.g. Shinn, 1986) and then, for an initial period, designated certain gatekeepers or guides (by attachment to existing institutions, by linkage to external examining bodies, or – in the case of the newest universities – by appointing independent planning committees to formulate the academic strategy and then to monitor the initial appointments and development). The crucial points, however, are that the initiative came from the institutions or, in the 1960s, the local committees anxious to promote a new institution, and that these universities and colleges, once established and accepted, have become autonomous and free from individual tutelage. The essential control lay at the threshold, in the selection or acceptance – thereafter only the most general forms of monitoring took place and of the newer on the same footing as of the older established institutions (members of which had exercised the original powers of choice and recognition). Put at its simplest, the procedure has been to select with care, and then to trust those selected to conduct their own affairs in a manner consistent with their newly acquired status.

Threshold control can be seen again if we turn to what is probably the single most important category of decisions for academic quality – the appointment (and promotion) of academic staff. At various points: initial appointment, the ending of probation, overcoming 'efficiency bars' to automatic salary increments, and promotion to the more senior ranks (senior lecturer and beyond) – at these points proposals are made by senior colleagues to some institution-wide committee or organ that decides, on the evidence of the performance and the judgement of colleagues and peers, whether to appoint, retain, or promote. In some cases the decision is merely about whether some criteria or standards are met, and in others – initial appointment and most promotions – there will also be important elements of competition (between candidates or for resources), but the basic pattern is the same in both cases: at these points academics select from amongst the initiatives of others. Especially for the more senior posts, individuals will often be encouraged or invited to apply, but such approaches tend to be informal and to occur within the framework outlined. Few British selecting committees operate quite like the more free-ranging American search committees.

The other striking feature of academic appointments – until the 1980s – has been the security of tenure from which most British academics have benefited from an early stage in their careers, and subject (for the most part) to dismissal only for 'good cause' (usually: gross incompetence or incapacity, or certain serious kinds of criminal or immoral behaviour). Economic pressures or academic organizational needs have not constituted 'good cause'. Moreover, there was traditionally little or nothing by the way of instruction in the arts of teaching or examining, and virtually no close monitoring. On the other hand, there had been the continuous *in*formal monitoring that sustains a reputation, and a keen interest by colleagues in results as measured by public writings and utterance or by the performance of one's students. In a relatively small country and system, word tends to get round at least about the more conspicuous examples of good and bad work, and on it promotion and recognition may depend. The way in which decisions are taken means that the academic profession is richer in rewards or incentives for the good than in penalties for the mediocre – hence some of the current pressures from the central government to increase 'productivity' (sometimes by means that are quite inappropriate for creative work), introduce more effective programmes for 'staff development' and, now being brought about by the new Education Reform Act, to modify (some say destroy) tenure. In the republic of learning, it is now more frequently being asked, who shall guard the guardians? – to which the only possible answer is 'other guardians'; but this is not the place to enter that controversy. My main point is simply that, as with institutions, so with staff, the traditional style of academic self-government encourages British higher education to select with care, and then to trust those selected.

Threshold control is also applied in the proposing and approving of new subjects or courses. Senates, faculties, or other academic bodies tend keenly to scrutinize (and frequently reject) subjects and courses at the point of entry – and scarcely at all thereafter unless faced with an undeniable problem or an unexpected shortage of resources. In this, universities are probably not unique. Studies of public expenditure and even of corporate budgeting suggest that the ideal system, in which every item is regularly appraised against every other, is much rarer than budgeting by habit and tradition modified only marginally by incremental change (e.g. Wildavsky, 1964 or Lindblom, 1968). Once again, therefore, the pattern is one of careful selection at the threshold followed by a substantial degree of laissez-faire towards those found (or deemed) to be trustworthy.

My final illustration is also a partial exception to the rule of 'select and trust'. In admitting students it is clear that British institutions apply a similar system of threshold control. Entry is selective and, at least in the past half-century, the most common experience has been one of having to turn away applicants who have not matched or exceeded the prevailing criteria for admission (including those relating exclusively to intellectual attainment or ability). The system is also characterized by concern about student failures or drop-outs, the 'wastage rate' as it used to be called (or 'retention rate' as Americans now seem to prefer to say). This stems at least as much from commitment (or even paternalism) and a feeling that high 'wastage' is a measure of subject or institution failure, as from external worry about the use of public money. The result, in any case, is to focus attention on careful selection at the threshold. Once selected, it is true, British students then benefit from the 'pastoral' duties of the teaching staff. But this monitoring, and sometimes even nurturing, of students is only a partial exception to the rule – and it has only been in the post-war period that Britain has witnessed the last (or is that over-optimistic?) of those formerly common figures in university society, the 'idle gilded youth' and the 'long-lifer' whose persistence alone sometimes led to eventual graduation.

Control over the quality of the 'end-product', which is to say of the assessment of students and the degrees awarded, provides the major exception to the system of 'select and trust'. As is pointed out elsewhere in this book (Chapter 3), in British universities there appears to be a marked *dis*trust of the academic-as-teacher when it comes to student examinations, in that outsiders are always involved in the assessment process as a check upon or, as in the case of the university colleges which taught for University of London degrees, substitutes for the internal teachers. These external examiners are almost invariably other academics and their role is as much a matter of ensuring fair treatment of individual students as it is of controlling quality through the maintenance of common standards among institutions, but this form of peer review is nevertheless a conspicuous departure from the pattern of threshold control found in the key areas.

Judgement at the threshold is nevertheless the principal occasion and method of quality control and is deeply entrenched in the characteristic style of academic government. Indeed it is part and parcel of the normal working life of academics. Sir Edward Parkes, then Vice-Chancellor of Leeds and a former chairman of the UGC, has pointed to the role of selection in that life. Writing in *The Independent* newspaper (27 July 1987), he pointed out that:

> Those of us who tend the production lines in the university industry spend a great deal of time in selection, and in encouraging selectivity by others. We sift applicants for admission, we mark essays, we grade course work and we set examination papers. In our research we choose between alternative hypotheses or alternative explanations of observed phenomena.
>
> We make judgements about our colleagues, choosing those who will be appointed, or promoted, and those who will not. Many of us carry our capacity for selective judgement into other universities, by acting as external examiners, or members of grant-awarding committees of research councils.

It is also a system that tends to exclude rather than to recruit and therefore must, other things being equal, help to restrict, or merely maintain, student numbers rather than generate a powerful recruiting drive – while those university academics who favour (say) the extension of opportunities for higher (or at any rate post-secondary) education to more people often look to other institutions for action.

These other institutions operate under a significantly more formal, collective, and centrally more co-ordinated system of quality control in which the key but not sole external body is the CNAA. Partly in furtherance of the aim to create, in the public sector, a form of higher education more directly responsive to local, public and social preferences, but partly also to provide a public warranty that the degrees and other awards 'are consistent in standard and are comparable in standard with awards granted and conferred throughout higher education in the United Kingdom including the universities' (to quote from Statute 9 (1) of the CNAA), all polytechnic courses have had to be approved and all awards be granted by the CNAA (or the Business and Technician Education Council for sub-degree courses). In addition, courses require administrative approval through a complex system, ultimately supervised by central government, to prevent wasteful duplication or unnecessary provision. To round off the system, all academic work is subject to monitoring through personal visits by HM Inspectors appointed by the Department of Education and Science (e.g. Gibson, 1986). The processes of evaluation and approval have always involved discussion between those responsible for the courses and outsiders (often from universities, especially in the early days). The style of the discussions has evolved from something like confrontation and cross-examination to a form of partnership and, most recently in the case of stronger polytechnics, to external participation in a largely domestic process. Throughout, however, the need to prepare for the discussion has resulted in elaborate procedures in each institution to ensure that new courses are proposed only after careful scrutiny of their design, objectives, staffing and resource implications, and are thereafter subject to regular review. Courses thus tend to be more the responsibility of teams of teachers, to be more explicit in their aims, and to be much more carefully constructed than has generally been the case in universities; though in all types of institution the quality of courses is a function, ultimately, of the quality of the teachers and facilities.

The precise details of the review machinery need not detain us here, but fuller accounts (e.g. Nixon, 1987; Jones and Kiloh, 1987; Church, 1988) refer to two concepts, the 'threshold' and 'peer review' that do deserve comment. In this context 'threshold' does not refer to the process of quality control discussed earlier in this chapter but to the aim of course review, namely, to ensure that a course qualifies by meeting a minimum standard. It does not, however, carry the implication that, once approved, no further attention is required; to ensure that the course meets acceptable standards is a continuous (or at least recurrent) responsibility. 'Peer review' deserves comment only because in this context it carries a special flavour in addition to the basic sense of judgement by one's equals. The point is that it is a review by *equals* rather than by superior levels in a hierarchy, and implies acceptance, as full members, by the academic world as a whole. It is particularly stressed, therefore, in connection with the CNAA's new policy (consequent upon the Lindop Report of 1985) of accreditation of the stronger polytechnics, that is, of agreeing with them the procedures by which they themselves carry the responsibility for self-evaluation and review, assisted by outsiders, but no longer subordinate to them. The institution as a whole and its procedures for quality control, but not individual courses, become the sole concern of CNAA. As Nixon has written, 'peer-group review, organized under the aegis of CNAA, is likely to become the prime means of assessing and controlling academic quality instead of, as hitherto, threshold validation of individual courses' (1987, p. 82). He might have added that this development also represents a move in the direction of that kind of threshold control typical of universities. And we must add that the development of these explicit and formal methods of 'quality control' in the polytechnics and colleges has generated considerable interest (in government as well as the polytechnics) in extending comparable procedures to universities whose more informal and inconspicuous methods (turning on reputation sustained by external examiners, external assessors for the most senior academic appointments, and the extensive system of peer review of publications and research funding) no longer command universal outside confidence. (We will not, here, speculate on the reasons for this external scepticism – but they do not seem to do only with proven lapses in academic quality (Moodie, 1988).) As a result, universities have moved towards greater formality and self-consciousness in some of their procedures (e.g. external examining, the supervision of graduate students, and the approval of new or revised courses), but are still reluctant to meet the high costs, particularly in man-hours, of adopting the elaborate systems for evaluation and review found in the public sector.

The two sectors of British higher education thus differ in their forms of government and their characteristic styles of 'quality control'. There is also some connection between the differences in the two areas. The sectors are alike, however, in having only limited control over access. They have some discretion about admitting entrants from outside the European Community, who by definition do not affect the issue, but student numbers are today largely a matter for the national government (through advice given to the Funding Councils) whose policies appear to be largely conditioned by the cost of student maintenance and direct teaching on the one hand, and by pressures from (mainly middle-class) parent voters and from industry on the other. For the institutions student numbers have followed resources rather than created them – but in the 1990s this will be modified to the extent that student fees are raised and become a more significant source of revenue.

Different institutions and subjects still attract student applicants at differential rates, and to that extent it might be said that market forces operate; but the main consequence, at least in the short run, is simply that the examination grades demanded for entry have become the 'price mechanism' to bring student demand into line with the supply of places laid down *for* each institution. (In the longer run, however, the 'grade price' is a factor taken into account by the Funding Councils when they make their differential grants, while a generally rising 'grade price' may create electoral pressure as it did in the late 1950s and early 1960s.) But as things now stand, decisions taken within and by institutions are largely irrelevant.

At the time of writing it is clear that relations between government, higher education and the market are about to change, but far from clear exactly how they will change. Ingredients in the new mixture will include: an attempt by the new Funding Councils to tie funding more closely and directly to performance in specified areas through systems of 'contracts' rather than grants; clearer statutory powers of direction for the Secretary of State for Education and Science; greater discretion to institutions in setting fees for students and a lesser dependence of students upon government money with which to pay those fees; encouragement to institutions to seek more non-government money; a sharp reduction in the size of the relevant age-group during the early 1990s, but business insistence that its need for graduate recruits will not diminish might lead to increased access expressed as a percentage of the population (e.g. Council for Industry and Higher Education, 1988). As yet, however, there is no consensus either on how precisely to implement these changes or on the wider changes in funding, in the kind (or, even more, kinds) of higher education on offer, and in the methods of selection and quality monitoring that any radical widening of access would entail.

References

Church, Clive H. (1988). The qualities of validation, *Studies in Higher Education* **13**(1), 27–43.

Council for Industry and Higher Education (1988). *Towards a Partnership: Supporting more Students*. London.

Department of Education and Science (DES) (1985). *Academic Validation in Public Sector H.E.* ('Lindop Report'). HMSO, Cmnd 9524.

Gibson, Alan (1986). Inspecting education. In Moodie, Graeme C. (ed.), *Standards and Criteria in Higher Education*. Milton Keynes: SRHE and Open University Press.

Halsey, A. H. and Trow, Martin (1971). *The British Academics*, London: Faber.

Jones, Stephen and Kiloh, George (1987). The management of polytechnics and colleges. In Becher, Tony (ed.), *British Higher Education*. London: Allen & Unwin.

Lindblom, Charles E. (1968). *The Policy-Making Process*. Englewood Cliffs, NJ: Prentice-Hall.

Moodie, Graeme C. (1988). The debates about higher educational quality in Britain and USA. *Studies in Higher Education*, **13**(1), 5–13.

Moodie, Graeme C. and Eustace, Rowland (1974). *Power and Authority in British Universities*. London: Allen & Unwin.

Nixon, Nigel (1987). Central control of the public sector in Becher, Tony (ed.), *British Higher Education*. London: Allen & Unwin.

Shinn, Christine Helen (1986). *Paying the Piper*. London and Philadelphia: Falmer Press.

van de Graaff, John *et al.* (1978). *Academic Power. Patterns of Authority in Seven National Systems of Higher Education*. New York: Praeger.

Wildavsky, Aaron (1964). *The Politics of the Budgetary Process*. Boston: Little, Brown.

7

The Campus Economics of Stringency in the United States

Michael J. Dooris and Kenneth P. Mortimer

Introduction

American colleges and universities have seen powerful changes in their world during the past 30 years. As described elsewhere in this book, political, social and economic forces from the 1960s through the 1980s have challenged US institutions of higher education with unprecedented upheaval. Amidst this upheaval, the quality of and access to higher education in the United States have become topics of lively debate. This chapter contributes a contextual point of view to that debate. The chapter places the push and pull of quality and access in the environmental context within which American colleges and universities have operated for the past 25 to 30 years.

The economics of stringency: Two central questions

This chapter focuses on how, after decades of explosive growth, American colleges and universities have responded to an era of stringency. The chapter addresses two central questions. First, *what* have been the most crucial shifts with which colleges and universities have had to cope over the past 30 years? Second, *how* have colleges and universities adapted to these forces?

The question of 'what' is the point of departure for a whirlwind tour of the relevant literature. In that literature, some especially potent environmental forces stand out: for example, economics, demography, and politics and government. The question of 'how' involves the way in which colleges and universities have adapted to the environmental challenges of the past three decades.

The diversity of 3600 colleges and universities cannot be captured in general comments such as those offered here. American higher education is a mosaic of unique institutions – each with an individual identity, traditions and experiences which influence how compuses confront the forces of external change. For example, economic vitality is more tightly linked to enrolments at non-selective private colleges than at other types of institutions. Concerns about institutional financial aid are more important to private than to public institutions. External fund-raising is traditionally a more critical consideration for private than for public institutions.

In addition to an overview of higher education's responses to stringency, this chapter provides an in-depth case study of a single public research university: The Pennsylvania State University. The study traces the various strategies by which that multi-campus research university adapted to the environmental turbulence of the past three decades.

The concluding sections of the chapter will return to quality and access, the concepts which undergird this volume. As colleges and universities have responded to the aggregate of external conditions, how and to what extent have quality and access been traded, compromised, defended, or enhanced? There is speculation, for instance, about whether colleges and universities can cut budgets and maintain quality. The chapter closes with a discussion of dilemmas such as these.

These are significant and timely issues. Just as the 1960s represented a time of profound change for higher education in the United States, we are facing another 'shift point' as we enter the 1990s. American higher education policy makers now know that colleges and universities are much more subject to external turbulence than people wrote about, or recognized formally, in the 1960s. Colleges and universities are beginning to realize that they can influence, if not control, their own destinies as they deal with this turbulence. The campus economics of stringency can be defined as the set of choices, including choices about quality and access, which have been or can be made in response to environmental contingencies. A clear understanding of those choices can help guide compuses as they cope with the unpredictable political, demographic and economic environments of the future.

Eight factors

It appears that eight factors will continue to shape campus economics for colleges and universities in the 1990s:

- Enrolment patterns.
- State appropriations.
- Financial aid.
- Regulation and accountability.
- Physical plant deterioration.
- Private fund-raising.
- The rising cost of knowledge.
- Commercialization and economic development.

Enrolments

The 1950s and 1960s were decades of rapid enrolment growth. The 1970s brought continuing increases but at declining *rates* of growth, while enrolments stabilized in the 1980s.[1]

During the 1960s total higher education enrolment in the United States doubled, from about 4 million students in 1960 to just over 8 million students in 1969. By comparison, total enrolments went from about 8.6 million in 1970 to 11.6 million in 1979, an increase of about one-third. During the 1980s, enrolments essentially reached a plateau – total enrolments nationally exceeded 12 million students for the first time in 1980, and ranged from 12 to 12.8 million through the 1980s. So while enrolments continued to grow after 1970, the *rate* of growth continued to decline substantially.

Student mix (by gender and ethnicity) and enrolments by institutional type have changed. Some of these changes have been sudden and, recalling the conventional wisdom of ten to twenty years past, many have been surprising.

It was not until 1978 that the number of female students equalled the number of male students. Just ten years earlier, men had accounted for 60% of total enrolments. Also, from 1967 to 1988, the share of enrolments accounted for by part-time students rose from 31% to 43%. In addition, ethnic composition is changing significantly, with white and black enrolments growing more slowly than total enrolments, and Asian and Hispanic enrolments growing vigorously. However, enrolment rates of racial and ethnic minorities remain a particular concern. In 1988, about 28% of white 18- to 24-year-olds entered higher education, compared to 21% of blacks and 17% of Hispanics.

Different sectors of higher education have experienced different patterns of enrolment growth. Over the past 25 to 30 years, 'market share' has shifted from four-year and doctoral institutions to two-year institutions, and from the private sector to the public sector. In 1963, two-year institutions accounted for about 18% of total enrolments; by 1988, two-year institutions accounted for about 38% of total enrolments. In 1963, private institutions enrolled 36% of students in the USA; by 1988, private institutions accounted for 23% of enrolments.

In sum, the overall enrolment trend since the early 1960s has been growth. Rates of growth, however, have been very different in the 1960s, 1970s, and 1980s, and the experiences of various sectors and sub-populations have likewise differed. In the past ten to fifteen years, some institutions experienced decline, but a more 'average' experience has been either stability or slight growth in enrolments.

Economics and state appropriations

During the same period that enrolment growth was levelling off, colleges and universities shared the sting of the general economic malaise of the 1970s – inflation, recession and unemployment – with costs outpacing revenues during those years. Higher education in general fell behind inflation in the early- to mid-1970s, and in more recent years has essentially been staying in place. For example, Zammuto[2] states: 'Overall, the revenue data indicate a clear slowing in the growth of institutional revenues between 1973 and 1982, particularly in the public sector.' More recent data show that nationally over the past nine years, overall state appropriations per student have just about kept pace with inflation as measured by the Higher Education Price Index,[3] although there has been great individual variation among the states.

As Leslie[4] points out, the real difficulty for many campuses was that the enrolment changes – for which there had been ample warning – were compounded in the early 1970s by the worst economic recession in forty years. It was difficult if not impossible for campuses to prepare for the interacting effects of enrolment instability or decline, the reduction in constant dollars in institutional revenues, and severe economic recession.

Financial aid

The declining rate of enrolment growth was mitigated by the massive growth in financial aid which began in the 1960s. Total financial aid from federal, state and institutional sources rose from about a half-billion dollars in 1964 to over $21 billion in 1986. Even in inflation-adjusted dollars, aid grew rapidly during the 1960s and 1970s – e.g. a tenfold increase between 1964 and 1976 – before falling by 3% from 1981 to 1986.

The mix of grants and loans also changed dramatically over this period. From 1964 through 1976, loans accounted for between 17% and 21% of total aid annually; by 1987, loans accounted for 50% of total aid. In constant dollars, federal loan (Guaranteed Student Loan) amounts per student have about held steady over the past twenty-five years, but major grants (e.g. Pell Grants) have declined on a per-student basis.[5]

In addition to changing financial aid policies there have been changes in the relationship between tuition, income and financial aid. In 1989–90, tuition rates outpaced inflation, as measured by the Consumer Price Index, for the eighth straight year. Tuition has risen a bit more rapidly for private than public institutions in recent years; from 1978 through 1989, tuition and fees rose at an average rate of 8% for four-year public institutions, and by 9% at private institutions.[6] However, tuition and financial aid have become intertwined to the extent that by 1988, higher education had 'become a discount business, with fewer and fewer people paying the sticker price as the price climbs'.[7]

Especially at private colleges, income from tuition increases has increasingly been used to replace federal funds and to supplement or replace financial aid for lower- and middle-income students. Consider the example of Boston College, which in fiscal year 1980 received $5 million in federal student aid and contributed $6.5 million of its own funds. In fiscal year 1987, Boston College received $4.6 million in federal aid and budgeted $15 million of its own moneys toward student aid.[8] This case is consistent with higher education's overall experience in recent years; between 1981 and 1986, inflation-adjusted aid from federal sources declined by 10% while inflation-adjusted aid from institutional sources increased by 26%.[9]

How does financial aid affect access to higher education? Integrating a number of studies, Leslie and Brinkman[10] found indications that the low-income population does not participate to the extent of middle- and high-income students, and that low-income students are under-represented in high-cost, prestigious institutions. None the less, they concluded that, overall, student aid does increase access, and that aid has been responsible in part for the increased enrolment of low- to middle-income students in recent years.

Regulation and accountability

The past twenty years have seen more and more regulation of colleges and universities.[11] This may be due to a general decline in confidence in public officials and a growing clamour for accountability, public and legislative dissatisfaction with the skyrocketing growth in higher education budgets in the 1960s and early 1970, and the argument that co-ordination and regulation can help eliminate waste and duplication among a state's colleges and universities.

The increased regulation of higher education by government can be illustrated by reference to several requirements mandated by federal and state agencies. In 1972 an executive order mandated affirmative action searches. A later executive order extended rights of access to buildings for physically disabled persons. The 1970s also saw a spate of public employee collective bargaining laws. More recently, state governments have moved to establish institutional assessment requirements. As of 1988, twenty-four states required programmes to assess what college students learn, and another twelve were debating whether to implement such programmes.[12] Generally institutions are expected to *absorb* the increased costs imposed by such legislation; there have been few, if any, special appropriations designed to buffer institutions from the increased costs of such programmes.

Physical deterioration

As colleges and universities struggled with the exigencies of the past two decades, one successful short-term coping mechanism was to defer the maintenance of physical facilities. The long-term dangers of this are only now beginning to surface. According to a 1987 study, 'among the most serious, and least recognized, of the problems currently facing institutions of higher education is the condition of their physical plants'.[13] Among the campuses included in that study, over half rated rehabilitation needs as extremely urgent or very urgent, with similar responses on the need for new construction or additions. One-third of the respondents planned on spending $25 million or more on new construction in the coming five-year period.

A 1988 report placed a $70 billion price tag on needed renovations to the nation's college and university buildings. Urgent repair needs alone were estimated at about $20 billion. The same report stated that colleges and universities defer about $4 in maintenance for every $1 they spend, with the net effect that the backlog of repairs is growing. In short, facilities are deteriorating faster than they can be repaired.[14] Such reports draw a discouraging picture of severely needed rehabilitation and new construction of classrooms, laboratory and research facilities, and office buildings.

Development activities

Colleges and universities have increasingly been looking to external fund-raising to cope with mounting financial pressures. As noted by Dunn,[15] 'There is no doubt about the growing importance of private fund-raising', with voluntary support outpacing both inflation and expenditure growth in recent years. Also, while independent colleges and universities have traditionally depended more heavily than the public sector on voluntary support, public institutions are now pursuing private gifts more and more aggressively.

From 1985–6 to 1986–7, private financial support of the nation's colleges and universities rose from $7.4 billion to a total of $8.5 billion, for the largest increase on record.[16] In the wake of tax law changes and a stock market crash, total fund-raising dropped to $8.2 billion in 1989–90, but institutions continue to raise their sights. In 1989, more than 65 colleges and universities were trying to raise $100 million in five years or less, and three universities – Boston, New York and Stanford – had announced goals of $1 billion.[17] However, this experience has not touched institutions of higher education uniformly; the leading twenty institutions typically garner one-quarter or more of the national totals, while for about two-thirds of American colleges and universities, development funds are essentially insignificant.[18]

The cost of knowledge

Simmons notes that the cost of education has been driven by explosions of knowledge and sophisticated technology, and by the concomitant need to keep pace on a much faster track. 'The nature of higher education is as different from that of two, three, or four decades ago as the computer is from the abacus . . . You no longer can teach laboratory science with Bunsen burners. This is the day of the electron microscope, the ultra-centrifuge, the high-performance liquid chromatograph, and of computers.'[19] Even library research has been revolutionized over the past decade, with the advent of computer networks and databases, electronic bibliographic systems, and sophisticated personnel able to use these resources. A labour- and capital-intensive infrastructure of people, facilities, utilities, insurance and so on, is needed to support up-to-date instructional and research programmes.

Commercialization and economic development

A recently emerging literature points out the blossoming involvement of universities in applied, often commercially oriented, activities – such as joint ventures with business, contract research for both industry and government, and economic development. For example, in 1988 Monsanto and Washington University (St. Louis) were in the midst of an eight-year, $62 million biotechnology venture; Carnegie Mellon and Stanford were investing in NeXt Inc. (a computer company); and Harvard was proposing to raise $30 million through a partnership involving its medical school faculty. More generally, from 1976 to 1986, industrial funding was by far the fastest growing component of funded research for large research universities. During those years, industrial funding grew at three times the rate of research sponsored by federal, state, or local governments.[20]

While the merits and dangers of commercialization are open to debate, it is clear that the involvement of colleges and universities in commercial ventures is being driven by vigorous economic forces. This involvement is both a response by colleges to changing societal expectations and needs, and a way for institutions to cope with the increasingly difficult financial considerations with which they have been confronted.

The evolution of institutional response

The external pressures cited above have not affected all types of institutions and all sectors of higher education to the same extent, or even in the same ways. This is in part due to the nature of different institutions, and in part due to the variety of potential combinations of external factors (e.g. growing enrolments and declining revenues, declining enrolments and stable revenues).[21]

But such trends, taken together, set the stage for describing the evolution of institutional responses to stringency. Leslie[22] noted that institutional responses to stress can hypothetically be categorized into sequential stages. The focus of that argument was slightly different from that of the present chapter (Leslie suggested how institutional behaviour moved from highly political actions to highly rational approaches in reacting to fiscal stress). None the less, the idea that the behaviour of colleges and universities in responding to environmental turmoil can be mapped onto identifiable, sequential phases is an appealing one. It is used here to structure the evolution of institutional response to the era of stringency which began in the early 1970s. Those responses are characterized into three phases: *horizontal reduction* (focusing on across-the-board retrenchment); *vertical reallocation* (shifting resources to meet priorities); and *strategy and choice* (deliberately establishing goals and working toward those goals).

Beginning an era of stringency

During the early 1970s many campuses moved from a perspective of managing growth to a perspective of managing stringency, or at best stability. Chaffee[23] called the early 1970s a 'shift point' in the management of colleges. Zammuto[24] said: 'The 1970s are generally thought of as the tail end of a period of rapid growth for higher education.' As characterized by Mortimer and Tierney,[25] the predominant theme for colleges and universities during those years changed from one of quantitative growth in enrolments, programmes and physical facilities, to qualitative growth – that is, the reordering of priorities based upon 'the three Rs' of reduction, reallocation and retrenchment.

Horizontal reduction

By the early 1970s, administrators and scholars were discussing the 'management of decline',[26] and many college administrators anticipated such radical changes as merger, consolidation, or closure, and in the case of some private institutions, the possibility of public take-over. Many in higher education were concerned about how to manage reduction and decline. Some institutional leaders were, of course, concerned with basic survival.

The initial response of many institutions to the early 1970s' plateau in resource growth was to attempt to hold the line or reduce expenditures horizontally. As described by Lozier and Althouse,[27] such across-the-board measures included position freezes, the collapse of vacant positions, and absolute budget cuts. This horizontal reduction can be an effective short-term budget tactic, but at some point 'it becomes unsound and irresponsible' (p. 239) to continue proportional, across-the-board budget reductions.

After a comprehensive review of budgeting strategies under conditions of decline, Mortimer and Tierney[28] concluded that across-the-board decremental budgets are difficult to maintain over several years. Internal political pressures build up to such an extent that administrative judgements and procedures are questioned and morale deteriorates.

Vertical reallocation

The 1975 Carnegie Foundation report *More than Survival*[29] was a milestone in the evolution of campus response to the stringency of the post-1960s period. Around that time, the focus seemed to shift from budget reductions as a means for survival, to the beginnings of a strategic approach. The Carnegie report noted that, in response to the new depression beginning in about 1970, many colleges and universities had 'joined the new management movement', employing tactics for 'holding down their expenditure growth, finding new sources of funds, and going from buying to selling in the student market' (p. 85). The report called upon institutions to advance from these tactical efforts to the development of an overall strategy.

That 1975 report prescribed campus strategies which would enhance an institution's flexibility to meet future changes. It suggested that administrative responses to the end of income growth focus upon built-in budgetary reallocation as the main source of flexibility, with corresponding attempts to ensure flexibility in the reallocation of facilities and personnel. Simply put, in the late 1970s and early 1980s we began to see a shift in emphasis from reduction and retrenchment toward reallocation and the setting of priorities as means to deal with financial stress.[30]

An illustration of how one institution, Penn State University, used this tactical approach – holding down expenditure growth while making selective choices about individual units and programmes – was provided in 1983 by Lozier and Althouse.[31] That case study described one university's adoption in 1977 of a rolling five-year budget planning process built around 'differentially applied' internal reallocations. The study, with its focus on reallocation through 'careful medium range planning', was characteristic of the state of the art of how campuses were responding to stringency – with a focus on tactics for reduction and allocation – in the mid-1970s and early 1980s.

Strategy and choice: The Penn State experience

In 1989–90 Penn State enrols 70,000 students in a network of 22 campuses across the Commonwealth of Pennsylvania. Approximately 37,000 students are located at the University Park campus; 25,000 at 17 two-year feeder campuses; and the remainder at the medical school, a four-year campus in Erie, Pennsylvania, and two upper division/graduate campuses. The university has a 1989–90 total operating budget of just over 1 billion dollars.

Penn State entered higher education's boom years of the 1960s after experiencing decades of steadily paced growth and diversification, in what has been termed an 'era of good feeling' for the university.[32] In fact, until 1953 Penn State was still called a college; it was probably the largest college in the country.

In the 1960s, however, the rapid growth in the number of college-age students rocked Penn State with an explosive influx of 'baby boom' enrolments. During the administration of a single Penn State president, from 1956 to 1970, the student population nearly tripled in size, from 17,000 to 48,000; the number of faculty members nearly doubled, from 1600 to 3000; and the total annual budget increased more than fivefold, from $34 million to $177 million; as did the state appropriation, from $12 million to $69 million.

The late 1960s in particular saw the Commonwealth of Pennsylvania scrambling to meet a burgeoning demand for access. In the years 1965 to 1969 Temple University and the University of Pittsburgh, both private, became public institutions; the state established fourteen community colleges; and Penn State opened an additional seven campuses to help meet the demand for public higher education. The Pennsylvania experience was not unique nationally. During this time, 'similar outcomes occurred in Ohio, Wisconsin, South Carolina, and

Table 7.1 Percentage increases in state appropriations to Penn State 1965–6 to 1969–70 compared to 1976–7 to 1980–81

Year	% increase	Year	% increase
1965–66	19.5	1976–77	3.9
1966–67	30.3	1977–78	0.0
1967–68	23.4	1978–79	4.9
1968–69	23.0	1979–80	7.3
1969–70	16.0	1980–81	5.8
Average	22.4	Average	4.4

Source: Office of Planning and Analysis, The Pennsylvania State University.

several other states, where . . . large public universities took the lead in creating satellite campus networks'.[33]

Just as much of higher education's enrolment growth was concentrated in the late 1960s, the economic prosperity of these years also brought generous financial support from the state and an abundance of federal moneys. The annual increases in the state's appropriations to Penn State for 1965–6, to 1969–70 ranged from 16% to 30% annually.

However, the prosperity of those years collapsed dramatically as the age of affluence, both for higher education and for Penn State, ended in the 1970s. By 1970, the Commonwealth of Pennsylvania 'had gone from a record budget surplus to the brink of bankruptcy'.[34] As national and world economic conditions worsened through the 1970s, the state's appropriations to Penn State actually declined in after-inflation dollars. During several budget years, the legislature was months late in passing the university's appropriation, and Penn State was forced to borrow millions of dollars for operating expenses in the interim. The annual increases in state appropriations for the late 1960s are compared to those for 1976–7 to 1980–81 in Table 7.1.

Entering the 1990s, the Commonwealth of Pennsylvania is firmly entrenched among states, many economically depressed, which have not adequately supported higher education. Pennsylvania's state and local appropriations per FTE student in 1987 of $3373 (compared with the national average of $4570) ranked the state forty-seventh in the nation. For Penn State, difficult strains upon already thin resources have worsened because enrolments have continued to mushroom (largely because of the university's 22-campus system). From 1970–71 to 1989–90 Penn State's student population climbed from 46,000 to over 70,000, an increase of fifty per cent.

The university has coped with this situation at a stiff cost to students. In 1970, for example, student tuition (at $675 per year) provided 31% ($36 million of $115 million) of Penn State's general funds budget. In 1989–90, student tuition (at $3754 per year) provided 52% ($278 million of $534 million) of the general funds budget. All expectations are that this trend will continue; in July 1989 the university announced its twenty-second consecutive tuition increase.

Penn State has been forced to cope with significant external stringency as an institution, but this has been exacerbated by difficult fundamental enrolment shifts within the university as well. For example, from 1971 to 1987, the percentage of students enrolled in engineering rose from 16% to 22%, and the percentage of students enrolled in business administration rose from 11% to 20%. Meanwhile, the percentage of students enrolled in education declined from 15% to 7%. Such shifts have forced the university to focus its attention on internal reallocation, not to meet overall economic and demographic constraints or to move toward strategic objectives, but simply to face up to difficult teaching-workload decisions. Simply put, the university has had to reallocate its instructional resources in response to marked changes in student preferences among academic majors.

Entering the 1990s, Penn State is not only representative, it is something of a standard-bearer among campuses in terms of the economics of stringency. The university has struggled with scant state appropriations – not atypical – to cope with unusually rapid and sustained enrolment increases.

Institutional responses

Lozier and Althouse described how Penn State responded to the challenge of matching income to expenses from 1971 to 1982. Beginning in 1971, Penn State implemented annual across-the-board annual budget reductions for all units. These cuts exemplify what was characterized earlier as the horizontal reduction approach of higher education in the USA in the early 1970s.

By the latter half of the 1970s it became obvious to administrators at Penn State that it 'made no sense to continue to assess the same level of budget reductions, for example, to the College of Engineering and the College of Education'.[35] Thus in 1977 the university began a process of selective internal reduction and reallocation. From 1977 to 1982, the average budget cut for all academic units was 4.7%, but individual budget allocations ranged from an increase of over 20% to a cut of 12.5%. These decisions were made by focusing on the basic needs of the university's various units, recognizing that some units were growing while others were declining. This recycling approach exemplifies what we have characterized as the second phase of institutional response: the vertical reallocation of resources.

In 1983, Penn State moved to the third phase of institutional response, when the Board of Trustees approved a comprehensive programme of strategic planning. That thrust integrated the existing planning and budgeting process with a broader strategic management process. That process retained the earlier concept of selective internal reallocation of resources. However, the strategic management programme was, in addition, driven by 'priorities . . . likely to propel The Pennsylvania State University to a place among the best comprehensive, public universities of the nation.'[36] The long-term focus of strategic planning was on achieving and enhancing institutional excellence. Faculty and administrators came to express this as the simple goal of becoming one of the best ten public universities in the country.

The strategic management programme was distinguished from earlier administrative approaches at Penn State because it deliberately established a goal of excellence for the university, and worked aggressively toward that goal. Compare this to the essentially defensive nature – primarily geared toward minimizing the erosion of important programme and units – of the earlier phases of recycling and reduction. Furthermore, Penn State has maintained its goal of becoming a top ten public university, even though state appropriations have continued to increase at minimal rates. Penn State averaged only a 6% annual appropriation increase for 1980–81 to 1989–90. While Penn State presses for more state funds, it is simultaneously pursuing the goal of increased quality.

Penn State's strategic planning programme was also distinguished by two other major departures: the process took a very external, open systems perspective, and it was based on the theme of building upon existing strengths. Both Penn State as a whole and each of the respective planning units (for example, each college within the university) initiated and have continued a systematic and ongoing evaluation of internal strengths and weaknesses, and of external opportunities and threats. Because the university's planning and budgeting process links strategic planning priorities to internal budgeting, resource allocation decisions are made in light of these ongoing evaluations.

Reallocation is still necessary at Penn State, but it is no longer from a defensive posture. Strategic enhancement of selected programmes through differential allocation of resources is a vital ingredient in the process. And in addition to guiding annual budget allocations, strategic planning has resulted in major initiatives such as the following:

- Creation of a new Biotechnology Institute.
- Creation of a new School of Communications.
- Creation of a new College of Health and Human Development.
- Completion of a $300 million private fund-raising campaign.
- Elimination of the department and programme in community studies.
- Establishment of a Division of Technology within the 'feeder system' of branch campuses.
- Initiation of a two-year comprehensive study on the status of women at the university.
- Reorganization of numerous other administrative and academic operations (e.g. student services and academic support programmes, academic computing, research and the graduate school).

Initiatives such as these reflect a shift from the horizontal reduction and vertical reallocation phases to a third phase, that of strategic choice. The strategic choices for Penn State are focused on the goal of becoming one of the top ten public research universities in the United States. That view of excellence is, of course, very heavily dependent upon increased prestige in graduate education and growth in funded research.

Stringency, quality and access

The Penn State drive to improve its quality typifies a current national movement in higher education toward strategic management and the enhancement of quality. As the decade of the 1990s begins, the meaning of a quality education has become the subject of a renewed debate.

The nature of the debate

Consider first three quite different conceptions of quality. Astin summarized two traditional views of quality, labelled the reputational and resource views.[37] The reputational view equates excellence with an institution's relative prestige (based, for example, on national surveys). The resource view is based on test scores of entering freshmen, the number of Merit Scholars, the number of faculty members in the National Academy of Science, the amount of expenditures per student, and so on. However, Astin argued that these traditional views do not serve us well, because they are not based on the fundamental purpose of higher education: the education of students.

For this reason, Astin argued for a third definition of quality based on educational effectiveness. A high quality education, in this third view, is one which maximizes the intellectual and personal development of students. The ultimate test of how well an institution performs would, by this definition, depend not on the characteristics of students *admitted*, but rather on their intellectual and personal development *while* they are students. A community college with an open-door mission may well be providing a better education than a selective college whose average SAT (i.e. aptitude test) scores for entering freshmen are much higher. The key judgement about a quality education must be made *after* students enrol, not before. Further, this judgement should reflect the diversity of institutional clientele and mission. The evaluation of the quality of education should not rely primarily on the attributes of students admitted to an institution but on the value added by the institution.

The debate over how to define quality is closely related to the issue of access, and at the national level, one can argue that higher education in the United States has chosen to support access at the expense of quality. For example, Astin[38] stated that although research shows that

> student involvement and development are enhanced by living on campus, attending a four-year rather than a two-year institution, and attending a small rather than a large institution, the major trends in American higher education since World War II have all been in the opposite direction. That is, the proportion of commuter students has increased, two-year colleges have proliferated, and institutions have grown steadily larger.

In essence, through the economies inherent in large campuses and non-residential community colleges, colleges and universities have been able to provide access – but only at the expense of the quality of the educational experience.

Similarly, the Southern Regional Education Board[39] noted:

> There is no question that the quality of undergraduate education is unacceptably low and needs to be raised . . . The reasons for the decline in the quality of undergraduate education are understandable. Chief among them was the pressure, beginning in the 1960s, for improved access to higher education for large numbers of students.

That report also noted that the issue of access has dominated higher education policy in the United States since the 1960s, and that quality – discussed in terms of admission requirements, standards for graduation, methods of assessing student progress, rigorous course and degree standards, and the like – became a secondary concern. The emphasis on educational opportunity is consistent with the value placed in the United States upon higher education as a means to promote equity, economic betterment and social justice.

Looking ahead: quality and access

The task as we close this chapter is to place the discussion of quality and access within the context of institutional responses to environmental turmoil.

This chapter has argued that in the United States, higher education is today poised at a potential shift point, and that we must be prepared to respond strategically to environmental challenges. Institutional experiences have shown that colleges and universities are learning that strategic choice, properly conceived, can lead to positive steps for a campus, even in a chaotic and sometimes hostile environment.

As noted, the United States has a long-standing commitment to access to higher education. A report of the American Association of State Colleges and Universities[40] decries serious problems of adult illiteracy, high school dropout rates, minority under-achievement, and inadequate federal support for higher education, and suggests that many of these are reflective of inadequate educational opportunities. The objectives of the 'Marshall Plan' recommended by that report address, in essence, issues of access: for example, the objective that at least 35% of American adults should have a college degree by the year 2001.

At the same time, others, as we have noted, have spoken strongly on the need for improved quality. Both sides of the argument are well-taken and persuasively made. In the end, we are left wth a series of dilemmas: What price is society willing to pay for quality? Who will pay? What do institutions trade off in terms of autonomy and control as they attempt to keep costs under control yet ensure quality programmes? Given the historical import of access in American higher education, quality cannot be increased by simply tightening admission standards – so how can access and quality be integrated as policy objectives?

We close with three basic questions about the quality–access debate and its relationship to economic considerations.

- What is quality, and how can it be measured in all of its diversity?
- To what extent are concerns about quality in competition with demands to increase access for under-represented or under-served portions of the populace?
- How can resource allocation decisions ensure improvement in educational quality, and how can they make programmes and institutions more responsive to external demands for accountability?

Notes and References

1. The discussion of enrolment trends draws heavily from the following: National Center for Education Statistics, *Digest of Education Statistics 1977–78* (Washington, DC: US Department of Health, Education, and Welfare, 1978); Center for Education Statistics, *Digest of Education Statistics 1989* (Washington, DC: US Department of Education, 1989); Center for Education Statistics, *National Estimates of Higher Education Statistics* (Washington, DC: US Department of Education, 1987); Center for Education Statistics, *Trends in Minority Enrolment in Higher Education, Fall 1976– Fall 1986* (Washington, DC: US Department of Education, 1988).
2. Zammuto, R. F. Managing decline in American higher education. In J. C. Smart (ed.), *Higher Education: Handbook of Theory and Research, Volume II*. New York: Agathon Press, 1986.
3. Halsted, K. *State Profiles: Financing Public Higher Education 1978 to 1987*. Washington, DC: Research Associates of Washington, 1987.
4. Leslie, L. L. (ed.), *Responding to New Realities in Funding*. San Francisco: Jossey-Bass, 1984.
5. College Entrance Examination Board, *Trends in Student Aid: 1980 to 1986* (Washington, DC: The College Board, 1986); College Entrance Examination Board, *Trends in Student Aid 1963 to 1983* (Washington, DC: The College Board, 1983); National Center for Education Statistics, *Undergraduate Financing of Postsecondary Education* (Washington, DC: US Department of Education, 1987).
6. Evangelauf, E. For most, cost of going to college outpaces inflation again, *The Chronicle of Higher Education* (16 August 1989), **35**(49), A1, A26.
7. Werth, B. Why is college so expensive? *Change* (March/April 1988), 13–25.
8. Simmons, A. Commentary on 'Why is college so expensive?' *Change* (March/April 1988), 16–17.
9. College Entrance Examination Board (1986), op. cit.
10. Leslie, L. L. and P. T. Brinkman, *The Economic Value of Higher Education*. New York: American Council on Education and Macmillan, 1988).
11. Mingle, J. R. Management flexibility and state regulation: an overview. In J. R. Mingle (ed.), *Management Flexibility and State Regulation in Higher Education*. Atlanta: Southern Regional Education Board, 1983.
12. 24 states found to require programmes to assess what college students learn, *The Chronicle of Higher Education* (10 August 1988), **34**(48), A19, A23.
13. Helpern, D. C. *The State of College and University Facilities: A Survey of College and University Planners*. Ann Arbor, MI: The Society for College and University Planning, 1987, p. 1.
14. US campus buildings may need $70-billion for renovations, *The Chronicle of Higher Education* (19 October 1988), **35**(8), A36.

15. Dunn, J. A. (ed.) *Enhancing the Management of Fund Raising*. San Francisco: Jossey-Bass, 1986, p. 1.
16. McMillen, L. 28-percent surge in alumni contributions lifts giving to colleges to $8.5 billion, *The Chronicle of Higher Education* (13 April 1988), **34**(31), A1, A34–A35.
17. McMillen, L. College fund raisers report high levels of stress as goals of campaigns reach new heights, *The Chronicle of Higher Education* (3 August 1988), **34**(47), A27–A28; Fuchsberg, G. Gifts to colleges off 3.5 percent, *The Chronicle of Higher Education* (3 May 1989), **35**(34), A1, A30.
18. Council for Financial Aid to Education, *Voluntary Support of Education*. New York: Council for Financial Aid to Education, annual reports.
19. Simmons, op. cit., p. 16.
20. Dooris, M. J. Organizational adaptation and the commercialization of research universities, *Planning for Higher Education* (1988–89), **17**(3), 21–32.
21. Zammuto, op. cit.
22. Leslie, op. cit., p. 94.
23. Chaffee, E. E. *After Decline, What? Survival Strategies at Eight Private Colleges*. Boulder, CO: National Center for Higher Education Management Systems, 1984.
24. Zammuto, op. cit., p. 46.
25. Mortimer, K. P. and M. L. Tierney, *The Three 'Rs' of the Eighties: Reduction, Reallocation, and Retrenchment*, AAHE-ERIC/Higher Education Research Report No. 4. Washington, DC: American Association for Higher Education, 1979.
26. Boulding, K. E. The management of decline, *Change* (June 1975), 8–9, 64.
27. Lozier, G. G. and P. R. Althouse, Developing planning and budgeting strategies for internal recycling of funds, *Research in Higher Education* (1983), **18**(2), 237–50.
28. Mortimer and Tierney, op. cit.
29. Carnegie Foundation for the Advancement of Teaching, *More than Survival: Prospects for Higher Education in a Period of Uncertainty*. San Francisco: Jossey-Bass, 1975.
30. Exemplary reports from the mid-1970s to early-1980s on concerns about coping with decline include Mayhew, L. B. *Surviving the Eighties: Strategies and Procedures for Solving Fiscal and Enrolment Problems* (San Francisco: Jossey-Bass, 1979); Boulding, op. cit.; Mortimer and Tierney, op. cit.; and Hyatt, J. A., C. H. Shulman and A. A. Santiago, *Reallocation: Strategies for Effective Resource Management* (Washington, DC: National Association of College and University Business Officers, 1984).
31. Lozier and Althouse, op. cit.
32. Bezilla, M. *Penn State: An Illustrated History*. University Park, PA: The Pennsylvania State University Press, 1985, p. 244.
33. Bezilla, op. cit., p. 227.
34. Bezilla, op. cit., p. 322.
35. Lozier and Althouse, op. cit., p. 239.
36. The Pennsylvania State University, *Strategic Planning Guide*. University Park, PA: Office of the President, 1984, p. 1.
37. Astin, A. W. Involvement: the cornerstone of excellence, *Change* (July/August 1985), 35–9.
38. Astin, op. cit., p. 39.
39. Southern Regional Education Board, *Access to Quality Undergraduate Education*. Atlanta, GA: SREB Commission for Educational Quality, 1985.
40. American Association of State Colleges and Universities, *To Secure the Blessings of Liberty*. Washington, DC: AASCU, 1986.

8

Financial Pressures and Quality in British Universities

Michael L. Shattock

1 A decade of cuts: 1980–90

British universities were well supported by the state during the later 1950s and the decade of the 1960s as student numbers grew rapidly, new universities were founded, and older universities expanded. But the decade of the 1970s saw a changing climate, a growing national disillusion with higher education, sharp fluctuations in financial support from government as a result of the oil crisis, and the loss of the quinquennial funding system. Student unit costs over this decade fell by about 10% but the effects were masked by a continued growth in student numbers and the fact that institutions were compensated for the effects of inflation. Universities were therefore slow to recognize the implications of what was taking place.

The arrival of the Conservative government in late 1979 brought a sharp change of atmosphere. The government was pledged to reduce public expenditure and its policies towards higher education were essentially 'expenditure led' rather than based on any particular view of the system. Its first step, taken within three days of assuming office, was to end the subsidy for overseas students and to require the payment of full-cost fees. This produced a saving of around £100 million over three years. Institutions with higher numbers of overseas students like the London School of Economics (LSE) and the University of Manchester Institute of Science and Technology (UMIST) suffered disproportionately. This was followed in 1981 by a further cut in grant of around 15% spread over the years 1981–2, 1982–3 and 1983–4.

The University Grants Committee (UGC) had decided, before the level of grant was known, to conduct a full-scale review of the university system with a view to allocating resources on a more selective basis than previously. The review was intended both to rectify historic anomalies in institutional grant levels and to introduce greater discrimination in funding on the basis of an assessment of research excellence and undergraduate quality. The effect of such a review, even if the promise of level funding had been maintained, would inevitably have had a differential impact on institutions but now it was catastrophic for some universities (Shattock, 1986). At one extreme Salford lost 44% of its recurrent grant over the period, four other universities, Aston, Bradford, Keele and UMIST, lost around 30%, and a further ten universities lost 20% or more. At the other extreme, a few universities received virtually no cut at all. At the same time the UGC reduced student numbers across the system as a whole by about 5%, but built in a small but significant switch of numbers to high-cost scientific, technological and vocational subjects thus reducing yet further the funding of arts subjects. The management of universities at all levels was placed under enormous strain by these decisions. Universities' continuing financial viability was in fact only achieved by the introduction of a government-funded early retirement scheme which enabled staffing levels to be reduced. The UGC criticized the time-scale of the cuts which it said created 'disorder and diseconomy' in the university system (Shattock and Berdahl 1984).

It had been expected that level funding would follow, but in 1985 the UGC had to advise universities that on the basis of likely public expenditure decisions, the university system would need to plan for a continuing fall in recurrent grant of 2% per annum for the period 1985–6 to 1989–90. The UGC carried out a further selective exercise in 1985–6 and made its allocations on the basis of a formula that distinguished between research and teaching, rewarding research distinction differentially but assuming broadly common unit costs for each discipline across the university system. The financial impact on individual universities was this time more difficult to assess because the actual allocations were only announced from year to year and were in any case obscured by the effects of a growth in student numbers in some disciplines and of transfers of staff and student numbers following subsequent UGC subject review and rationalization exercises. Nevertheless it is clear that across the system as a whole the impact was almost as great as in 1981. A 'safety net' system had to be established by which the most successful universities were taxed to provide support for the less successful and at one point there were between 15 and 20 universities and colleges on the UGC's 'sick list' of institutions which were potentially likely to encounter serious financial difficulty. Two institutions, University College, Cardiff and Aberdeen University, had to be bailed out by the provision of loans or additional recurrent grant. University College, London confessed to a bank overdraft of £5 million and appeared to be heading for a formidable accumulated deficit.

Once again a government-funded early retirement scheme was used to reduce staffing levels. But following severe criticism of its operation in the previous funding period by the Public Accounts Committee of the House of Commons, the UGC was compelled to exercise greater control over university expenditure under this heading. The demonstrable failure of university management in the case of University College, Cardiff (Shattock, 1988) provoked further pressure by the Public Accounts Committee to ensure that the UGC, and its successor the Universities Funding Council (UFC) adopted a significantly more robust role in ensuring universities' accountability. This manifested itself in a requirement that universities submit academic plans (against which UGC-funded early retirements could be judged), statements about how they were improving their processes of management in response to the recommendations of the 'Jarratt Report' (CVCP, 1985) and financial plans extending over the next five years. Discussion within universities as to how to respond to this plethora of questioning undoubtedly had the effect of heightening their recognition of the need for improved management and decision-making, although too often the conclusions which institutions drew represented somewhat unsophisticated compromises between the previous consensual form of university government and a new slightly macho form of authoritarian leadership by the vice-chancellor.

As occasional palliatives to the prevailing tightening of the financial screws the decade saw the launching of a number of new initiatives sponsored by government: the 1983, 1984 and 1985 'new blood scheme', the Biotechnology Initiative, the Engineering and Technology Programme, the Manufacturing Systems Engineering scheme, the Professional Industrial Commercial Updating Programme (PICKUP), and via the research councils, the Link programme, the Teaching Company scheme and the Interdisciplinary Research Centres (IRCs). These initiatives brought new resources into the university system in areas where the government had special priorities. They required competitive bidding by universities and success tended to reinforce the differentiation which was already emerging from the successive selectivity exercises. By 1989 the university system seemed to be entering a period of greater, though still underfunded, stability. Only in London where it was announced that the total indebtedness of the University and its colleges now amounted to £46 million did there remain a sense of crisis. In 1990, with the passage of the Education Reform Act 1988 which incorporated measures to dispense with academic tenure for reasons of financial exigency, the early retirement scheme was brought to an end, leaving universities more self-reliant, but probably also less adequately financed compared to the tasks expected of them, than at any time since the mid-1950s.

2 Selectivity and rationalization

Reductions in budgets drew attention to the diseconomies of the British university system. On the arts and to a lesser extent on the science side there were too many small academic departments attracting too few students. On the science and technology side the costs of major research, and the pressure to link university-based research more effectively with development and the needs of the national economy required a greater concentration of research in large better-focused departments (Shattock, 1989). This requirement has given the research councils a much greater role in policy making and *A Strategy for the Science Base* (ABRC, 1987) spelled out an organizational interpretation of the pressures on science suggesting a restructuring of higher education into three layers with research universities at one extreme and purely teaching institutions at the other. Although the formal realignment of institutions into a tiered system was ultimately rejected by the government the impact of the UGC 1986 and UFC 1989 selectivity exercises taken together with the policies of the research councils have led to a much greater differentiation between major research universities and the rest.

Both arts and science rationalization remained, however, in the hands of the UGC which developed review mechanisms to look at the needs of minority languages (classics, Spanish, Italian) on the one hand and major science subjects (earth sciences, physics and chemistry) or minority sciences (for example, meteorology and oceanography) on the other. In classics, for example, the result of the review was the closure of classics teaching in 10 universities and the reinforcement of 12 others by the transfer of staff and funded student numbers. In Earth Sciences 13 departments were selected for mainstream teaching and research, 8 more were advised to restrict themselves to inter-disciplinary or joint degrees with only specialist postgraduate work and four were recommended for closure. This represented a review of a major subject with a large-scale transfer of resources from university to university and a reserve fund of £17 million for new equipment needs. The impact of such exercises could be, if anything, as great as the overall cuts in recurrent budget. In every exercise there have been winners and losers, with the losers facing disruption, loss of morale, and a reduction of their funding base. From a subject point of view, however, the exercises have often provided a new security and for the institutional winners, the results have frequently represented the realization of long-frustrated ambitions for growth and a better funding base.

3 The impact of selectivity at the institutional and departmental levels

University governance in Britain has stressed the dominance of decision making by committees and the sovereignty of the senate in all academic matters. Over the period of the 1960s and 1970s resource allocation within institutions was student-number-based and was largely formula-driven (the formulae varying between institutions) (Shattock and Rigby, 1983). Cuts in recurrent grant and more stringent guidance from the UGC in the period 1981–5, and the more explicit UGC research selectivity policy implicit in 1985–6, have inevitably put institutional resource allocation machinery under great strain. The general regard for equity in the distribution of scarce resources, and the unwillingness to mete out cuts differentially could not be reconciled with the requirements of the UGC. On the other hand, for universities to take decisions which had the effect of extinguishing whole departments, or groups within departments, was to impose severe tests on collegiality.

Even more serious was the feeling that such selectivity had been externally imposed against criteria, which while possibly justifiable nationally in terms of external academic judgements, were less clear-cut at the institutional level. Internal jealousies could easily surface when some departments, most notably those in the sciences or in business studies, were explicitly earmarked by the

UGC for expansion, while smaller and less obviously fashionable subjects must lose posts or be rationalized out of existence. Institutional priorities often therefore seemed in conflict with national priorities. External measures of quality, based on quantitative assessments of uncertain validity, seemed much less compelling to institutional resource allocation committees which were concerned not to measure quality in a single discipline across the whole country but to weigh up the claims of unlike departments within a single institution. Local knowledge can too easily encourage indecisiveness but it can also recognize shadings of opinion which are not picked up at the national level.

By contrast one effect of the UGC subject reviews was often to sow discord between university central authorities and the departments concerned. Whole departments negotiated their transfers to other institutions behind the backs of their vice-chancellors and senates, ignoring the academic consequences on the institution they were leaving. Cloak and dagger transfer deals struck in haste over the telephone have not in the past been the basis of university decision-making and, while the end result may ultimately strengthen the university system, it can be seen as seriously weakening the machinery of institutional self-government.

4 The impact of differentiation at the departmental level

The increasing concentration of research grants, expensive equipment and leading researchers in fewer departments and universities means that in the long term many departments are likely to find themselves without postgraduates, without an externally recognized research role, and perhaps without an undergraduate degree programme they can call their own. In some universities, poorly rated (for research purposes) mathematics, physics and chemistry departments have had their role reduced to 'service' teaching for other degrees. Such ratings raise large questions for the future. What are the career development prospects for their staff? How do members of staff, particularly younger members, develop individual research programmes when both the institution and the external funding agencies are concentrating resources elsewhere? What effect will this have on their teaching and on the morale of their students? The danger must be that such departments will become caught in a spiral of disapprobation so that they lose staff, they are unable to recruit replacements, they become less attractive to students, and their student numbers decline, making further cuts in staff inevitable. Conventional wisdom suggests that one response to the loss of research rating should be to seek to excel in teaching, but if teaching is not rewarded on the same basis as research, or if research excellence remains the dominant theme of the institution's or the system's culture, then such a strategy lacks conviction.

Strong departments that have benefited by the UGC or UFC selectivity exercises may also suffer if related departments in the same institution have been downrated. Strong departments buttress one another in facilities, cross-disciplinary activities, complementary research interests and attractiveness to students. In the end, even if they can continue to capture an appropriate level of resources within their university, strong departments will be fatally weakened if the departments with which they relate are not of adequate strength. A weakening of one department may then lead to a weakening of others and the loss of key members of staff.

5 External pressures to expand applied/industrial/vocational subjects

Even without the explicit encouragement of government and the UGC/UFC the climate was clearly right to expand certain vocational subjects to respond to student demand for example in engineering, computer science, business studies, law and accountancy. The problem however was to find staff of the right calibre, at salaries the universities could afford. Universities thus face the danger of building up large departments of low research capability in these fields in order to respond to UGC initiatives and to attract additional recurrent grant, and run the risk of having them downrated in future selectivity exercises. In some priority areas, notably in the sciences and engineering, departments suffered from a growing shortfall of good undergraduate applicants so that entry levels declined, and departments failed to fill their places.

By contrast some non-vocational subjects which have suffered cutbacks in intakes, notably English and History, faced growing pressure from well-qualified applicants which they could not meet. From an institutional point of view such policies are hard to justify, especially when arts departments can point to their students' good employment records in the present boom period for graduate employment, and to the fact that a high proportion of expensively trained graduates in science and engineering are currently turning to jobs in accounting, merchant banking and the City instead of following the careers which their courses might seem to have mapped out for them.

At the postgraduate and post-doctoral levels the reduced career prospects in universities served as a disincentive to postgraduate research and many highly rated science and engineering departments are failing to find an adequate number of research students and post-doctoral researchers to sustain their research effort.

Within these fluctuations in priorities, problems of institutional subject balance can become acute. Already some arts faculties have contracted at an alarming rate, a process accelerated by the pressure on older staff to take early retirement and the effects of the UGC/UFC rationalization programme. The result is a feeling of injustice and persecution in the arts which can inhibit new ideas. But problems of balance are thrown up within all faculty areas between, for example, pure and applied subjects in science or between vocational and non-vocational subjects in social science or simply because of the narrowing of student choice. Too often the requirements of the UGC, or other external bodies, were seen within institutions as destroying academic balance and lowering academic quality even when the policy objective was to raise quality and obtain a better national academic balance.

6 The effects of changes in the pattern of student demand

The problem of shortfalls in candidates in some science subjects and in engineering seems likely to worsen because of the low quality of science teaching in the schools and the national shortage of science teachers. The problem, however, is compounded by the fall, compared with the 1982 peak, of about thirty per cent in the number of 18-year-olds by 1995. The fall in qualified applicants to universities will not occur at the same rate but some decrease seems inevitable, and will accentuate the fluctuations in the ratio of applicants per discipline. Logic suggests that to survive some disciplines have the choice either of lowering their standard of entry or of looking for a new clientele of mature candidates. In either case the narrowly based single-subject degree will need to be broadened. There are sound educational arguments for doing so but the dominant motive in a period of budgetary reductions may be a concern to resist a further fall in funding levels.

There are positive signs that universities, perhaps a trifle uncertainly, are beginning to respond to these pressures. While there is only slow progress in the reform of degree syllabuses for full-time students there is evidence (see, e.g., Chapter 11) of some movement towards greater modularization and a grudging acceptance of credit transfer. Increasingly universities are entering the field of part-time degrees for local students, thus breaking out of the constraints imposed by the three-year full-time degree structure. The highly traditional extra-mural departments are beginning to find a new, though for many of them distinctly uncomfortable, role in contributing to this more diverse student clientele.

In the first half of the 1980s the government was inclined to resist calls for an expansion of higher education chiefly for reasons of cost. But as the economy grew it became apparent that rather than there being a danger of overproduction of graduates, the nation faced a probable shortfall. Treasury arguments that a demography-led fall in students needed to be paralleled by a reduction in staff were now stood on their head by the evidence marshalled by the Council for Industry and Higher Education that the fall in numbers must be reversed rather than seen as an argument for further reductions in recurrent grant. The government has, therefore, encouraged an improvement in the Age Participation Rate from around 14% to up to 23% and has urged strongly that universities should actively seek out a greater number of mature students. It seems intrinsically unlikely, however, that such students will necessarily be in the field of science, technology and vocational studies which the government has made a priority.

The government's strategy for encouraging expansion has been to transfer a proportion of recurrent grant into increased fee levels. This has the double effect of encouraging institutions to take additional students because of the resource implications and forcing institutions to adopt a more market-orientated approach to student recruitment. Such a policy represents a complete volte-face from the policy adopted in 1982–3 when, under pressure from the Treasury, the undergraduate fee was halved so as to prevent universities from over-recruiting to mitigate the impact of the 1981 cuts, and to close off the open-ended Treasury commitment to pay maintenance grant to every British student admitted to higher education. Two other innovations taking effect in 1990 and 1991 complete the picture: the first is the freezing of the maintenance grant and the introduction of student loans and the second is the bidding system introduced by the UFC where universities bid for student numbers on the basis of competitive pricing of student places. The working out of these policies is outside the time-scale of this chapter, but it is fair to say that cumulatively they represent a revolution in attitudes as compared to the more negative approach adopted in the early 1980s.

7 The competing pressures of research and teaching

Since the 1986 selectivity exercise universities have been enjoined to discriminate in the allocation of resources in favour of departments or research groups within departments which they judge to be particularly distinguished in research. In 1989 the secretary of state decided that the UFC should separate its allocation to each university for research from the rest of its allocation to emphasize the importance attached to universities being properly accountable for the element of their grant which was intended to support research.

From an ABRC point of view it is readily understandable that there should be concern that universities might be propping up weak departments with grant intended to provide the 'well-found laboratory' or its equivalent for departments with strong research records. The problems on the ground are more difficult. At the departmental level the division of staff effort between research and teaching becomes increasingly important. The easy logical approach would suggest that departments should take decisions which reduce the teaching hours of outstanding researchers and increase them for those less successful in research. Unfortunately the best researchers are often the best teachers and are much in demand by students and the less successful researchers are often as committed to research as their more successful colleagues. One danger of the UGC and UFC's selectivity exercises is that higher-rated departments may feel justified in concentrating on research at the expense of teaching.

At the institutional level the same dilemmas arise. Research is expensive and the allocation of resources to particular departments can not only foreclose resource allocation decisions in regard to other departments, but can make decisive impacts on the personal advancement of staff. In many disciplines research requires expensive facilities, research support, library and computing back-up far in excess of the requirements for teaching. Successful research departments therefore look more opulent than primarily teaching departments and have more favourable student–staff ratios. Their quality ratings are also easier to measure. The danger is that the 'teaching' departments simply look like less successful departments.

There is little research evidence that unfavourable student–staff ratios have much effect on the quality of teaching, though common sense would suggest it. From a resource allocation point of view it is therefore difficult to know where to draw a line on the extent to which staff numbers may be allowed to fall in given departments especially when every positive decision must be taken against a background of financial stringency. There is an inevitable pressure to reward research excellence, because this is recognized in the UGC formula. Against this there is a reluctance simply to accept that a department cannot be rescued from a poor rating by additional support. Since there are no ratings for good teaching and no satisfactory indicators of good teaching performance, teaching generally comes a poor second in the resource allocation process.

8 The emergence of the UFC

Many scholars argue that the replacement of the UGC by the UFC represented a political act symbolizing the antagonism of the government to the academically dominated UGC. I tend to take the different view that the change owes a great deal more to shifts in Whitehall thinking about accountability and the merits of hiving off certain activities (Shattock, 1988). It is, of course, too early to speculate on the change from the point of view of its impact on quality. Undoubtedly it is possible to argue that the abolition of the subject committees and their replacement by single academic advisers can be seen as a less concensual approach to vetting standards, but the subject committee system was itself widely criticized as erratic and ineffective in 1981 and as being unreliable in making comparable assessments over several subjects in 1986.

More significant is the gradual shift of the UGC/UFC system from concern about subjects and disciplines to concern about institutions. In 1981 the Chairman of the UGC made it clear that his first concern in the allocation exercise had been the support for subjects, and the impact on institutions had only been of secondary interest. By 1986 the formula-based allocation system distinguished between selective funding to recognize research excellence and formula funding for undergraduate teaching, but a safety net was created to protect institutions in the hardest-hit category. By 1989 the UFC had replaced the UGC but chose not to disturb the UGC research selectivity exercise which was in midstream. However, it has radically changed the basis of funding undergraduate teaching by the introduction of the bidding process and its chairman has made it clear that he regards the funding of subjects as much less important than the funding of institutions. In this he appears to be echoing the conclusions of the Leverhulme Study (1983). The UFC approach relies much more on market mechanisms than the UGC's: this may be expected to encourage greater enterprise and flexibility, qualities that were not encouraged by the UGC system of the 1970s, but could perhaps do so only with some loss of the guarantee of quality which the old UGC approach tended to provide.

9 The effects of income generation

A main plank of government policy has been to encourage universities to generate additional income both to make up deficiencies in recurrent grant and to diversify universities' sources of funds. Many universities have addressed themselves seriously to the problem simply as a means of survival. Others have seen it not only as the only means of breaking out of the syndrome of annual budget cuts, but as an opportunity to broaden the baseline of university relationships.

(a) Overseas students

When, in 1979–80, government eliminated the subsidy for overseas students and insisted that they should pay full-cost fees there was a sharp fall in overseas student numbers. A decade later, however, the numbers in universities exceed their 1979–80 levels. It was feared that institutions would lower their standards to recruit overseas students, and while this has undoubtedly happened in some, and at the margins in many, the academic implications do not appear so far to have been serious. More care is now taken in the recruitment of overseas students, selectors have taken the trouble to become much more expert in the evaluation of overseas qualifications and sensitive to their academic needs; on-campus welfare provision for overseas students has generally been drastically improved. In 1987–8 overseas student fees generated over £158 million (or over 6% of its total income) for the British university system. Since in most universities a proportion of the fee income goes direct to the academic department, departments have acquired a new and welcome freedom to allocate resources according to their own priorities.

On the other hand over-reliance on overseas fee income has been criticized by the UGC and the UFC and clear evidence is emerging that universities are being optimistic in their expectations. Competition from other countries like the USA, Canada and Australia, and between British universities and polytechnics, suggest that academic standards may be under threat particularly when marketing and recruitment programmes are energized by the consciousness of falling numbers.

(b) Contract and applied research

Universities have become much more positive in seeking out research contracts from industry. Concern has been expressed that this will distract university researchers from fundamental research and encourage them to undertake low-level industrial development projects because of the financial inducement; but the evidence does not point to that. On the contrary what one hears about is the range of interesting, often multi-disciplinary problems, that emerge from industrial research. Many would argue that a longer-term trend to change the balance between pure and applied research is merely redressing a serious imbalance in British academic life. At the research council level the increasing support for 'strategic research', that is, research in fields where exploitation may ultimately be of importance, as exemplified in the IRCs, is bringing university research much more closely in touch with industry and groups of companies are now more willing jointly to fund pre-competitive research. There have been examples of the 'enterprise culture' adversely affecting the operation of university laboratories in fields like biotechnology, but there is little sign that the new emphasis on the exploitation of intellectual property is acting as a deterrent to university research.

(c) The creation of special teaching programmes for industry

When funding came only, or predominantly, via the UGC there was little incentive to mount special teaching programmes in conjunction with industry and commerce: this is not to say that they did not take place but they were usually on a small scale and not on a self-financing basis. There are now a growing number of programmes at the master's or post-experience levels, usually in science, technology, or business studies, which are specially provided for groups of companies where the companies participate in the planning and the teaching. From an academic point of view this has been good for the university system: it has made considerable inroads into departments' insularity and stimulated them to look outwards; it has forced them to become genuinely involved in understanding the needs of industry and commerce, and it has encouraged a more positive attitude towards universities by companies. While there must remain the risk that quality is forced down by rampant consumerism the evidence suggests that such programmes are instrumental in breaking down barriers to understanding between universities and industry and are assisting the building of long-term relationships from which new kinds of collaborative teaching and research partnerships are emerging.

British universities are in the early stages of facing up to the need to generate external income, cultivate alumni and take account of the market-place. In doing so they are returning to the roots of the modern university system in the nineteenth century. A recent account of the establishment of some of the civic universities, while it emphasizes the difficulties in surviving without government support, does not suggest that institutions readily compromised their principles in seeking external support (Jones, 1988). The most salient criticism of the post-Robbins university system is that in becoming over-reliant on the UGC the universities tended to become homogenized by a single source of funding. The search for new sources of income and new clients has made universities more interesting places and has acted as a stimulant to fresh thinking and new kinds of activity. It is, however, too early to assess whether the reductions in university budgets have so weakened the universities that in seeking new sources of finance they are merely exchanging one form of dependence for another.

10 University management under conditions of financial stringency

Until the 1980s it was inconceivable that British universities could or would be allowed to go bankrupt or to close. In 1981–2, in the months before the government-funded early retirement scheme was established, there were serious questions about whether Salford and some of the other hardest-hit universities could survive, but it remained more a question of how than whether. Since 1985–6, however, the prospect has entered the realms of the possible as reductions in university funding continue and the capacity of universities to manage their affairs is put under yet further strain. So far the one example of an institution reaching the verge of bankruptcy, University College, Cardiff, occurred not because of the cuts, but almost entirely because of the spendthrift approach of its management.

Slipping into financial difficulty, as several universities have now done, sets severe tests for those concerned to maintain quality because short-term decision-making inevitably concentrates on survival rather than the maintenance of recognized strengths. The best academics immediately look more sympathetically on offers from elsewhere, and are not replaced; companies and research councils ask questions when large research contracts have been won as to whether the institution's financial situation is sufficiently secure to justify a substantial investment; undergraduate applicants apply elsewhere. Academic strengths built up over 10 to 15 years can be destroyed in a frighteningly short time as academic confidence ebbs away from an institution in trouble. If there was a single message for those concerned with quality in higher education it was that when an institution faces a time of acute financial difficulty, policies simply for institutional survival are not enough. Universities in trouble need speedy rescue or the costs and effort of restoring them as high-quality institutions may be beyond the resources of the university system and permanent damage may have been inflicted.

The threat of financial difficulty has imposed sharp changes on the way in which universities are run (Sizer, 1987). The need to act quickly, the complexity of financial planning, and the volume of decision making has had the effect of weakening the traditional structure of university governance and strengthening the position of the vice-chancellor and his senior officers in line with the recommendations of the Jarratt Report. However, these pressures have militated against the reinforcement of lay control through university councils which was also recommended by Jarratt except in instances where controversial financial decisions have had to be made. The government's decision to amend university statutes to allow tenure to be broken on grounds of financial exigency potentially opens up a new area of decision-making by university council.

11 The effect on performance of institutions and of the university system

Because about three-quarters of any individual university's budget goes on salaries and wages the cuts have had to fall heavily on manpower. Between 1981 and 1985, 4500 academic staff either took early retirement or left British university employment and were not replaced. Forecasts for the period 1986 to 1990 suggest further large losses. Such losses have been painful and have been achieved at domestic and human costs which cannot be evaluated. The losses have particularly affected staff over the age of 55 and the inability to recruit replacements at the younger end is producing a bunching effect in the 35–55 age-group which will have serious academic implications in the 1990s.

In the post-war years the British university system had increasingly isolated itself from societal needs; it had concentrated on highly selective relatively specialized degree programmes, it had assumed that all institutions were equally capable of research and demanded that they be funded accordingly, and it had become inward-looking and self-regarding. The early retirement programme has had the effect of providing an exit for many less productive staff and there is evidence that the level of research has significantly increased. Indeed the selectivity exercises have probably had the effect of spurring on staff to increased research output. But the system has also lost many outstanding staff to other countries, most notably the United States, and some who have simply chosen to retire rather than face the disruption and turmoil into which many departments and universities have been thrown.

All the selectivity exercises, whether in 1981, 1986, or 1989 were criticized for dubious methodology and faulty assessments but it is clear that on the whole the weaker universities and departments were the hardest hit. No one would argue that Salford is not an immeasurably more lively, more distinctive and a 'better' institution now than before 1981. The effects have however not been uniform: some institutions have certainly improved their performance under the stimulus of external threat and greater competition for funds, others have been gravely weakened. Taking the system as a whole some institutions have become more outward-looking, more research is funded from non-government sources, more effort is being put into continuing education of various kinds and more institutions are finding ways of taking decision more quickly and realistically than in the past. But this must be balanced against the loss of morale in many parts of the system and the real and prolonged financial difficulties into which some institutions appear now to be plunged.

Moreover there is little to suggest that universities have learnt the harsh lesson that if they are to have the public on their side they must find ways of more obviously serving the public good. Too many universities remain self-regarding and ultimately self-pitying. On the other hand the long-run restructuring of the system that is now in progress must ultimately shake out the institutions which cannot cope with the changes imposed upon them. University campuses have lost their complacency but this has yet to be replaced by a confidence in the future. Concern for survival and managerial effectiveness too often take precedence over quality.

References

ABRC (1987). *A Strategy for the Science Base*. London: HMSO, DES.
Committee of Vice-Chancellors and Principals (1985). *Report of the Steering Committee on Efficiency Studies in Universities* (the Jarratt Report).
Jones, D. R. (1988). *The Origins of Civic Universities*. London: Routledge.
Leverhulme Study into the Future of Higher Education (1983), *Excellence in Diversity*. Guildford: Society for Research into Higher Education.
Shattock, M. L. (1986). The UGC and standards. In Graeme C. Moodie (ed.), *Standards and Criteria in Higher Education*. Milton Keynes: SRHE and Open University.
Shattock, M. L. (1987). The last days of the University Grants Committee, *Minerva*, **25**(4), pp. 471–85.
Shattock, M. L. (1988). Financial management in universities: the lessons of University College, Cardiff, *Financial Accountability and Management*, pp. 99–112.
Shattock, M. L. (1989). Higher education and the research councils, *Minerva*, **27**(2–3), pp. 195–222.
Shattock, M. L. and Berdahl, R. O. (1984). The British University Grants Committee 1919–1983; changing relationships with Government and the universities, *Higher Education 13*.
Shattock, Michael and Rigby, Gwyneth (1983). *Resource Allocation in British Universities*. Guildford: Society for Research into Higher Education.
Sizer, J. (1987). *Institutional Responses to Financial Reductions in the University Sector: Final Report to the DES*. (Duplicated.) Loughborough University of Technology.

9

The British Binary System and its 'Missing Link'

Robert E. Cuthbert

Introduction

Making sense of the UK system of post-secondary education is always difficult. There are different systems, with different arrangements for governance and funding, in Scotland, in Northern Ireland, and in England and Wales – and the English and Welsh systems have increasingly diverged in recent years. Few if any of the people who work and study in the various parts of these various systems have a reliable understanding of all the constituent parts and how they are connected. It is hardly surprising that access, progression and credit transfer have long been crucial issues in the development of the post-secondary sector.

This chapter aims to describe and analyse some aspects of the structure of British, mainly English, post-secondary education, with particular reference to the non-university parts of the so-called 'binary system'. We will consider the idea that there is a 'missing link' in the process of evolution of British higher education (HE) and examine the claims of further education colleges for filling the alleged gap.

Trow's (1974) distinctions between élite, mass and universal systems of higher education were first presented and have become accepted not as mere typology, but as part of a theory of the evolution of higher education systems. Seen in these terms, the British system has shown a stubborn refusal to 'evolve' beyond its élite stage, prompting endless attempts at explanation of this phenomenon of blocked evolution.

In these circumstances it is not surprising that the editors should have coined the title 'The binary system and its missing link' for an account of some structural differences between UK and US systems. Though happy with the brief, I at first resisted the title: British higher education was perhaps never a system, and is decreasingly binary. But the displaced concept of 'missing link' seemed more appropriate: an entity whose existence had always been in doubt, but was necessary to sustain the prevailing theory of evolution.

The 'link' in the USA between high school and university can be said to be the community and junior college system, open to all for all kinds of educational purposes, including preparation for college or university. Martin Trow (1987), in a compelling analysis, has argued that the British further education (FE) system holds the key to the evolution of higher education towards a mass system and beyond:

> What is still lacking is a general recognition that all degree-granting higher education is only a part, albeit a central part, of a broad system of post-secondary and continuing education, marked by a diversity of standard, mission and cost, which has as its mission the advanced education of a whole society and not just its leadership.
>
> (Trow, 1987, p. 268)

Sir Christopher Ball (1987), when Chairman of the Board of the National Advisory Body which planned non-university higher education in England, has described non-advanced further education (NAFE) as the 'royal road' to higher education in the future:

> if wider access is to be achieved, it is this sector which will deliver it. It is the FE sector which holds the key which will unlock demand from non-traditional applicants, from part-time and mature students, from those seeking a second chance, and from that myriad amongst us who have never been made aware of their own potential. We shall have to learn not to call such students 'non-traditional' applicants to higher education any longer. I believe that NAFE will shortly provide the royal road to AFE, and offer a route at least as well worn as the old path for 18-year-olds from school to higher education.

Can we say, then, that FE is the 'missing link' in the evolutionary chain for British higher education? If we accept, for the time being, the evolutionary hypothesis, we should still confront the other implicit premiss in this question: that comparison will be instructive rather than destructive. There must at least be some dangers in comparing a system built on egalitarian principles from the top down (colleges appearing before schools – Trow, 1987) with a system evolving much more slowly with élitist values from the bottom up. The more comprehensible structures of the US system seem to allow many possible routes between recognizable entry and exit points. There are various 'links' between high school and the upper echelons of the higher education system, accessible and intelligible to the individual student. The British system, by comparison, is a jungle of criss-cross paths with unexpected entrances and exits, where even experienced guides have only incomplete maps. The best-known route, still regarded as the norm, involves a step straight from school to university, with no 'link' at all. Other routes are still generally regarded as deviant or second best. Clearly we must tread carefully in comparing two such different systems.

The chapter is divided into four main parts. First comes an attempted simple parallel between the British system and American structures such as that of New Jersey. The reasons for the failure of the parallel are instructive and carry the argument forward to a treatment of history and mission in British higher education. This is followed by a brief appreciation of size and scope, leading to a final section which suggests some changes which will need to follow the recent restructuring of the British system if the system is indeed to evolve beyond its élite stage.

A failed parallel

Higher education in American states has a set of readily identifiable elements: major state-funded universities of national and international standing; major private universities and colleges also with international reputations; state university systems and colleges; the community colleges; vocational–technical institutions; and alongside them other private colleges. Post-secondary education in Britain has some apparently similar elements: the autonomous universities, sometimes referred to as the 'private sector', but largely supported by public funds; the polytechnics, major and prestigious institutions with a national role but with stronger local links than many universities; colleges and institutes of higher education which for the most part are teaching institutions without major research programmes, some having a religious affiliation; and colleges of further education, variously titled FE colleges, technical colleges, colleges of technology and so on.

It is tempting to draw a simple parallel with a fairly typical US state such as New Jersey, in which

Princeton (an élite 'Ivy League' institution) Rutgers (the 'flagship' of the state system)	=	universities and polytechnics
State university colleges Private colleges	=	polytechnics and colleges of higher education
Community colleges	=	colleges of further education

Though different aspects of this 'parallel' might appeal to different parts of a British audience, as was indicated in Chapter 1, it cannot be sustained. Princeton invites Oxbridge comparisons, but Rutgers too is a major research university; though the former is private and the latter a public institution, they enjoy similar proportions of support from public sources. Although British universities and polytechnics are publicly funded (with one exception), different institutions would define their catchment and mission quite differently, with varying emphases on research and teaching, public and private sources of income, international, national and local service, and so on. The colleges of higher education are an even more heterogeneous group, some being polytechnics in all but name, others being liberal arts colleges, others deriving from religious foundations, some being specialist 'monotechnics' such as colleges of art and design, still others providing a mix of craft, technician and higher level work. The colleges of further education have some similarities with community colleges and vocational–technical institutions, but differ fundamentally in that many of the FE colleges' students are in the 16–18 age-group.

The parallel thus breaks down at many points, for reasons which for our purposes can be divided into three:

  (i) There is no ready international equivalence in the missions of institutions in the different subsectors. The pursuit in Britain of the 'gold standard' of the single-subject honours degree, what Trow (1981) called the 'nothing but the best' syndrome, ensures a hierarchy of esteem without a hierarchy of mission. Many polytechnics and colleges strive to become more like universities, at least in their patterns and types of work, if not always in their educational philosophies. It follows that the pursuit of excellence, so notable a feature of the New Jersey system at every level, is translated in Britain into the pursuit of élitism.

 (ii) There are major differences in the proportionate scale of provision – the differences between an élite and a mass or universal system of higher education.

(iii) There are important differences in the client groups for which the different institutions provide.

The simple parallel confuses more than it explains. It is necessary to examine the British system more closely in terms of mission, hierarchy, scale and clientele to develop a more illuminating comparison.

History and mission

British further education fulfils the first criterion for a 'missing link': it existed long before most of today's HE institutions, many of which can indeed trace their origins to FE institutions. The mechanics' institutes and the nineteenth-century polytechnics were the forerunners of many of the technological universities and the polytechnics which have been 'created' in the last thirty years but can be seen as evolving from their antecedent institutions. The process has recently repeated itself at approximately ten-year intervals: the technological universities in the 1950s (Burgess and Pratt, 1970), the polytechnics in the 1960s (Pratt and Burgess, 1974), the colleges and institutes of higher education in the 1970s, all developing higher-level education work from a further education foundation, until they were ready for redesignation as a fully-fledged HE institution.

The theory of 'academic drift' developed to account for this process (Pratt and Burgess, 1974) was qualified by Locke (1978), who showed how institutions' development can be explained by the framework of incentives and constraints defined by funding mechanisms, as well as by the lure of prestigious and more intrinsically rewarding higher-level work.

This process of drift, punctuated at intervals by system-wide restructuring, created a plural system which became generally labelled 'binary' in the late 1960s after secretary of state Anthony Crosland's speeches at Woolwich Polytechnic in 1965 and Lancaster University in 1967. On one side of the binary line were the universities; on the other, a range of polytechnics and colleges. The latter were subject to control by local education authorities, later co-ordinated by a National Advisory Body (now abolished by the Education Reform Act, which has removed the polytechnics and colleges of HE from local authority control). Though the polytechnics and some colleges developed research programmes, their primary purpose was as teaching institutions; in addition to full-time courses at higher diploma, degree and postgraduate level, they also dominated the provision of part-time higher education opportunities.

Peter Scott's review of the binary policy for the Leverhulme Studies (Scott, 1983) warned against the 'misleading habit' of referring to a binary system:

> It implies a system neatly and symmetrically divided into two homogeneous sectors ... The non-university sector in particular is a heterogeneous collection of institutions which have little in common with each other except the fact that none is a university in the rather precise constitutional sense which we have adopted in Britain.
>
> (Scott, 1983, p. 169)

The binary policy can be said to have failed in some of its stated objectives (Scott, 1983), but nevertheless to have succeeded in catering for the expansion in student numbers throughout the 1970s and 1980s, at a declining cost per student in real terms. The steady absolute and relative expansion of the lower-cost 'public sector' system of polytechnics was by 1987 exerting great pressure on university funding through the increasingly open debate about costs and outcomes on the two sides of the 'binary line'.

The 1987 White Paper *Higher Education: Meeting the Challenge* proposed new structures and a restated philosophy for the development of the HE system. The unvarnished instrumentalism and vocationalism of the 1985 Green Paper was polished and smoothed, but its emphasis remained. The 1988 Education Reform Act (ERA) implemented the White Paper's proposals in almost every detail. In the restructured system the university sector remained unchanged in its membership, with 45 UK institutions recognized for separate funding by the Universities Funding Council. The Open University remained separate and directly funded by the Department of Education and Science. In England 29 polytechnics and 45 other colleges came within the ambit of the Polytechnics and Colleges Funding Council. There remained more than 450 further education colleges in England funded and controlled by local education authorities.

Before the Act a quiet restructuring in Scotland had transferred large colleges in Glasgow and Edinburgh from local authority control to become central institutions, with some small specialist central institutions travelling in the opposite direction. In Wales the structure of higher education was left virtually unchanged, apart from (and some would say because of) a merger between University College, Cardiff and the University of Wales Institute of Science and Technology after the former's much-publicized financial difficulties. In England the 1988 Education Reform Act rewrote the administrative boundaries and, for the first time, defined further and higher education (FE and HE) as mutually exclusive categories, by reference to the level of work in each. The similarities in funding and control between universities, on the one hand, and polytechnics and colleges, on the other, became more marked, to the point where a merger of the two new funding councils is widely expected. A clean administrative line separates the institutions within each of these subsectors. Beyond the PCFC line lie the colleges of further education, still funded by local government rather than a central funding council, but guaranteed more managerial autonomy by the Act.

But the administrative line does not exactly fit the contours of the system. Some colleges have torn themselves in two, or shrugged off their FE courses, to create an institution which meets the arbitrary administrative criteria written into the Act for inclusion in the polytechnics and colleges sector. Many more, while not meeting these criteria, retain a little work at higher level; for this their local authority must 'contract' with PCFC to continue to receive funding. Educational and social needs give way to administrative convenience, and the ultimate victory of the Department of Education and Science view that higher education should be concentrated in relatively few, relatively large institutions. As further gratification of this concentration philosophy, the period just before and after the passing of the Act has seen a rash of proposed mergers: between colleges, between polytechnics and colleges, between universities, and between universities and colleges.

In the outer darkness of FE, the colleges struggle with the paradox of weighty DES circulars spelling out in detail how they shall be freed from detailed control. In the new ERA, colleges of FE must reconstruct their links with polytechnics, colleges and universities, and hope that access courses will not fall foul of new funding rules.

Even in the complete reform of the education system undertaken in the ERA, further education was something of an also-ran. While schools and HE had their White Papers, FE had to settle for a green-covered consultation paper (DES, 1987). The FE colleges have always been the least understood part of the education system. Though there are major differences in emphasis between different colleges, in general FE colleges are relatively comprehensive providers of: vocational training for craftspeople and technicians; general education and academic preparation for HE for people of all ages, including 16–18-year-olds, as an alternative to the schools; and cultural and leisure activities. There is also a network of separate adult education centres and 'evening institutes' offering cultural and leisure activities alongside some general education programmes; in some areas the adult education provision is separate, in others integrated with the FE colleges. There is a relatively small but currently flourishing private sector of FE, mostly concentrated on academic programmes at GCSE and A-level for British and overseas students.

Perhaps the most significant change of the last ten years has been largely outside this system, though closely linked with FE. The national Training Agency (formerly the Manpower Services Commission) has initiated a bewildering series of training programmes for adults and for young people. The largest is the Youth Training Scheme (YTS), at first a one-year programme for 16-year-olds, later a two-year programme for those aged 16 and 17, aimed in particular at those who would otherwise have left school at 16 and become unemployed. Massive investment in YTS expanded participation to over 430,000 at the end of 1987, bringing within the scope of a recognized training scheme many young people who would otherwise never have been involved in further education or training. The YTS is for the most part a work-based programme involving some periods of college-based education, organized by 'managing agents' allocated funds for each trainee. This stimulated the growth of private training providers, either as managing agents or as rivals to the FE colleges in providing the educational components of the scheme. Some of these private providers also look to adult clients, whether for training funded by the Training Commission or otherwise.

The British 'system' is thus a patchwork of elements which arose at different times in response to different pressures and needs, which has been subject to periodic attempts to tidy up the structures, usually by putting an official stamp on structures which had already evolved. Just as some commentators have seen a common element at HE level in the 'gold standard' of the honours degree, so it has been argued that in FE: 'The system is held together as a national system by the central examining and validating bodies, which ensure a sufficient national consistency of content and level of education of students holding identical certificates' (Russell, 1985, p. 18).

The schools' examining bodies outside Scotland have recently coped with the replacement of GCE O-level by the General Certificate of Secondary Education (GCSE), meant to provide certification of attainment for a broader range of school-leavers. The government has rejected the 1988 Higginson Report proposing the replacement of the relatively specialized and narrow A-levels, the traditional preparation for HE entry, by a broader curriculum; this despite (or perhaps because of) virtual consensus within secondary and higher education in favour of the change. Many vocational and technician qualifications now come within the scope of the Business and Technician Education Council, which validates and moderates many certificate and diploma courses at 'national' and 'higher national' level. A two-year Higher National Diploma can be seen as broadly equivalent to the first two years of a three-year undergraduate programme, and most polytechnics offer a range of HND courses alongside their CNAA degrees. Many courses in FE and in the polytechnics are also validated by the independent professional bodies; these together with the City and Guilds of London Institute, which is the pre-eminent body for craft-level examinations, constitute perhaps the most influential element of a small private sector in British post-secondary education. Many of the rationalizations and innovations in FE can be seen as creating the conditions for future innovation in HE.

The new structures and funding arrangements for HE enacted in 1988 virtually guarantee that there will be no major new developments of higher education outside the university/polytechnic and college sectors. But the new autonomy offered to FE and HE institutions by the Act may facilitate innovation on a wider scale, especially when driven from the higher education side by increasing competition for declining numbers of students – at least, of those arriving through the present channels. There will no doubt be new kinds of link between further and higher education. To develop the comparison between these and the community college 'link' in the USA it is necessary to get a sense of scale in each case.

Size and scope

Enrolment comparisons, even year-on-year in the UK, are bedevilled by recent rapid changes and the difficulties of comparing like with like. This brief section attempts no more than a sketch for the purposes of orientation.

It should be noted first that compulsory schooling ends at age 16 in Britain, and many of the students in further education are in the 16–18 age-group. In 1984 there were 2.7 million 16–18-year-olds in Britain. Of these about one-third were in full-time education (17% in school sixth forms, 14% in FE); about one-third (34%) were working or were unregistered unemployed; one-sixth (17%) were registered unemployed; 9% were working and also attending part-time day release classes; and 10% were on Youth Training Schemes of various kinds, mostly work-based with some college experience included. Thus over half (51%) of this group of young people were not in any form of post-secondary education or training (Source: Russell, 1985, Appendix C). The 'missing link' starts here. By comparison, in the USA in 1985, 93% of the 14–17-year-old population was enrolled in grades 9–12 of high school; 7% of 16- and 17-year-olds and 14% of 18- and 19-year-olds were high school dropouts; overall 12% of those aged between 14 and 34 were dropouts (Source: *Digest of Education Statistics 1987*, pp. 50, 86). Plainly Britain loses many more people earlier from its education system than the USA.

The consequences for enrolment in higher education are readily apparent: enrolment in US higher education was 12.2 million in 1985, about 5.1% of the population; in Britain it was just over 0.9 million, about 1.5% of the total population. Total expenditure on all US HE institutions, public and private, in 1984–5 was $90 billion (at 1984–5 prices), about 2.3% of GNP (Source: Digest of Education Statistics, 1987). In Britain in 1985 the total expenditure on HE was £3.0 billion, about 0.9% of GNP (*The Government's Expenditure Plans 1985–86 to 1987–88*). Of course, this is not a comparison of like with like. Some of the work in American community colleges, included in these HE statistics, is analogous with that in British FE colleges, not included here. But FE colleges also include many 16–18-year-olds who do not feature in community college enrolments. In 1984–5 there were about 1.7 million students enrolled in British FE, of whom about 0.7 million were in the 16–18 age-group. Total spending on FE institutions was £965 million. Even if we were to count the whole of British FE, including 16–18-year-olds, and adult education, as part of the HE system, spending as a proportion of GNP would be no more than 1.2%. The debate about 'access' to HE in Britain is sometimes conducted as if the transition from an élite to a mass system can be achieved by the expansion of non-traditional routes, the creation of Ball's 'royal road'. But plainly the problem dwarfs marginal tinkering with numbers.

These simple numbers beg many important questions, including those of what to count and when and how to measure it (whether in credits, enrolments, full-time equivalent numbers, or whatever). But the general scale of the differences between British and American systems is clear. At the Oxford and Princeton seminars which preceded this book, some of these differences became clear for the first time to some of the American participants. Their disbelief was summarized by one who said 'If one half of the people are paying for the other half's education, why don't the first half organize?'. The answer lies in political and sociological explanations which are partly beyond the scope of this chapter, but must at least be touched on here.

Tyrrell Burgess once said of the English system that 'Vocational training is the higher education of the working classes, and higher education is the vocational training of the middle classes'. Edwards (1979, 1982) built a comparative theory of HE expansion around the notions of social class and status. He argued that the growth of the middle classes, their valuation of graduate status, and the increasing application of knowledge to 'production and social provision', were sufficient to explain the patterns of expansion of HE in most Western countries during much of the twentieth century:

> The dynamic of past development has been the valuation attached to HE by sections of the population who already had a high perception of its nature and a high confidence in their ability to participate in it if they chose. The main internal inertia to a more rapid advance in demand for HE has been the failure to develop any real perception of its nature and possibility among the majority of the population.
>
> (Edwards and Roberts, 1980, p. 37)

Edwards sought to account for HE expansion in terms of two contrasting trends: the explosion of factual knowledge, congruent with the dominant academic ethos of knowledge for its own sake; and the expansion of student numbers and spending on HE, driven by middle-class pressures and the increasing application of knowledge. Halsey develops the sociological argument:

> universities have always played a role in social stratification, controlling access to highly valued cultural elements, differentiating the capacity of individuals to enter a hierarchy of labour markets, and therefore being intrinsically inegalitarian institutions.
>
> (Halsey, 1985, p. 131)

Alongside this we can set two strands of orthodox economic argument, that HE serves as vocational preparation, and/or as a filter (Arrow, 1973, p. 194: 'higher education serves as a screening device, in that it sorts out individuals of differing abilities, thereby conveying information to the purchasers of labour').

Such instrumental considerations have been given high priority in recent policy statements such as the 1987 White Paper *Higher Education: Meeting the Challenge.* The distinction between vocationalism and the pursuit of knowledge for its own sake has also been used to differentiate between the purposes of polytechnics and universities, from the first statements of the 'binary policy'. Though there is no doubt that such distinctions have substance, and may be passionately argued by people in HE, it also seems clear that polytechnics and colleges fulfil a social stratification function just as universities do. The binary policy is about the divisions within the élite.

This argument would be abhorrent to those in polytechnics who cling to the radical alternative which Eric Robinson (1968) once outlined for the polytechnics as 'the people's universities'. But such views have become un-fashionable, as majority opinion in polytechnics seeks to blur the binary line, favouring such symbolic trappings as the establishment of a polytechnic professoriate and (though opinion on this is more evenly divided, and the DES has so far resisted the change) the redesignation of polytechnics as 'polytechnic universities'.

These issues, familiar to observers of British HE, have important con-sequences for the 'missing link'. Their impact was clearly analysed by Fulton (1981), summarizing the Leverhulme seminar on the theme of access, who concluded that: 'rather than a wholesale and centrally dictated reform of existing opportunities, what is needed is far greater diversity and freedom to experiment' (p. 20).

It may not be too optimistic to suppose that the Education Reform Act takes us substantially nearer some of these freedoms. While there can be no doubt that there is a problem of scale, and that more expenditure is needed to achieve the transition to a mass system, history teaches us that funds have often followed innovation rather than stimulated it. The final section will consider some recent innovations, which may help to provide new links, and finally returns to questions of mission as the key to future evolution.

Making the connections

The Education Reform Act might, only slightly unfairly, be characterized in its HE proposals as a managerialist charter and a licence for instrumentalism by students, teachers and institutions. Yet from such unpromising material might come just the kind of experimentation needed to transform British HE from its élitist stage towards Trow's 'broad system marked by a diversity of standard, mission and cost'. The new arrangements for governance in HE have prompted first some restructuring and merger proposals. As panic subsides and institu-tions become more self-confident in their new status then polytechnics and colleges will be freer to experiment in terms of mission and philosophy. Such experiments will be driven by demographic decline, which may also engage some universities in radical reviews to ensure a continuing flow of students and the funds they bring with them.

There have already been a series of experiments with new kinds of HE provision. The Open University, despite world-wide acknowledgement, remains curiously unfavoured and starved of funds, perhaps because of the oddly British undervaluation of part-time HE (Tight, 1987). Almost unnoticed outside FE there has been a significant development of open and distance learning programmes offering alternative routes to both established and new FE qualifications. There have been higher-profile failures such as the Manpower Services Commission's Open Tech programme. A group of polytechnics are trying to establish an Open Polytechnic which will complement Open University provision and use different delivery modes. Repeated attempts to establish a nation-wide Credit Accumulation and Transfer Scheme to facilitate student mobility are making slow but noticeable progress. In different parts of the country FE and HE institutions are forming links either to promote post-secondary education jointly, or to design access routes for local students through FE courses onto university or polytechnic degree programmes. In different ways such innovations are creating some of the conditions necessary for systemic change, which when or if it comes will almost certainly be driven by demand rather than supply-side changes. Halsey (1987) has argued that:

> The European university has passed through four main phases of dominance of the curriculum since its medieval origin. They are (1) priestly, (2) aristocratic, (3) professional, (4) democratic. Vestigial remains of (1), (2) and (3) are still with us and (4), the rise of student/consumer sovereignty, has implications which the British universities still fail to accept. We need universities for the scholarly few and higher education, pluralistically funded, for everyone.
>
> (Halsey, 1987, p. 341)

British institutions are surely at the rear in this European shift, but the rise of consumer sovereignty will sooner or later be accelerated by the widespread introduction of student loans in addition to, or alongside, grants. This will not be the final piece in the evolutionary jigsaw, but it may at the margins encourage consumer-driven experimentation by institutions, to provide as a matter of choice rather than necessity a range of courses other than honours degrees. Alternatively or in parallel the FE colleges may also develop new kinds of programme, or more likely repackaged versions of existing courses, more attractive to students with a sharpened appreciation of the kind of educational experience and terminal qualification they want, or are allowed to pursue by the terms of their financial support. The binary system will be long gone, replaced by an emerging hierarchy of sectors with more clearly differentiated purposes: the major research universities; the universities and polytechnics with some major research programmes and a stronger emphasis on teaching; the teaching universities, polytechnics and colleges, divided according to philosophy, geographical catchment, religious affiliation, or howsoever. In such a system the boundaries between FE and HE, so recently defined sharply for the first time, would be much less significant.

It follows that the next restructuring should see the creation of some kind of national funding body for further education (Cuthbert, 1988), along with the merging of the UFC and the PCFC. This would make it possible to establish as a next step regional structures for funding and control of all post-secondary education. Such structures, allied with consumer-driven funding, might be sufficient to overcome the élitist instincts of the present HE system.

The changes at the margin of the system would need to create their own groundswell of support, fuelling political demands for the extension or transfer of financial support to that half of the population who currently only pay for the higher education of the other half. The new students and the institutions they attend would indeed finally provide the 'missing link' which could bring about a mass system. It would at last be realistic to think of that 'higher education for the whole society' with its 'diversity of standard, mission and cost', which British HE finds so attractive to embrace as an ideal, but so difficult to pursue in practice, because it strikes at the roots of its current existence.

References

Arrow, K. J. (1973). Higher education as a filter, *Journal of Public Economics*, **2**, 193–216.

Ball, C. J. E. (1987). *The future provision, of AFE in colleges, with a substantial amount of non-advanced work*. Paper for the Summer Meeting of The Association of Colleges for Further and Higher Education, Norwich, 4–5 June 1987.

Burgess, T. and J. Pratt (1970). *Policy and Practice: The colleges of advanced technology*. Harmondsworth, Middlesex: Allen Lane/Penguin.

Crosland, A. (1965). *Speech by the Secretary of State for Education and Science*, Woolwich Polytechnic, 27 April 1965.

Crosland, A. (1967). *Speech by the Secretary of State for Education and Science*, Lancaster University, 20 January 1967.

Cuthbert, R. E. (1988). Reconstructing higher education policy. In Eggins, H. (ed.), *Restructuring Higher Education*. Milton Keynes: Open University Press/SRHE. Selected proceedings of the 1987 SRHE Annual Conference.

Department of Education and Science (DES) (1985). *The Development of Higher Edcuation into the 1990s*. HMSO, Green Paper, Cmnd 9524.

Department of Education and Science (DES) (1987). *Maintained Further Education: Financing, governance and law*. London: DES, Consultation Paper, August 1987.

Digest of Education Statistics 1987. US Department of Education, Office of Educational Research and Improvement, Center for Education Statistics.

Education Reform Act 1988. Ch. 40.

Edwards, E. G. (1979). Towards a relevant university, *International Journal of Institutional Management in Higher Education*, **3**(2), 253–70.

Edwards, E. G. (1982). *Higher Education for Everyone*. Nottingham: Spokesman.

Edwards, E. G. and I. J. Roberts (1980). British higher education: long-term trends in student enrolment, *Higher Education Review*, Spring, 7–43.

Fulton, O. (1981). Principles and policies. In Fulton, O. (ed.), *Access to Higher Education*. Guildford: Society for Research into Higher Education. Leverhulme Programme Report 2.

The Government's Plans 1985–86 to 1987–88. London: HMSO, HM Treasury, January 1985, Cmnd 9428.

Halsey, A. H. (1985). The idea of a university: the Charles Carter Lecture 1984, *Oxford Review of Education*, **11**(2), 115–32.

Halsey, A. H. (1987). Who owns the curriculum of higher education? *Journal of Educational Policy*, **2**(4), 341–5.

Higher Education: Meeting the challenge (1987). White Paper (Cm 114) HMSO.

International Financial Statistics Yearbook 1986. Washington, DC: International Monetary Fund Bureau of Statistics.

Locke, M. (1978). *Traditions and Controls in the Making of a Polytechnic: Woolwich Polytechnic 1890–1970*. London: Thames Polytechnic.

Pratt, J. and T. Burgess (1974). *Polytechnics: a report*. London: Pitman.

Robinson, E. E. (1968). *The New Polytechnics*. Harmondsworth, Middlesex: Penguin.

Russell, T. J. (1985). *Further Education and Industrial Training in England and Wales*. Blagdon, Bristol: Further Education Staff College. Comparative Papers in Further Education Number 12, Revised Edition.

Scott, P. (1983). Has the binary policy failed? In Shattock, M. L. (ed.), *The Structure and Governance of Higher Education*. Guildford: Society for Research Into Higher Education. Leverhulme Programme Report 9.

Tight, M. (1987). The value of higher education: full-time or part-time? *Studies in Higher Education*, **12**(2), 169–85.

Trow, M. A. (1974). Problems in the transition from elite to mass higher education. In OECD, *Policies for Higher Education*. Paris: OECD. General Report, Conference on Future Structures of Post-secondary Education 1973.

Trow, M. A. (1981). Comparative perspectives on access. In Fulton, O. (ed.), *Access to Higher Education*. Guildford: Society for Research into Higher Education. Leverhulme Programme Report 2.

Trow, M. A. (1987). Academic standards and mass higher education, *Higher Education Quarterly*, **41**(3), 268–98.

10

The American Modular System

Sheldon Rothblatt

Modularity: Introduction

The world's first democratic nation is also the world's first mass-access higher education system. The special characteristics of American higher education regarded as a *system* are market discipline; diversified sources of funding; competition for students, faculty and resources; strong presidents and boards and comparatively weak academic senates; a process of 'articulation' allowing students from one kind of college or university to 'transfer' to another without loss of time; and the absence of a common 'idea' of a university except 'service' to 'society'. In the public segment, government action is often intrusive; but it is also confused, contradictory and divided, since government itself is subject to multiple and self-cancelling pressures arising from an unpredictable electorate and shifts in 'public opinion'.

American higher education is also characterized by a great variety of types of institutions and standards and a certain hesitation to proclaim one intrinsically superior to the other, even within what may be defined as the élite sector. A report to the Board of Harvard Overseers written in 1886 cautioned that it was 'well . . . that young men in college should become used to the standards which prevail in the world outside, where a man's rank among his fellows is determined by many different considerations, and anything approaching the mathematical inaccuracy of a college rank list is unknown'.[1] By contrast, the nineteenth-century history of Oxford and Cambridge is characterized by precisely such an effort (especially at the latter) to rank undergraduates by order of merit.

Most of the cardinal features of the American higher education system are captured in the organization of the curriculum, which, with several exceptions, is modular in form. The modular system can only be appreciated as a special creation of American history and society, importing local and national tensions into colleges and universities while also providing for alternatives and digressions.

While a remarkable artefact, the American modular system is virtually taken for granted. It is assumed to be axiomatic, a basic and timeless feature of higher education, although few are conscious of its origins and functions. The system does not even possess a common name. The word 'modular' – at least as applied to the American courses structure – is not in everyday use. Possibly it was first used in connection with the lower levels of the education system; but it may well be a British import, or an import subsequently exported, for in Britain the word is assumed to be American in origin.[2]

In the 1930s, the designations 'unit system' and 'college hour system', or more pejoratively, 'time-exposure system', were used. Americans today frequently say 'course system', but in Britain the word 'course' is more akin to the American academic word 'programme'. The British use of the word 'course' is monotheistic, but the American is polytheistic. Monotheism, it has been said, is characterized by rigour, jealousy and exclusion, while polytheism is relaxed, tolerant, careless and inclusive. Recently, designations like 'credit-unit' or 'course-unit' system have been employed, but neither of these is very precise. (Nevertheless, the University of East Anglia adopted the language 'course-unit system' to describe its teaching.) The word 'modular' is not necessarily less vague. While conveying the necessary meaning of a structure of detachable, separate parts and distinct pieces, its use is nevertheless fraught with semantic difficulties. It may, for example, suggest standardized units of study where none in fact exist. In some respects the word is actually misleading, implying intensive not concurrent units of study, as in the bloc 'modular' inter-sessional curriculum of Colorado College, Colorado Springs.

In so far as any kind of degree programme may be chopped into modular bits, the word 'module' does not automatically convey the American meaning of a degree programme that is actually built upward from the bottom of the curriculum. The degree itself is little more than a container for collecting modules from different parts of the study list, such as the 'major', free electives, and choices from a range of breadth and proficiency requirements. By itself, modularity suggests nothing about 'articulation', early twentieth-century educational jargon used to describe the process by which the module as a unit of exchange facilitates the working of transfer mechanisms. From this feature of American higher education modularity acquired the designation 'credit transfer' system. But if no single word or phrase provides a shortcut for understanding the essential nature of the American higher education curriculum, 'module', 'modularity' and 'modularization' (when properly qualified) will have to suffice.

Modularity: History

That much abused notion 'system' does in truth describe the American curriculum, which is composed of many separate elements of different origin linked together over time. In the beginning (for our purposes) was the old unified (and interdisciplinary) collegiate curriculum or 'class system' influenced by Scottish practice and carried over from the later eighteenth century.

Undergraduates were divided into distinct cohorts by year, and the subjects for each year's cohort were specified. The class system persisted right up to the middle of the nineteenth century and beyond, but beginning in the 1820s (or perhaps earlier) a number of institutions began to experiment with alternatives, usually in the form of parallel subject tracks providing students with elective choices. The introduction of electives has been called 'the central educational battle of nineteenth-century America . . . the question which aroused the greatest amount of controversy [and] inflamed passions as no other educational issue was able to do'.[3] The issues were legion: the value of collegiate versus professional or 'university' education; the definition of a liberal culture; the place of religion in the curriculum; character formation versus knowledge for individual consumption and use; discipline versus self-motivation; curricular innovation versus the old-time college class system.[4]

Consumer choice with respect to curriculum is an aspect of the transformation of American society from a grouping of colonies in a virgin wilderness to a self-governing federal union increasingly urban, and what subsequently became known as the 'elective system' was intricately connected to the making and remaking of American society.[5] The exact historical origins of electives are vague. Conceivably electives originated at Edinburgh University in the very early eighteenth century where they were called the 'voluntary' system. Thomas Jefferson, credited by some historians with introducing electives to America, had a Scottish teacher at the College of William and Mary in Virginia, and it was at colonial William and Mary that several scholars find traces of an elective principle in the late eighteenth century. But despite the undeniably great influence of the Scottish university on post-1750 American education, the evidence for a Scottish modular precedent is slight and the specific example fleeting.[6]

Indigenous ideas of democracy and a belief in individual self-reliance were factors in the kind of elective system introduced by Jefferson and the Jeffersonians in the University of Virginia founded in the mid-1820s. Support for variety in the curriculum could also be obtained from German sources on the freedom of teaching and the freedom of learning which penetrated Harvard in the 1820s and resulted in the introduction of a limited amount of choice. In general, many different ideologies associated with voluntarism and consumerism existed in nineteenth-century America, many different ways in which electives could and were used, many different types of elective systems were in operation: systems with no restrictions, with partial restrictions, with choice among alternatives, or choice in some sectors of the curriculum but not in others, or partial or full choice in some undergraduate years but not in others. Choice could exist in sequences and timetabling but not in actual courses. Where introduced, 'parallel' tracks allowed for the coexistence of older programmes of study and curricular experiments, and some tracks led to new types of degrees. As in Victorian Britain, separate degree programmes were used to protect the historic BA standard, but mixtures are also in evidence: compulsory with optional modules or tracks, providing full, limited, or no choice in some tracks. Almost all of the typical curricular forms in use in the United States

today – mandatory foundation-year courses, capstone courses, two-year collegiate 'seminars' – were known and experimented with in the last century.
Americans have never ceased to tinker with combinations of electives and
requirements, with ways of joining or separating modules, ever since that
famous (or infamous) day on which the diversified curriculum of the present
first revealed its educational and administrative potential.[7]

However, the story of the voluntary curriculum or electives, unquestionably
important to the history of undergraduate education, is only one part of a larger
development. First, elective parallel tracks had to be completely broken into
discrete parts (the American 'courses' of today) in order to become self-
contained modules where teaching and examining were combined. As this
occurred, degree examinations – the oldest type of American college examinations, extending back into the seventeenth century – diminished in importance.
Examinations were more or less uncoupled from the degree and instead
attached to modules, where every kind of evaluation was possible. Examinations were also scheduled at the convenience of the individual professor, as
happened at the state university of Michigan as early as 1833, and the net effect
of this transfer was a reinforcement of the practice of continuous assessment,
consisting of frequent exercises, quizzes, recitations and examinations. As
American higher education did not yet sit atop a lower system of feeder schools,
the college and university environment continued to resemble a school. Not
until the influence of the graduate school of the twentieth century was felt in the
undergraduate curriculum did the core letters and science college become more
like a university.

A second and essential step was providing for articulation, so that students
could move modules from one kind of institution to another, generally to
improve their social or career opportunities. (The migratory American student
is not and never was the *Wandervogel* of German romance, pursuing knowledge in
and for itself.) If the student transferred, but without modular credits, then
obviously the time to degree as well as expenditures increased, and such
prolongation of the years of higher education was unacceptable to families of
modest means. Furthermore, to encourage upward academic mobility, it was
essential to have institutions of very great variety, of different academic
standards, levels of cost and geographical location, responsive to very different
kinds of educational markets. Otherwise, no useful service was performed in
having the student exchange one kind of educational experience for another.

Very likely in the 1870s, or soon thereafter, modules were assigned an
arithmetical equivalent connecting the separate capsules of teaching to hours of
instruction, thus creating the banking or trading-stamp system that character-
izes the administration of nearly all American modular arrangements. The
employment of units of credit appears to have been exclusively internal to begin
with, a form of domestic book-keeping to provide some means of determining
the relative weighting of modules. Severed from parallel course tracks, modules
threatened the higher education system with chaos, and among the list of
concerns was the fear that unless limits were assigned to student work loads,
undergraduates would be overly taxed. The whole vexed problem of defining a

work load was in fact beginning to puzzle the American academy, and credit units were therefore a functional substitute for some kind of overall administrative co-ordination of a curriculum transformed into a riot of courses.

The use of units to define transfer work is a feature of the Progressive Era, the period from about 1900 to the First World War, and enters public debate in tandem with calls for standardized testing. Much of the surviving literature from the period is concerned with units principally as a means of bringing order into the typical disorder of American lower education and of stabilizing the curriculum in secondary schools, whose enormous variability was continuing to trouble a higher education community preoccupied with the problems of regularizing the process of university admissions. Because the newly established Carnegie Foundation for the Advancement of Teaching was particularly active in promoting the idea of a common national measure, the unit of credit became known as the 'Carnegie Unit'. At the time of their introduction, units were frequently attacked as a device for measuring classroom quality and the value of academic work,[8] but such was never the intention of their creators, and units have remained quantitative indicators only, a means of tabulating the amount of time presumably spent in studying a particular subject. A number of years elapsed before a universally recognized definition of unit did in fact take hold.

The history of units is fascinating but essentially obscure. Aetiological detail and how units became entangled with a method of evaluation called 'grade points' are missing from historical narrative and remain puzzling.

It is not absolutely necessary to assign numerical work load equivalents to courses for purposes of transferring modules. The system would work if transfer credit were simply given for whole or half courses, although the problems of defining a 'course' stubbornly remain. Today, some aspects of articulation are actually conducted through courses rather than credit units; but units provide more flexibility, permitting the accumulation of many kinds of partial courses as well as numerical fragments and allowing for the simple calculation of an overall average measure of achievement.

Over a period of approximately half a century, the various elements of the American educational system – electives, modules, units, grade points, transferring, continuous assessment, teaching combined with examining, articulation – grew together to form the everyday curricular structure so familiar today. Accompanying that process, indeed caused by it, was the growth of a complex body of regulatory academic legislation which is often a nightmare to administer; and in the wake of legislation, as only to be expected, came a body of faculty and non-faculty administrators.

A connected account of the origins, growth and variations of the interesting and important history of the expansion of the American modular system does not exist. But after all, the story may not appear so interesting and important to potential readers and auditors. It is administrative history, a tiresome account of tiny details congealing into a system, slowly without an identifiable master artificer carefully shaping a massive educational structure. No heroic personalities combat nearly insurmountable odds. No social classes contend for mastery of the economic machine. No threats of revolution hang in the air. The story is humdrum. Yet the American modular structure is a way of life for millions of young persons and for the entire academic profession. It is the means by which a culture attempts to fulfil the life aspirations of its energetic citizenry, aspirations that range from mere getting-on to happy dreams of personal fulfilment and renown. It is a playing out on the stage of universities and colleges of the story of how the United States has accommodated egalitarian pressures and distributed satisfactions in the form of educational access and opportunity, while attempting to retain – where such attempts are made – examples of excellence, merit and originality which by definition cannot be indiscriminately bestowed.

Modularity today: Merits

The merits or advantages of the American modular system as it has evolved in conjunction with other features such as articulation, the combining of teaching and examining in one person, and consumer demand, may be identified as flexibility and *Lehrfreiheit*. Flexibility refers to the capacity of the modular system to alter the curriculum with comparative ease and to accommodate diverse student interests and levels of preparation within a single institution. Programmes and courses for an élite group of students can and do exist side-by-side with courses taken by the majority. The liberal arts, professional and technical studies are all provided for in one fashion or another. Just as the existence of a public sector of higher education in America protects the private sector (by absorbing pressures for admission and expansion), so does the availability of ordinary courses protect and guarantee more demanding courses for a smaller number of high-achieving undergraduates. Rigorous methods of assessment intermingle with routine evaluation. Courses can usually be added to or substracted from the overall curriculum without fuss, provided they are not compulsory and have the imprimatur of a recognized teaching unit.

Modular flexibility also rather directly furthers the American concern for social mobility by allowing for the entry into classrooms of non-traditional students who can be given special assistance or encouragement as time and attitude permit; and the system allows (and sometimes forces) the instructor to adjust the pace of learning to the perceived ability level of the class. Modularity provides a fairly simple solution to the controversial question of admitting underprepared students. Remedial courses can be added without disrupting the 'coherence' of the curriculum because, as critics mockingly notice, the American modular system has no coherence anyway. No course needs to be removed to make room for another, but such seeming generosity has a farcical side. Courses are listed that are seldom taught, and in some institutions many listed courses are never given at all because the resource base is weak. But the fiction is maintained to legitimize the curriculum, especially if the title 'university' has been claimed and the institution feels beholden to the mission of disseminating 'universal knowledge'.

Part-time attendance is possible under a modular system, although an institution may wish to control this traffic with a minimum progress-to-degree rule. The number and variety of courses can be co-ordinated with the admissions policy and adjusted to demand, sometimes quite suddenly, as in the teaching of foreign languages or sections of mathematics, that is to say, wherever prerequisites are essential.

By *Lehrfreiheit* (the word has important historical associations for Americans, for the earliest generations of course reformers were always conscious of the German example) is meant the relative freedom of faculty to create and teach in modules and to assign the corresponding student work load. The content of book lists, lecture presentations and discussion sections can be altered at will, as can certain aspects of the student work load, e.g. the number of intermediate examinations, quizzes, critical essays and term papers. Assignments can be revised, reduced, increased, adjusted; marking standards can be modified en route and so on. However, the changes must not be seen to be sudden or unfair, for students enter the classroom assuming instructors have agreed to a social contract based on the course description distributed in advance.

Because the single instructor is rarely asked to teach to a syllabus designed by a civil service ministry or government agency, a board of studies, or even an academic department composed of peers, the American modular system is *professorial* in the classic Oxbridge sense. Lectures are not linked to a degree examination. Research results can be incorporated into the course without delay, so the connection between teaching and research is as strong as the instructor desires. The only substantial external control on the actual content of a course derives from peer pressure, the internalized standards of the discipline, or student complaints too vociferous to ignore. It is in the hiring of faculty that an institution attempts to assure itself of the quality of teaching, although some further assessment occurs at critical review steps in the academic career ladder. Recently, the members of some state legislatures have raised the possibility of different kinds of assessments, but no debate has yet occurred comparable to the discussions over 'value-added' measurements that took place in the Britain of the 1980s.

Just as modularity can exist without articulation, so can it thrive without continuous assessment, but the two are natural allies and together strengthen the instructor's control over the classroom. The utility of continuous assessment is well understood, especially when contrasted with its customary opposite, the single-subject degree course. A student's progress is easily measured, encouragement and warnings are given on a frequent or regular basis, and because of the instructor's autonomy in the classroom, grades or marks can be adjusted according to a teacher's understanding of improvement. Assignments can be weighted as to their importance (usually progressively, but a final grade can also be awarded on the basis of the two or three best pieces of work the student has done). Compensatory work can be allowed if students are desperate for a second chance. Unlike the single-subject honours degree in Britain, assigned after exhausting combat with unseen questions drawn from 'papers', continuous assessment in modular form allows for a poor performance to be counterbalanced by a more successful one. Mistakes are not fatal. An unfortunate experience is soon over with few lasting consequences. *Amour-propre*, that pleasant cherub, is always to be found lurking on the premises. There is no Judgement Day. For these same reasons, success in examinations does not carry quite the cachet in America that it does in Britain. An 'A' student never acquires the glamour attributed to a 'First-Class Mind', since some of the modules contributing to the 'A' record may have been breathers, inserted into the game to allow even star players a chance to gain a second wind.

In Chapter 11, Oliver Fulton points out that critics of the British terminal honours examination system argue that undergraduates have too much time on their hands and are inclined to be idle until the period of count-down commences. Preparation for examinations should be steady and regular, whereas in reality it is no more than cramming. Learning acquired at the last minute is just as readily lost.

Perhaps; but preparation for examinations is always at the eleventh hour in any country, even where continuous assessment exists. For that reason, nineteenth-century teachers spoke about the educational superiority of critical essays or term papers. However that may be, it is a fact of history that 'wasting time' has often been a feature of Anglo-American élite systems of education. Learning takes place within a carefully structured environment where a peer-group culture is as important as classroom instruction. Students are supposed to learn as much from one another as from teachers – this feature is 'designed' into the system. The rationale is clear. Leisure is required to promote peer interaction, to allow students an opportunity for self-discovery, wide reading, and valuable extra-curricular activity, such as acting, journalism, music, games and further networking and contacts. If *Lehrfreiheit* describes the American modular system, then a particular kind of *Lehrfreiheit* describes the single-subject honours degree.

Comprehensive terminal examinations on unseen papers with blind marking can only be usefully employed where undergraduates are known to have the requisite skills and necessary self-discipline to acquire a certain amount of proficiency on their own. Continuous assessment on the American model actually suggests a lack of faith in the ability of undergraduates to work independently, to examine material critically, recognize contradictions, define problems, read widely, or pursue subjects of special interest to them. Wherever faculty direction is obviously loose, student educational choices in America tend to be governed by advertising and fads, the classic means of influencing consumer choice. The 1960s student demand for a wholly elective curriculum on the grounds that the consumer was the best judge of his own interest was not a call for educational freedom so much as another instance of American market economics. But the relatively weak elementary and secondary structures of education in the United States invalidate most student claims to intellectual independence.

Taken together, American modularization and continuous assessment describe a system of higher education that combines student demand with professorial self-interest. Both partners to the teaching relationship have an opportunity to express preferences. Students have a chance to select individual classes, and student preferences are most respected where a campus is particularly vulnerable to market discipline. The faculty have an opportunity to more or less teach the courses they choose in a manner they choose according to methods they select without undue concern for continuity or syncopation with their neighbours' modules.

A signal feature of American forms of modularity is their place in furthering the objectives of a second- and third-chance society, one that attempts to minimize both the actual and perceived results of failure. Where access is universal (or nearly so), the risk of failure is always present. The modular system breaks the fall. Despite students' fears, rarely do their educational or career opportunities rest on the outcome of a single academic adventure. Life generally begins again with another module. While certain courses may weigh more heavily in a given programme of studies than another, in general it is the grade-point average that matters. Students rely upon the invisible hand of the academic market-place to smooth out the aberrations, compensate for the errors and correct the overall academic record. The system is self-adjusting: a poor performance is balanced by a better one, although by the same token a strong showing in one module is compromised by a weak one in another.

Modularity today: Drawbacks

No higher education system can meet every objection, nor satisfy every criticism, and each must surely contain drawbacks when compared to another. The drawbacks to modularity are many: they are expense, administration, scheduling, work-load definition, the absence of common standards of achievement and measurement, the burden of uniting teaching with examining, the difficulty of establishing effective academic advising procedures, and competition for the student vote arising from the pressure to attract numbers whenever institutional income is threatened.

The old college or class system with its prescribed and limited curriculum confidently rested on the teaching of a few generalists and could survive considerable faculty turnover. Indeed, such turnover was built into the college system as a means of cost control, younger faculty replacing older ones. But modules require specialists, and free electives imply a great range of subjects and large academic (and non-academic) staffs; and since the fixed costs of higher education depend largely on the investment in people, the expenses associated with modularity are substantial, especially as the knowledge base grows and sub-specialization occurs.

Administrative costs are high. Bringing the modules together into some sort of relationship however tenuous and providing even minimal external co-ordination absorbs the energies of department heads, senate committees, deans and their staff. Evaluating transfer equivalents from several thousand different institutions and educational programmes, keeping track of credits and grade points, making exceptions to the rules, advising students on the myriad of regulations that have accumulated around modularity and hearing appeals require a staggering amount of time and energy. The modular system is also a scheduling nightmare. Generated by the American concern for flexibility, modules are often created but rarely destroyed, and this soon leads to problems of classroom space and competition for hours.

As a measure of learning, the assignment of credit units on a basis of classroom contact hours is meaningless, and on a basis of student work load, arbitrary and nonsensical. Neither uniformity of input nor of output is possible. Substantial writing assignments exist in some social science and humanities courses but not in others. Some faculty are dismayed by student prose, others are satisfied with ball-park approximations. The pace of learning and absorption differs radically from student to student, and faculty demands upon student energies and abilities are so varied as to make even the idea of a common measure nearly ludicrous.

Like any legal or taxation system that is unenforceable as written, the credit-unit system will continue to produce elaborate fictions and evasions. The *mythos* of a standard measure is maintained while in practice students manipulate study lists and negotiate exceptions with equally frustrated or sceptical faculty. Since there is no effective immediate outside control on the internal quality of a given course, there is really no practical means of preventing downward academic drift in a certain number of courses. (Conversely, there is no external constraint on higher standards if the traffic is willing.)

The very same diversity of achievement levels which permits a flexible overall pedagogical response is also the bane of a single classroom teacher's existence. In a 1980s survey of Berkeley faculty, 90% of the respondents identified uneven student preparation and ability as a hindrance in teaching large lecture courses. Should lectures be designed to bring up the bottom, reach the 'average' student, or attract the ablest?[9]

No feature of the American modular system so disturbs critics as the absence of coherence in the curriculum. Building-block sequences are the natural exception. Connections are strongest in foreign languages and mathematics, weakest in the social sciences and humanities. Hence a perennial cry has been for 'coherence and integrity' in the curriculum.[10] The proposed solutions – team-teaching, interdisciplinary courses, separately housed programmes, or mini-colleges – ironically defeat their intentions, since such innovations are seldom compulsory. Consequently, they merely increase the number of choices, compounding the difficulties of the existing course structure.

Modularity exacerbates tensions in the teaching relationship. Faculty are pulled between different role conceptions. Are they liberal arts teachers responsible for forming character, encouraging learning, inculcating discipline and drawing out the innate powers of the mind, a mixture, that is to say, of academic and 'humane' objectives? Or are the professors patient but stubborn representatives of the Higher Criticism, committed to the very best standards of scholarship and science, unwilling to suffer fools gladly? Is the student only a mind upon which is inscribed bold, soaring and sophisticated ideas, or also a person, distinct and special, if momentarily buried beneath alluvial deposits of academic sediment and bureaucratic dust? Such ambivalences make faculty vulnerable to student plea-bargaining for grades and exceptions. They also interfere with efforts to establish informal and personal teaching relationships, such as those existing in systems where teaching and examining are strictly partitioned.

No system of pedagogy is perfectly free of conflict, if simply because some element of coercion is always present in a process of socialization; but the conflicts are greatest where authority is the most visible. However they may feel about their education – and all the available recent survey data indicate that undergraduates generally approve of the ways in which they have been taught – American students often behave as if their college and more especially their university is a collection of obstacles to be overcome, from impersonal record-keeping officers conspiring to prevent their graduation to faculty who are sometimes defended as themselves the victims of a mysterious bureaucracy. But since a university bureaucracy does not itself examine and assign marks, blame can only be laid upon teachers, whose classroom autonomy is so manifest.

The graduate student instructor adds yet another layer of confusion to the teaching relationship. The instructor enrolled for a degree is an intermediary also caught between roles, being neither a regular member of the faculty nor just a student – an ambivalence that in some institutions is addressed by the formation of collective bargaining unions for graduate students to secure benefits, increase independence and improve status.

A major defect of modularity is the difficulty of establishing a really satisfactory mode of academic advising. There is no lack of trying. Different methods are continually juggled, discarded, reintroduced and modified. The problem is less acute in the major, but even there undergraduates struggle to obtain reliable inside information on courses and faculty. Outside the major, chaos reigns. Modularity in conjunction with specialization has created such a bewildering variety of separate courses that no single adviser can have first-hand information on more than a handful, and much of the information is accidental. Furthermore, suiting the student to the course is even more fitful. Mass-education institutions in the United States have such poor staffing ratios that few undergraduates are well-enough known to teachers to receive tailor-made advice.

Conclusion

The flexibility and openness of the American modular system, those very features which allow it to speedily adapt to new conditions, are also the same reasons why the organization of teaching in America resembles the Ptolemaic cosmology of the later Middle Ages. It too works. It accounts for the backward movements of planets and other puzzling phenomena discernible to the naked eye; but it upsets the rationalist who dislikes fictions, is offended by evasions, demands simplicity, and wants a clear-cut statement of principle to govern the operation of complex systems. Whatever its drawbacks – and these are substantial when viewed both in comparative perspective and against some of the historic objectives of American undergraduate education – the modular system is genuinely popular. It is certainly 'unnatural' for American faculty to consider alternatives to the combination of teaching and examining characteristic of the self-contained module, and students understandably are not aware of other systems. No practical objection to modularity exists. The reasons are clear. Faculty prefer the classroom autonomy provided by modules and electives, and students prefer choice to compulsion.

One argument must be refuted, the argument of current (and past) reformers that modules are wholly or mainly the result of ('narrow') specialism and the departmental organization of faculty. While it is true that modularity is inconceivable in the absence of specialization, and that modules and the departmental organization of disciplines have prospered in tandem, a more accurate explanation of the success of autonomous courses lies within the structure and values of American society generally. Modular courses made a mass market for higher education possible, 'solved' the problem of access by 'solving' the problem of remedial education, made transferring possible, and thus provided a brilliant means of accommodating a very large number of quite different but potent social and political pressures. Modularity evolved and survived (and shows no signs of disappearing) precisely because it possessed the widest possible kind of educational reference in a deepening plural culture.

The contradictions of the modular system are those of American society generally. Its merits are its defects, and its defects its merits. But modularity is not a mere reflection or 'reproduction' of a convenient notion called 'American society'. It is a special compromise within that society, an agreement to tolerate the coexistence of radically different aspects of education. It is a system of trade-offs (not all of equal value) and exchanges that are constantly renegotiated as social and economic conditions change. An account of those renegotiations would itself be a major contribution to our understanding of the actual functioning of institutions; but for the moment we must be satisfied with a descriptive and structural analysis of the purpose and place of modules in American history and culture.

Acknowledgements

My colleague Martin Trow has provided me with his customary assistance and insight.

Notes

1. Mary Lovett Smallwood, *An Historical Study of Examinations and Grading Systems in Early American Universities*, Cambridge, Mass., 1935, p. 84.
2. I am indebted for these remarks to an unpublished paper by Clive H. Church of the University of Kent on 'Modular courses in British higher education: a critical assessment'. An earlier published version appears in the *Higher Education Bulletin*, 3 (1975), 165–84.

3. John S. Brubacher and Willis Rudy, *Higher Education in Transition*, 3rd edn, New York, 1976, p. 100.

4. *Ibid.*, pp. 100–101.

5. The same cannot be said of the present British interest in modules, an interest about thirty years old, but this judgement may be challenged by the events of the 1990s. In the 1960s modules were used in the Science Faculty of the University of London and in the Open University. They are now prominently featured in the curricula of the polytechnics and colleges of education (see Church, *ibid.*), but without the extraordinary range of applications possible in the United States.

6. Sir Alexander Grant, *The Story of the University of Edinburgh*, I, London, 1884, p. 277. As well as in Brubacher and Willis, useful remarks on the history of the elective principle appear in R. Freeman Butts, *The College Charts its Course*, New York and London, 1939; William T. Foster, *Administration of the College Curriculum*, Boston, 1911; G. W. Pierson, 'The elective system and the difficulties of college planning, 1870–1940', in *Journal of General Education*, **4** (April 1950), 165–74. Documents appear in Richard Hofstadter and Wilson Smith (Eds), *American Higher Education*, II, Chicago, 1961, pp. 697–747.

7. It has been estimated that between 1870 and 1940 Yale University attempted 'at least seven rather substantial reorganizations – to say nothing of a long series of minor adjustments and experiments' (Pierson, *ibid.*, p. 168).

8. Howard J. Savage, 'The Carnegie Foundation and the rise of the unit', in 43rd *Annual Report* of the Carnegie Foundation for the Advancement of Teaching (1947–48).

9. Robert C. Wilson, 'Berkeley faculty opinions on teaching quality in large lecture classes' (1985).

10. E.g. Ernest L. Boyer, *College, The Undergraduate Experience in America*, New York, 1987; Robert Zemsky, *Structure and Coherence, Measuring the Undergraduate Curriculum*, Association of American Colleges, 1989.

11

Modular Systems in Britain

Oliver Fulton

Introduction

The American modular system which Sheldon Rothblatt describes has the qualities of a truly functional arrangement. Its advantages have sufficiently outweighed its defects, in the particular circumstances of mass higher education in American society, to give it a virtually unchallenged acceptance and a taken-for-granted historical inevitability. The same cannot be said for its counterpart in England and Wales,[1] the 'traditional' university system of the single-subject honours degree course, planned – and examined – as a three- or four-year whole by the collective enterprise of a department or a faculty. No doubt the latter has plenty of life left in it, but it has faced repeated challenges since the Second World War, and an opponent might even claim that its end is in sight. Certainly the number of examples of modular courses in Britain is growing very fast.

The previous chapter has set the scene. The fundamental question which Rothblatt poses is the functional one: what is it about our societies that has sustained the particular organizational structures and the cultural and pedagogic assumptions within which we admit young, and not-so-young, people to our universities and colleges, and determine what and how to teach them and how they are to be assessed? I shall argue here that part of the answer, at least, lies in our respective attitudes to and opportunities for access: it is surely not an accident that the single-subject honours course in Britain was first challenged by modular arrangements in the 1960s,[2] and that modularity began to increase much faster and more steadily in the mid-1980s. The tension between access and 'quality' expresses itself in many forms, but the creation of new institutions in the 1960s, when participation rates were rising sharply, and the recently revived concern with access are undoubtedly connected with the move away from traditional course structures. I return to this point in due course.

The traditional English degree structure

The dialectic which Rothblatt and I have adopted as our method has already indicated the essential qualities of the traditional 'English' system. But it may, none the less, be helpful to underline them. The first is specialization, beginning quite early in the secondary schools. In our traditionalist institutions, newly arrived first-year undergraduates have already long abandoned large areas of knowledge, and there is no question of a student of the humanities or social sciences studying even a smattering of science in college, polytechnic, or university: probably they last did so at the age of 15. The typical undergraduate course (using the word to cover the whole three or four years' experience) is restricted to a single discipline, taught within a single department: choice is confined to certain 'electives' (the term is exclusively American, however) or areas of specialization within the discipline: historical periods, say, or topic areas corresponding closely to the specialist interests of particular members of the teaching staff. But there is always a large core area common to all students in the department. Breadth or interdisciplinary study are ruled out.

A basic assumption is that any choice by students can permit variations only in topic and not in level. We do not find the kind of specialist options to which Rothblatt refers, which provide extra opportunities and challenges for the most able students, or safety nets for the weakest. There are of course inexplicit differences between the standards expected in different options, and it is part of the student's task of mastering the hidden curriculum to discover which options, or which staff members, are most highly regarded academically, or which will require the least effort, depending on their own ambitions and needs. But the principle of common standards for all is crucial.

The second element of the traditional system is assessment. The standard form is the final honours examination, set and marked by the faculty, school, or department as a whole, or by their representatives in the larger universities, to be taken in the last term of the course in a whole series of three-hour examination papers consisting of essays on previously unseen questions. Although most papers cover particular sub-areas of the discipline, they will not necessarily be set, and will certainly not be marked, exclusively by the teachers of these specialisms. In the purest form, choice is catered for not by a choice of papers but by a choice of questions within each compulsory paper, and staff take pride in the ingenuity with which they ensure breadth of coverage across the discipline. This diet is still on offer in many British universities – and many polytechnics – today. It is symbolized in the language of prospectuses for potential students which describe the (three- or four-year) course in terms not of topics to be covered but of papers to be sat in the final summer term.

The justification is academic – a belief in the indivisibility of the essential core of the discipline, and a fear that even for final-year students cross-fertilization and continuity between sub-areas of a discipline do not happen spontaneously. So there must be 'general papers' to encourage students to synthesize their separate specialisms into a coherent view: to examine piecemeal would encourage a magpie approach to the acquisition of knowledge. But like the American modular system, the English system also embodies a set of more basic values about the nature of knowledge, the process of learning, and the relations between teacher and taught, as well as the social role of higher education in training and selection. For example, it proclaims a strong belief in the *uniformity* of students' experience – both during the course and before they join it.

As far as the course itself is concerned, the English (and now, generally, British) predilection for 'quality' here shows itself at its strongest. In practice, I suspect that nowadays the main preoccupation is no longer the protection of the unity and coherence of a disciplinary perspective, important though that is to many academics; rather, it is the problem of fairness. Rightly or wrongly, British academics see themselves as members of a strongly meritocratic profession; and they are acutely aware that the society (or at least the specific professions and occupations) into which their graduates will go takes the degree classifications which they apply extremely seriously. There are undoubtedly some quite troubling problems with any of the assessment systems applied by higher education; but whatever their blind spots, British academics are devoted at a rhetorical level to the principles of meritocracy and fairness. And fairness is enshrined not only in elaborate examination regulations, frequently consulted, but in the whole idea of competition against universally applied criteria in a curricular experience which is common to all.

But the uniformity stretches back well before enrolment. The whole system is also predicated on a homogeneous student body, capable – financially as well as academically – of studying at the same pace, and coming from a common background of preparation. Hence the attachment to full-time study and common, high entry standards – a point to which I return later.

As for teaching and learning, the implication is that learning takes place best when untainted by (continuous) assessment. At Oxford or Cambridge 'tutors' teach, and provide informal feedback on essays which they do not grade: lecturers, drawn in rotation from among tutors and others, examine – without partiality, since they do not know the students.[3] In the jargon of evaluation, the 'formative' and 'summative' tasks of the teacher are completely distinct: tutors wrestle, formatively, with individuals, and deal with their personal as well as their intellectual development and problems; lecturers examine, without reference to personal circumstances and without the pressure from students that Rothblatt describes.

Defects of the traditional system

To these attitudes and values there are, of course, rejoinders, and even without the preceding description of the American system it might be possible to deduce the main lines of attack. For attacks, or at least experiments with alternatives, there have long been.

The call of interdisciplinary courses

The most longstanding criticism has been aimed at the narrow coverage of the single-subject degree. Excessive and premature specialization has been a central theme of educational reformers, in secondary as well as higher education, for many years. Many of the arguments are familiar enough on both sides of the Atlantic – they correspond to the American debates over liberal or general education: the need for a broad education for citizenship (that is, for both political and cultural participation); the needs of the labour market (many of the criticisms have come from employers of graduates, who recruit more administrator–manager generalists than they do research and development personnel); and, of course, a desire to find failings in the education system on which national economic decline, materialism, ecological disaster, the subversion of the media, or football riots can plausibly be blamed.

Attempts to develop less specialized undergraduate curricula stretch back to the introduction of Greats at Oxford in the nineteenth century, in close parallel with the introduction of broadly based entrance examinations for the home and Indian Civil Services. Particular examples have varied considerably in their emphasis on, on the one hand, combinations of useful disciplines and, on the other, the analytic and integrative skills which interdisciplinary work might develop, regardless of content – 'developing the general powers of the mind', in the Robbins Report's useful phrase. But pleas for reduced specialization have recurred regularly, notably in the Robbins (1963) and Leverhulme (1983) Reports, in the comments of the UGC in the 1960s, and in those of employers' organizations – only to be offset by calls for rigour, depth, high standards and continuity from much the same quarters as the wheel of educational fashion revolves.

But there are other causes than fashion. For one thing, the balance between research and teaching has changed. By the 1960s an increasing number of graduates were being recruited back into higher education as teachers, but the Ph.D. had not yet been adopted as the standard form of training or the required qualification. Thus the first degree began to be expected to bear the brunt of specialist research training for the brightest students, at a time when most academics' own interests in research as opposed to tutoring were in any case growing fast. Proclamations of the need for interdisciplinarity and the dangers of over-specialization at this time were thus also a reaction by those who cared mainly about teaching to what they saw as a deteriorating situation.

Another element was provided by the growth in demand for higher education in the 1950s and 1960s, and in particular by the UGC's decision to meet it in part by creating new universities. These institutions, needing to establish themselves quickly in their own right, looked for some form of distinctiveness with which to attract good students and staff. If the new crusade was in favour of interdisciplinarity, and against the traditional 'redbrick' model in which the department was sovereign, the new universities appointed themselves as its leaders. With self-conscious references to Scotland, and even to 'Balliol-by-the-Sea', they set out to 'redraw the map of learning'.[4]

Student choice

If a preference for interdisciplinarity was partly imposed by staff, there was also – perhaps more strongly after the events of 1968 – an acknowledgement of the desirability of giving students greater freedom of choice. The political challenge to the unquestioned authority of the teacher was reinforced by the resurgence of 'progressive' learning theory – across the age-range from primary schools onwards – which suggested that students' motivation and indeed their intellectual development and comprehension could be enhanced by giving them greater control over the shape of their own curriculum; and by the sense that the increasing competitiveness forced on secondary education by the rising demand for a limited supply of places had damaged students' capacity for self-direction and discovery.

In the 1960s and their aftermath, student choice was proposed in the causes of improving learning and re-humanizing the university. By the mid-1970s, however, the philosophy of the market had begun to erode the confidence of providers of higher education that, as producers, they knew best what not only the students but the nation needed. A rising, politically orchestrated dissatisfaction with 'standards' began to suggest that it was only through consumer power that the entrenched professions could be forced to respond to the popular will. In a situation where real resources were declining fast, institutional leaders began to flirt with the idea of using consumer (i.e. student) demand as a weapon for claiming extra funds, or simply of shifting existing allocations around their institution. Modular structures, with free student choice, began to look attractive: what better reason for closing a course or disposing of an unwanted staff member than failure to recruit viable numbers?

At a more modest level, modular systems at least allow for greater flexibility and responsiveness to external change. It is not so much that curricular flexibility is a great virtue as that inflexibility is an obvious vice – and there have been notorious cases of atrophied curricula in great universities. The modular system, by allowing small-scale, piecemeal development, enhances the potential responsiveness of courses to changes in science and scholarship.

Alternatives to assessment by examination

The third main strand in the web of change was the attack on the traditional assessment system. One element was indeed the sheer dislike of many students for the gruelling three-hour honours examinations: brutal, impersonal (a vice, this, not a virtue in the 1960s) and rigid, putting an unfair premium on performance in a single week at the end of the final year and creating a huge strain for all but the most phlegmatic students. Many staff, too, were at least half-convinced by the occasional catastrophes that these examinations were more of a lottery than was acceptable. The best defence of end-of-course examinations is that there is no alternative: as soon as more humane and flexible possibilities were on the agenda, traditional systems were left with few friends.

These humanitarian considerations were considerably bolstered by psychological research (mainly at school level, but the implications for higher education were obvious) which suggested that this kind of examination rewards or encourages certain kinds of cognitive and intellectual skills at the expense of others – most damagingly, that far from promoting a wide-ranging synthesis at the end of three years of increasingly sophisticated work, it may in fact reward rather primitive types of rote learning; and that 'first-class minds' turn out to possess a rather narrow range of personality traits. Sociologists were quick to add that the later success of those with better classes of degrees was not conclusive evidence that the labels had been, objectively speaking, correctly applied.

Thus 'continuous assessment' began to find its way into higher education. By now the technical arrangements vary considerably, not only between institutions but between departments or even individual teachers within them; and much ingenuity, and not a little confusion for students, is involved in the multiplicity of schemes combining elements of both terminal and continuous assessment. Now in practice continuous assessment is expected to perform a large number of incompatible functions: providing both formative feedback and summative judgement, monitoring progress and, not least, penalizing lazy or disorganized students. The essentially humane motives which led to its adoption are not the whole story. If cunningly devised, it can also be a powerful method of control over students' work styles and indeed motivation. Everyone who endured the traditional system knows of people who devoted most of their student career to the extra-curricular attractions of university life. Sanctions against all but the most grossly idle were informal at best, and largely unenforceable. Continuous assessment tightens the screws. It probably saves quite a few students from the worst consequences of their own character defects, and it also assures the taxpayer that public money, which includes student maintenance grants, is not being frittered away. Rothblatt's defence of 'wasting time' cuts little ice with the promoters of efficiency studies, or those who propose to fit the British near-standard of 90 weeks' residence for a first degree into two calendar years instead of three. The American lack of faith in students has spread as the size of the British system has grown.

Changes in the recruitment of students

It is not only the public's perception of students that has changed as the system has grown: academics, too, have felt compelled to respond to the changing composition and changing preparation of university and polytechnic entrants. Keele University, founded in the late 1940s with an innovative design of a common 'foundation year' followed by major/minor specialization, based its plans not only on the needs of graduates but also on its hopes of attracting students from weaker schools, which could not provide as good a liberal arts foundation as the traditional recruiting ground of élite grammar and public schools. By 1970, the Open University faced the need to develop appropriate introductory courses for its ostensible[5] prime target group of older people with, potentially, no formal qualifications; and in the 1980s large parts of the system, notably the sciences and technology, faced a severe shortage of applicants qualified with the appropriate A-levels, and again had to devise new preparatory courses.[6]

Modular structures as a solution

This brings us back to modularity and its relationship to access. Britain has been uniquely slow, not so much in expanding its system (that is at least a subject for debate) as in adapting it from an élite to a mass character; even at present participation levels of almost fifteen per cent of the 18-year-old age-group (a figure which, not incidentally, refers only to full-time participation) there are many respects in which we are still operating an élite system on a surprisingly large scale. The effect is well represented by the now well-known 'efficiency' of British higher education, indicated by very high and very fast graduation rates by international standards. Nowhere is the élite character better demonstrated than by the assumption, built into course structures, student support systems and so on, that the British student will not be a *Wandervogel*: the norm is still one of continuous full-time attendance at a single institution.

It is, to repeat, not an accident that a modular course structure was pioneered by the Open University, which was created to cater solely for part-time students without 'normal' entry qualifications. I suspect that careful enquiry would show that the introduction of part-time courses was a major inducement to modularity in institutions of all kinds. The other components have, no doubt, all played their parts in specific cases: some modular or 'combined studies' courses at polytechnics, for example, have interdisciplinarity as their main goal. On the other hand, not all modular courses are continuously assessed by their teachers: the Open University is a monument of collective enterprise from course design right through to assessment. But both the presence and the needs of 'mature' and 'non-traditional' students are increasingly preoccupying most institutions; and notable among these are alternative modes of study, credit accumulation and credit transfer. Attempts to graft these onto the traditional system are clumsy and off-putting to all concerned.

If one were to make facile comparisons, it is undoubtedly the polytechnics which look most American in the senses described by Sheldon Rothblatt. In the last few years (up to the point when they gained independence from local government in April 1989) most of them have been strongly pressed by their political controllers to respond to local community needs. Many have developed strong equal opportunity policies, aimed at recruiting members of the various under-represented minorities in their immediate catchment area. And it is the polytechnic sector which has been the driving force behind increased participation in general. Whether out of philosophical commitment or in response to strong financial incentives which national governments first failed to control and then belatedly took credit for, the polytechnics have very substantially increased their enrolments during the 1980s, partly by finding space for students who might earlier have expected to find places in universities, but mainly by creating a new clientele for themselves. Like all British higher education institutions, they suffer from the tension between their desires for market responsiveness and status enhancement. But in the 1980s they almost managed to square the circle.

It would require a substantial research project to establish the present state of play on the various dimensions of modularity: university and polytechnic prospectuses are frequently inexplicit, and certainly inconsistent in the amount of information they provide. But I doubt if one could find a single institution with the range of 'electives' that even a small American college purports to offer: even so-called combined studies courses generally turn out to have a fairly restricted focus. And British institutions go in for much bigger units: the Carnegie unit may be 1/120 of a degree and Berkeley's 1/40, but the Open University's is 1/8: far less freedom here. The ideology of student choice is heavily constrained by subject-based academics' prescriptive instincts; and interdisciplinarity seems only precariously in fashion at present, the wheel having revolved another half-turn in the last few years.

On the other hand, government policy, as well as that of most – but not all – institutions in the face of demographic decline, is tilting in favour of mature students and their needs; and credit accumulation and credit transfer seem to be coming in on a slow but irresistible tide. In a research project on admissions policy Susan Ellwood and I discovered that modularization was indeed growing fast (Fulton and Ellwood, 1989). A substantial number of institutions – smaller colleges and polytechnics, but also a few universities – had either already modularized all or part of their courses or were planning or contemplating doing so in the fairly near future. One pressing reason was financial: in contrast to the American experience, modularization can in the early stages bring considerable economies as duplication of courses is reduced and class sizes are increased. The extra administrative burden, though real, is not yet seen as serious enough to threaten this economic rationale. But the main reason given to us was indeed the demand for greater and more varied access. The system allows institutions to take in a wider clientele with much more varied levels of specific or general preparation; it facilitates part-time study; and it creates the possibility not only of admitting students with credit transferred from elsewhere but of giving partial credits, generally certificates or diplomas, for intermediate years, which are portable to other institutions and have a value on the job market.

In a sense, the motives in Britain are more pragmatic than egalitarian: not for us the ideology of upward educational mobility, of the Ph.D. lurking in the book-bag of the remedial student at the community college. Transfer is mainly horizontal (i.e. within the same sector of the system), not vertical, and primarily permits geographical and career mobility in response to new needs for retraining and continuing education. But if we do not (yet) need upward mobility, it will be odd if every institution succumbs. There is already a university–polytechnic divide, with most of the recent developments on the polytechnic side. Quite where the line will be drawn is hard to predict; but I suspect that truly élite status will continue to imply many of the features of the historic English system. (Not, however, traditional examinations. Continuous assessment seems already to have taken over the vast majority of courses.)

Rothblatt has argued that it is external pressures, mainly for access and all the advantages it brings with it, that have been the motive force behind modularization, and not the interests of the academic staff. Modular courses, continuously assessed, undoubtedly put greater control in the hands of individual lecturers, even with all the British paraphernalia of double marking, external examining, validating and moderating that is described elsewhere in this volume. My impression is, however, that in our debates in Britain we have concentrated mainly on the benefits for students and for learning, and not on the rights and privileges of staff.[7] Perhaps undergraduate education is still seen as an appropriately collegial enterprise, one where individualism is less admired. It is more likely, however, that we have fudged, or failed to notice, the distinction between the 1960s' ideal of *inter*disciplinary teaching – which is time-consuming and difficult and makes great demands of teachers as well as students – and *multi*disciplinary opportunities for students, of which modularity is the essence. Here academic staff may well offer their special subjects with little regard for what their colleagues are providing, and it is up to students themselves, sometimes aided and sometimes hindered by administrators and their regulations, to make sense of the result. The levels of collegiality and collaboration which characterized the genuine interdisciplinarity of the 1960s were a reaction against the growing research ethic, and they have been increasingly squeezed as the dominance of research has asserted itself. Cutting up the map of learning is more amenable to busy researchers than redrawing it.

The traditional English system has few defenders. Confusing and confused though some of the newer alternatives may be, it is difficult to regret the changes. We are a long way still from a system which will fit the requirements of mass higher education. Most of our modules, where they exist, are too big to provide crevices for remedial coursework: instead we still insist that every entrant must be fully competent to pass the course before first enrolment, and we pack off doubtful cases on 'access' courses which are provided elsewhere, with neither the cachet nor the financial support which higher education brings with it. Our inflexibility is both a product of, and reinforces, understandable but quite excessive worry about entry standards (Fulton, 1988; Fulton and Ellwood, 1989). Exit standards, too, have been distorted by the traditional system. Collective course design and the quest for integration lead too easily to inertia – the failure to adapt curricula in response to new scholarship or to students' needs. The fixed disciplinary menu has done no better at rounding out our graduates than the laissez-faire cafeteria of the United States: each system has its own pathology. We cannot and certainly will not trade our system piecemeal for the American – but ours is more obviously dysfunctional, and change is in the air. One thing is clear: loose talk about quality and standards, defined by structure and not by process, is not going to get us very far.

Notes

1. The 'traditional' honours degree pattern is specifically English in origin. It has also prevailed in Wales. The old Scottish university tradition – which has been increasingly, but not totally, assimilated to the English pattern – is less specialized and more accessible. In this chapter, references to the tradition use the terms 'England' or 'English', and to current trends and events use 'Britain' or 'British'. (See, also, the general Note on British National Terminology in the preliminaries to this book.
2. See Church (n.d.). A further, authoritative account which dates the main impetus to the early 1970s is given by Squires (1986).
3. This has not, however, entirely protected them from claims of discrimination – against papers with women's names on them, for instance.
4. These two phrases come from the first years of Sussex University. See Daiches, (1964).
5. Ostensible, because in practice it recruited very largely in the early years from people with substantial sub-degree qualifications (such as school teachers with non-graduate Certificates of Education).
6. See Fulton and Ellwood (1989).
7. Academic freedom is probably far less discussed in Britain than in Germany or the United States, where there is a history of more serious conflict; here it tends to be equated, uncritically if not downright tendentiously, with the mere presence of tenure in academics' contracts of employment.

References

Church, C. H. (n.d.). Modular courses in British higher education: a critical assessment. University of Kent, mimeo.

Daiches, D. (ed.) (1964). *The Idea of a New University*. London: Deutsch.

Fulton, O. (1988). Elite survivals? Entry 'standards' and procedures for higher education admissions, *Studies in Higher Education*, **13**(1).

Fulton, O. and S. Ellwood (1989). *Admissions to Higher Education: Policy and Practice*. Sheffield: Training Agency.

[Leverhulme] (1983) *Excellence in Diversity: Towards a New Strategy for Higher Education* (The Leverhulme Report). Guildford, Society for Research into Higher Education.

[Robbins] (1963) *Report of the Committee on Higher Education*. London, HMSO, Cmnd 2154.

Squires, G. (1986). *Modularisation*. Manchester, CONTACT Paper No. 1.

12

The Disciplinary Contexts for Quality Judgements

Tony Becher

Introduction

Viewed in the context of its parent volume, this contribution is anomalous in two main respects. First, it focuses on the question of the quality of research as much as on that of teaching, and has no direct concern at all with the management of individual institutions or of higher education as a whole. Second, its contrasts are not so much between Britain and the USA as between one disciplinary or sub-disciplinary milieu and another. Indeed, in the context of research, there is scarcely a cross-national contrast to be drawn, since judgements within a particular field are largely independent of their particular geographical settings. Nevertheless, as the chapter will go on to argue, there are a great many other variables to be taken into account in considering the question of excellence both in the provision of undergraduate programmes and in the pursuit of academic enquiry: it is their very abundance which makes the judgement of standards a delicate and far from straightforward matter.

The account begins with a relatively brief discussion of how undergraduate provision is assessed, and what diversities underlie that process. A more lengthy discussion is then offered of the different forms of knowledge and the varied types of associated research communities which constitute the domain of academic research. This leads into a consideration of peer review as a mechanism for quality control in research, and a brief appraisal of its strengths and weaknesses. The concluding paragraphs suggest that, despite its evident limitations, it is strongly preferable to the current attempts to develop quasi-objective performance indicators which might be assumed to apply across the whole range of intellectual disciplines and specialisms. In both teaching and research, it can be held that quality is a proper subject for qualitative judgement rather than for quantitative measurement.

Qualitative variation in the undergraduate curriculum

Notions of quality, and of the maintenance of standards, are – as previous chapters have made plain – endemic in British undergraduate education in a way that they are not in American. But beneath the carefully sustained mythology of the gold standard for university degrees, the variation in their currency, even in Britain, is in practice quite substantial. Understandably, when recruitment is from a very narrow band of academic ability (however that elusive term may be defined) the range of such variation is less considerable than when it is from a much broader cross-section of the population. But my initial purpose is to offer a reminder of the ways in which, in both systems, the quality of undergraduate education is subject to fluctuation not only across institutions but also across disciplines.

There are three readily identifiable elements in any exploration of the level of excellence of initial degree programmes: namely input, process and output. Beginning with the first of these, distinctions may be noted between high-ranking and less sought-after subject areas as well as between élite and less prestigious institutions. The divergences in levels of student intake between a leading research university and a college of modest pretensions are evident enough to need no elaboration in both the UK and the USA. On closer scrutiny, similar market principles can also be seen to operate strongly across subject departments in Britain and across the corresponding course units in America. Although the organizational framework differs between the two systems, in that the characteristic pattern is of a single-subject specialist degree in the former, and of a modular course-credit pattern in the latter, the substantive issue applies to both.

Selectivity of intake is high when demand for a place in a department in the UK, or a course in the USA, is greatly in excess of the available supply. In the name of equity, selectors for pre-medical programmes in both countries are under pressure to admit only the very brightest and the very best. In contrast, scrutiny of the initial qualifications of applicants is less rigorous when the supply of places noticeably outstrips the demand. In subject areas which are currently undersubscribed – such as philosophy or physics – admission policies tend to be generous enough to admit anyone who can be given the benefit of the doubt: 'motivation' and 'relevant life experience' come more strongly to the fore than previous examination performance in the discussion of allowable entry criteria.

The attractiveness to applicants of undergraduate courses in a particular discipline or field may have little to do with the intrinsic merits or demerits of the courses themselves. One obviously relevant issue arises from the content of the upper secondary school curriculum. Where a school subject is seen as being 'mainstream' rather than 'minority' – English literature, say, as against German – the number of potential candidates for university places is likely to be large; applicants from marginal subjects will necessarily be fewer.

Another factor concerns the quality of provision in schools. If the subject is well taught – as history often is (since many of the more able history graduates go into school teaching) – its attractiveness as a degree subject will be further enhanced. If it is badly taught – as chemistry often is (since few of the more able chemistry graduates go into school teaching) – its attractiveness as a degree subject is likely to be diminished.

But there are also many disciplines which are not taught in schools at all, and whose marketability may be subject to a variety of other considerations. Vocational relevance is likely to loom large in a period of relatively high graduate unemployment – at least part of the current boom in information technology, business studies and other commercially orientated specialisms may be ascribed to this factor. Another equally uncontrollable and unpredictable factor may be the current climate of intellectual fashion, which led to a glut of sociology courses in the 1960s and 1970s, and which has more recently favoured subjects such as linguistics and anthropology.

As in all imperfect markets, supply takes some time to adjust to fluctuations in demand. There are always likely to be some subject areas which have over-expanded and are struggling to avoid the drastic effects of contraction by lowering their sights; and some which enjoy the luxury of choosing well-qualified applicants before new courses emerge to cash in on the surplus. Again, in certain cases – especially in those professions which operate an informal but highly effective *numerus clauss* – the places available may be adjusted to ensure that the applicants healthily outnumber the places for them, and so to inflate initial qualification levels in relation to competing subject fields. In others – especially academically low-status areas such as fashion or sports science – the self-fulfilling prophecy operates in the inverse direction, ensuring that it is largely those with weaker qualifications and lower ambitions who apply.

Alongside such evident, but not very widely discussed, differentiations between the acceptable level of input to undergraduate courses, there are also process variations – that is, distinctions in the quality of learning experience which students may be expected to undergo. One feature which has already been remarked upon is the extent to which a given subject is assumed to have been taught in secondary schools. For example, in mathematics a degree-level course will normally take for granted a reasonable level of sophistication in the subject – a knowledge at least of the basic elements of algebra, trigonometry, geometry and calculus. In undergraduate courses in archaeology, the basic grammar and vocabulary of the subject will normally have to be learnt *ab initio* before any more advanced level work can be embarked upon: and the same will be more literally true of the early stages of Arabic or Russian. It would seem to follow that there is a higher initial platform, and hence a more exacting overall level of intellectual demand made, in subjects which are a central part of the school curriculum than in those in which degree courses have to begin at the beginning.

A further qualitative difference may be identified in the type of knowledge which is in question. It is commonly held that the most abstract and theoretical subjects are the hardest to learn: on this count, courses in mathematics, theoretical physics and philosophy would call for the exercise of a different order of intelligence from subjects where the rote learning content is high, or where the main emphasis is on the acquisition of practical skills. Such distinctions can be highlighted by an analysis of the different types of examination questions which are posed in one subject area as against another: though this type of analysis can reveal some interesting surprises (see, for example, Thompson, 1979).

The teaching traditions within a discipline are related to both these issues – assumed entry level and general nature of learning activity – but may none the less be seen as a further source of differentiation between one subject and another. Much as it may be said, in a very rough-and-ready way, that good teaching is a more respected and better rewarded activity in some types of institution than in others (small colleges of higher education in the UK, long-established liberal arts colleges in the USA, as against upwardly mobile research-orientated universities in either country), so too it may be claimed in an equally rough-and-ready way that academics in 'hard' subjects – quantitative, scientific and technological fields such as chemistry and engineering – tend to make fewer concessions to the learning needs of their students (and tend indeed to be less aware of them) than teachers in 'soft' subjects such as history, literary studies, or achitecture. In some applied fields, the apprenticeship model – watching and attempting to emulate the expert – looms large; in others, an effort is made to improve the academic status of the course by emphasizing the intellectual high ground, concentrating heavily on theory at the expense of practice. The variety of different forms of learning demanded of a student, not only across disciplinary boundaries but even within individual disciplines, is sufficiently extensive to call in question the idea of a definable level of intellectual capability which all students on undergraduate courses are expected to attain.

The contrasts in input and process to which attention has already been drawn are matched by similar contrasts in output. As Chapters 10 and 11 make plain, assessments of the learning outcomes of undergraduate courses manifest themselves in a great diversity of shapes and sizes. Even with the apparent safeguard of the elaborate external examiner system enshrined in Reynolds (CVCP, 1986), there can be no strong claim to uniformity in Britain, as a recent enquiry has made plain (ESRC, 1990). The accreditation system in some subject fields in the USA invokes a similar analogy of a fig-leaf called in to lend an air of decency to an otherwise questionable phenomenon.

The relative standing of a degree from one particular institution as against another is acknowledged explicitly in the American higher education system and implicitly (for all the formal insistence on inter-university comparability) in the British. The assumed quality of a British undergraduate course or an American course credit in one particular academic area as against another is more often a matter for tacit than explicit comment in both countries. However, student folklore is able readily to distinguish 'Mickey Mouse courses' from those which are 'tough going': and there is little doubt about the academic credibility of, say, a qualification in classics in comparison with one in catering science. As if to underline these deviances, there can be found in Britain – as the statistics which accompanied the 'Robbins Report' (Committee on Higher Education, 1963) were able to show – remarkably stable historical differences in the proportions of degree classes awarded not only across institutions but also across subject fields.

Such considerations suggest that, in so far as the notion exists of some identifiable, objective standard which all degree-level work is called upon to achieve, that notion is of greater symbolic than operational significance. To point this out is not in any sense to ague that there are no differences in quality between higher education and any other sector of the educational enterprise; it is merely to maintain that the boundary is a more imprecise one than is commonly allowed, and that what lies within the boundary area is less uniform or homogeneous than is often suggested. For all their other dissimilarities, the higher education systems of Britain and the United States have in common their internal heterogeneity, in that both embrace a number of different forms of knowledge, and of the varied academic cultures associated with them. The wider implications of these differences for the definition and control of research quality will form the central theme of the argument which follows.

The heterogeneity of knowledge forms

Forms of academic knowledge may be conveniently charted along two main dimensions: the hard–soft continuum and the pure–applied spectrum. Between them, these mark off four broad knowledge categories: hard pure, soft pure, hard applied and soft applied (see Becher, 1989, for a fuller analysis). At a high level of generality, these roughly correspond with the more familiar distinctions between the natural sciences and mathematics, the humanities and social sciences, the science-based professions and the social professions (Kolb, 1981). Under more detailed examination, however, the equivalences can prove somewhat misleading.

Hard pure subject areas may be characterized as having closely defined boundaries, focusing on quantitative issues, and possessing a well-developed theoretical structure, strong explanatory connections, generalizable findings and universal laws. Hard pure knowledge allows for a process of breaking down complex ideas into simpler components. It is relatively impersonal and value-free. It is cumulative, in the sense that new findings may commonly be seen as linear developments from the existing state of awareness: the criteria for establishing or refuting such findings are usually clear-cut. It may be metaphorically described as growing like a crystal or branching out like a tree.

In contradistinction, soft pure knowledge domains have boundaries which are loosely defined and permeable; they are predominantly qualitative, lacking much scope for patterning and reproducibility, and demanding complex judgemental forms of reasoning. Soft pure knowledge is not readily amenable to reductionist analysis: it embraces complexity and embodies a holistic, synthetic approach. It allows room for intentionality, and hence for the personal and value-laden. It is recursive or reiterative, in the sense that academic work often traverses ground already explored by others: criteria for the acceptability of claims are diverse and non-consensual. It may be pictured as evolving like an organism or meandering like a river.

The nature of applied knowledge has been less well explored than that of pure (an interesting exception is the recent work of Schön, 1983, 1987). But it can be observed that hard applied fields are amenable to heuristic, trial-and-error approaches. They are not necessarily cumulative (though depending from time to time and area to area on the techniques and findings of hard knowledge), nor altogether quantitative (since application will always involve some element of qualitative judgement). Hard applied subjects are concerned with ways of mastering the physical world, so the activities to which they give rise are generally directed towards some practical end, and are judged by purposive and functional criteria. Their primary outcomes are products and techniques.

Soft applied knowledge, in contrast, is built up to a sizeable extent on case laws. It draws on soft pure knowledge as a means of understanding and coming to terms with complex human situations, but does so with a view to enhancing the quality of personal and social life. It is not as stable as, and has a less evident sense of progression than, hard applied knowledge. Its primary outcomes are protocols and procedures, whose validity is judged mainly in pragmatic and utilitarian terms.

These categories are not to be seen as neat pigeon-holes, sharply distinguished one from another, into which all knowledge can be neatly and unequivocally sorted, but rather as a means of characterizing the wide domains adumbrated by the two ranges, mentioned earlier, between the hard and the soft and the pure and the applied.

The purpose of attempting to portray academic knowledge in this way is to bring out something of the richness of its internal variation, and hence to suggest that questions about what constitutes excellence in intellectual enquiry are not likely to be amenable to very simple answers.

The variety of disciplinary cultures

Disciplines, and the specialisms which are their component elements, have social as well as cognitive aspects. That is to say, they are associated not only with certain forms of knowledge, but also with particular kinds of academic community. We may again conveniently map out their main features along two broad dimensions, which may be labelled as convergent/divergent and urban/rural. Since these terms are likely to be less familiar than the ones introduced to discuss the variety of knowledge forms, it will be necessary to offer a separate account of them here.

The first set of contrasts – between convergence and divergence – is most readily characterized by the extent to which a given disciplinary community offers a commonality of intellectual values and a coherence of cultural assumptions. To say of such a community that it is convergent is to say something about the world view that binds constituent subgroups to one another; to say that it is divergent is to imply a collectivity held together not by a strong sense of cultural affinity but by the weaker bonds of historical or social circumstance. In this respect, the degree of convergence of a broad academic grouping is analogous with the sense of nationhood accorded to the inhabitants of a particular country. Convergence can be related to the maintenance of reasonably uniform values, standards, conventions and procedures governing the work of a given intellectual nation-state, marked by the existence of 'intellectual control' and a 'stable élite' (Mulkay, 1977). Those engaged in divergent disciplines lack such features, tolerating a greater measure of intellectual deviance and in some cases degenerating into self-destructive disputation.

While the notions of convergence or divergence apply to the broad collectivities which we choose to define as disciplines, or more loosely as general fields of enquiry, the categorizations of urban and rural modes of research activity relate to the narrower groupings engaged on a particular specialism. To characterize any such academic network as urban or as rural is to say something about the intensity and nature of the interaction between the individuals who comprise it. The defining feature of the rural/urban dimension is the people-to-problem ratio – the number of researchers engaged at any one time on a particular problem or constellation of problems. Urban researchers tend to occupy a narrow area of intellectual territory, and to cluster round a limited number of discrete topics which appear amenable to short-range solutions. Their rural counterparts span a much broader area, across which problems are thinly scattered and within which they are not sharply differentiated: articulating the solutions to such problems is often a lengthy business. Teamwork and close interaction across the research community as a whole is more characteristic of urban than of rural research, as is a concern with plagiarism, priority and rapid publication.

The distinctions between convergence and divergence and between urban and rural research styles are – it should be reiterated – at different levels of generality. It is possible to aggregate patterns of research, and hence loosely to describe disciplines as predominantly urban or rural: but the disaggregation of convergence and divergence and their application to subdisciplines makes no sense (any more than it makes sense to ascribe nationhood to the constituent subgroups of a nation, except in so far as any one of them aspires to secession as an independent national entity).

Combining and applying the categories

A number of interesting patterns may be discerned when these various categories – hard and soft, pure and applied among the epistemological aspects; convergent and divergent, urban and rural among the social – are put to work in describing disciplinary groupings.

For example, at the subdisciplinary level, it can be noted that instances of urban research – high-energy physics offers a good case in point – are to be found exclusively in hard, and predominantly in hard pure, knowledge fields. However, only a relatively small subsection of hard specialisms generates this style of research: for the most part, patterns of research activity tend to be rural, or at best suburban. Yet curiously, it is this minority of hard, pure, urban arenas that has attracted the most attention in writings about academic modes of enquiry.

At the more general level of disciplines or fields, there is a rough correspondence between the epistemologically hard and the socially convergent, and a comparably rough one between the soft and the divergent, though there are also many anomalies. It can for instance be argued that chemistry, though predominantly hard, is also discernible divergent; and that history, though it has to be classified as a soft discipline, is none the less quite strongly convergent. Moreover, hard applied subject areas such as engineering tend to be divergent, perhaps because external influences make for rather looser ties between their academic communities and the fields of knowledge they study.

While the academic world may be viewed from a distant external perspective as a fairly homogeneous entity, it can thus be seen on closer inspection to embody a large internal diversity of characteristics. There are few disciplinary groupings which do not contain within themselves elements of hard and soft, pure and applied knowledge. Even physics, as a prototypically hard pure discipline, has its soft edges in the complexities of meteorology as well as its applied elements in such subfields as optics. Within the mainly hard applied subject area of engineering, design is soft and fluid dynamic theory relatively pure. Again, sociology – predominantly a soft pure area of enquiry – incorporates relatively hard components such as demography and applied ones such as welfare or development studies. Education may be typified as a soft applied field, but within it cognitive psychology aspires to be hard and the philosophy of education may be categorized as pure.

Taken as a whole, then, the domain of academic knowledge may be divided not only into distinct and characteristically different disciplinary groupings but within these into an even more heterogeneous collection of subspecialisms. The epistemological abundance has its social counterparts in a diversity of disciplinary cultures (some at the convergent end of the scale, some at the divergent, and others at various intermediate points); and of subdisciplinary modes of activity (ranging from the hectic and urban to the measured and rural).

Many of these differences emerge in the collective activities of academics (see Becher, 1989). They include the contrasting validation processes associated with particular disciplinary areas (depending primarily on coherence with existing knowledge in mathematics, correspondence with the available evidence in empirical science, 'resonance' with the interpretations of others in the humanities, and utility and functionality in applied fields). They also embrace differences in the ways in which reputations are established, disciplinary élites identified, eminence recognized and power exploited. There are systematic deviations in language and style, modes of competitiveness, the nature and incidence of collaboration, and the consequences of controversy.

In terms of individual experience, there is again a great divergence in recruitment procedures, modes of choice of specialism, forms of doctoral supervision, mobility between research fields, peaking in research productivity and achievement, and intensity of involvement in work. Indeed, the whole way in which an academic career is lived out will differ not only from one discipline to another but even between different specialisms within the same discipline.

Quality control in a context of diversity

These arguments suggest that the notion of what constitutes 'academic excellence' is subject to extensive variation from one intellectual setting to another. In other words, the criteria by which the quality of research may be judged are not constant across knowledge fields or their associated academic communities, but are instead highly idiosyncratic and context-dependent. It is accordingly difficult for someone outside a given subdisciplinary milieu to make an authoritative judgement about the intrinsic merits or demerits of the work done within that particular environment: though extrinsic assessments of 'usefulness' or 'relevance' may be – and often are – more readily proffered.

The conventional form of quality control, namely academic peer-group judgement, has evolved in response to such diversity. It is related to the exercise of a number of key evaluative functions (Zuckerman and Merton, 1971) performed by suitably selected members of a body of reasonably close colleagues. It forms the basis of the grant-awarding process in the case of many research-funding bodies and is also used in assessing articles submitted for journal publication and in determining eligibility for the membership of learned societies. Senior members of the peer group may be invited to act as external examiners for degree awards, to participate in the process of appointment to senior posts, and to offer comments on candidates for promotion within an institution.

The principle of mutual judgement by informed specialists seems well founded. In terms of research activity, as Mulkay (1977) argues,

> trustworthy assessments of the quality of a given piece of work can only be made by those who are working on the same or similar problems and who are known to be capable of producing results of at least the same level of quality. There can be no separate formal hierarchy of control in scientific research. All participants, as they use, modify or disregard the results communicated to them, are continually engaged in judging the adequacy and value of their colleagues' work. As a result of those judgements, recognition is allocated and reputations are created; not only for individual researchers, but also for research groups, university departments and research journals.

Peer review, it may be said, serves to maintain overall standards as well as to recognize individual capability.

But like many useful social mechanisms, the peer group has its drawbacks. One is that those who have already earned reputations tend to be favoured at the expense of those who have not (Cole *et al.*, 1977). Another is that in the more highly specialized areas, the selection of referees may have to be made from those whose professional acquaintance with the field is only indirect (and whose judgements will in that sense be amateur) or from the few people with shared expertise who may wish to protect their own standing against rival claims. A third limitation is the commonplace one that experts often fail to agree, so that their judgements may be mutually inconsistent; a fourth is that in retrospect, those apparently in the know may signally fail to predict winners (Cole, 1983).

Moreover, peer review tends to operate unevenly between different knowledge areas. Some communities would appear to be more tolerant of divergence than others. Even within the same discipline, different speciality groups may be seen to adopt different standards of academic rigour (the deviations often being related to their ranking in the intellectual pecking order).

Because the peer groups concerned with establishing standards in what we have seen to be a wide diversity of knowledge areas are faced with dissimilar tasks, it is unsurprising that they have to tackle them in different ways, and that breakdowns in procedures may be traced to different sources of weakness. Sharp practice or plagiarism are typical causes of complaint among hard scientists, pure as well as applied. There are legendary stories about eminent referees who have caused others' submitted papers to be rejected or long delayed, and who have then proceeded themselves to publish suspiciously similar findings. In soft knowledge domains this form of corruption is uncommon, because few people are working on the same issues, and even if they are, their interpretations of them are very rarely identical. On the other hand, there is more room in such fields for the venting of personal preferences or antipathies. Any member of the peer group may be open to the accusation of 'log rolling' for friends and protégés – by treating their efforts more kindly than they deserve – or of 'doing down' enemies and rivals – by unmeritedly harsh criticisms of their work. The deliberate freezing-out of contributions which are seen as in some way threatening (usually because they purport to undermine an established ideology or school of thought) is not confined to any one knowledge area, manifesting itself from time to time with equal partiality in every kind of discipline.

The limitations of the exercise of peer judgement are easier to discern in the more or less publicly accessible arena of book reviewing or the refereeing of journal articles – where opinions are at least open to being challenged or appealed against – than in the closed world of making appointments and promotions, approving grant proposals, according honours, or awarding prizes. Here the only recourse against the suspicion of unfairness is to try one's luck at another time or in another place, with the attendant risk that one or more of the same unfavourable referees will be employed. Where the achievement of a coveted goal is open to strong competition from people in a diversity of fields, the problem of making a just choice is all the worse. Faced with an array of well-supported, highly qualified candidates from disciplines whose standards are not easily comparable with one another, the temptation to lapse from the niceties of intellectual judgement to the coarser pursuit of political bargaining can become intense, as many of those who have been involved in such situations may be prepared in their unguarded moments to acknowledge.

But although such complaints about the peer-review process serve a useful purpose in signalling familiar pitfalls to be guarded against (e.g. by including 'outsiders' from closely related specialisms on review panels), or in suggesting modest reforms in current practice (e.g. 'blind refereeing' in which the author's name is not made known to those sitting in judgement), they cannot be allowed to constitute a major indictment against the system as a whole. Arguably, the exercise of peer-group judgement must be tolerated, for all its admitted faults, because no one has yet come up with an approach to academic evaluation that would not be discernibly worse.

Conclusion

The considerations advanced in this chapter, in relation both to the quality of undergraduate provision and to the judgement of research excellence, would seem strongly to call into question the search for generally applicable performance indicators. To be fair in their discrimination, such indicators would have to be sensitive to the variegated shades of excellence in a wide range of curricular contexts when assessing teaching programmes, and in a comparable diversity of forms of enquiry when judging the merits of research. To be workable, they would have to be reasonably unequivocal in their application – which means that, in all likelihood, aspects that could be easily quantified would triumph over those that called for qualitative appraisal.

In considering how the standards of undergraduate programmes are calibrated it is evident that even when some apparently uniform yardstick is introduced (as it has been in Britain), the device serves only to obscure the actual variation in inputs, processes and outputs across the range of disciplines and institutions. In research, as in teaching, determining the extent of excellence is a matter for subtle and relative judgement rather than for simple and absolute measurement. For all its acknowledged inadequacies, the peer-group system has, in relation to assessing the calibre of research, the great advantage of responsiveness to the variety and idiosyncracy of all that can be counted as a legitimate part of the academic enterprise. No set of apparently objective indicators, however well constructed, could conceivably be versatile enough to do the job better.

In short, along both the curricular and research dimensions, the identification of quality is amenable to the careful and particular case-by-case procedures of the common law, but not to the kinds of rigorous and universal requirement that can be laid down by statute.

References

Becher, T. (1989), *Academic Tribes and Territories*. Milton Keynes: Open University Press.
Cole, S. (1983). The hierarchy of the sciences, *American Journal of Sociology*, **89**(1), 111–39.
Cole, S., Rubin, L. and Cole, J. R. (1977). Peer review and the support of science, *Scientific American*, **237** (Oct), 34–41.

Committee of Vice-Chancellors and Principals (1986). *Academic Standards in Universities*, Reynolds Report. London: CVCP.

Committee on Higher Education (1963). ('Robbins Report') HMSO, Cmnd 2154.

Economic and Social Research Council (1990). *The Role of External Examiners*. London: HMSO.

Kolb, D. (1981). Learning styles and disciplinary differences. In Chickering, A. W. (ed.), *The Modern American College*. San Francisco: Jossey-Bass.

Mulkay, M. (1977). The sociology of the scientific research community. In Spiegel-Rösing, I. and D. de S. Price (eds), *Science, Technology and Society*. London: Sage.

Schön, D. A. (1983). *The Reflective Practitioner*. New York: Basic Books.

Schön, D. A. (1987). *Educating the Reflective Practitioner*. San Francisco: Jossey-Bass.

Thompson, N. (1979). The assessment of candidates for degrees in physics, *Studies in Higher Education*, **4**(2), 169–80.

Zuckerman, H. and R. K. Merton (1971). Patterns of evaluation in science, *Minerva*, **9**(1), 66–100.

13

Quality and Access as Interrelated Policy Issues

Robert O. Berdahl and Irving J. Spitzberg, Jr

For those able to attend both Anglo-US conferences in Oxford and Princeton, the rewards in the form of enriched understanding of the two central terms, quality and access, seemed very apparent. Never again should we see these terms in a simplistic fashion, for the more we discussed them, the more we came to realize how interrelated they are in a context of educational, social and financial policy.

Readers of this volume may or may not already have come to the same understandings, but in any case it remains for this concluding chapter to restate the main themes, necessarily painting with a broad brush and relying on many insights gathered from earlier essays. Essentially we will be suggesting the following major points:

1. There *is* some rough truth to the generalization that British universities tend to do a better job of protecting quality and American universities a better job of promoting access; but in each case important qualifications must be added.
2. In the case of quality and British universities we will want to discuss both the need to compare 'like with like' and the implications of accepting a broader definition of quality to include the notion of 'value-added'.
3. In the case of access and American universities we will want to discuss both the need to compare like with like and the implications of putting notions of attrition (or 'wastage' as the British call it) alongside those of access.
4. Three contextual variables face each country and make the quality/access issues more crucial than ever to consider. These are those relating to the need to develop healthy diversity, the need to improve the country's ability to compete in an increasingly international market, and the need to accomplish the preceding elements without major additions of national resources.
5. Finally, it is time for both educational and political leaders to recognize that policy decisions should not be made for either issue as a separate matter; rather each notion should be examined in terms of its impact(s) on the other. If each country, using only limited new resources, is to achieve a healthy

social diversity and viability in international markets, there will be many smaller decisions 'at the margin' where quality and access trade-off consequences should be examined together. Until recently we have not seen many examples of the broader policy analyses recommended here.

Let us now provide more detail to some of these general points.

Access and quality: Differences and similarities

Access

The most striking evidence of the apparently different choices made by the British and the Americans is found by comparing the percentage of the age-cadre participating in any way in post-secondary education. In Britain, if one looks at both the university and polytechnic sectors, approximately 15% of the age-cadre attends higher education. In the United States approximately 60% of the age-cadre attends some form of post-secondary education, including the two-year community colleges but excluding the large proprietary (run-for-profit) sector.

However, this surface difference hides more similarities than meet the eye. Although 60% of the American age-group attends at least one year of higher education, a far smaller percentage continues through to the successful completion of a first degree. In many states the community colleges enrol over half of the students in the first two years, with only a minority of them later transferring to a four-year college. We are suggesting, then, to compare 'like with like' that the non-transfer community college students in the USA (who *are* counted as higher education students) are really more comparable to British students enrolled in vocational training or FE (who are *not* counted and who cannot transfer credits to a university or polytechnic).

Furthermore, as mentioned briefly above, when attrition (or wastage) is taken into account, the huge American superiority in access needs further reduction, for a higher percentage of British college students graduate from their first-degree programmes.

While both of these caveats require some modification of the generalization about 'the American side doing a better job on access', participants at the two conferences and writers of the preceding essays on the whole have found the statement correct in its essentials.

Quality

On the flip side of this issue, it was widely accepted that the British were doing a better job at quality control. After all, their students constituted the top 15% of graduates from a fairly élite secondary school system; and the 'gold standard' of first and second class honours degrees, etc. is strongly defended by a system which uses external examiners.

Yet, to compare 'like with like', when one looks closely at the American system and controls for the top 15% (of institutions, faculty, or students) the quality standards will not be so dissimilar from the British. Both American academics who teach British students in the USA or the UK and British academics who teach Americans generally agree on the comparability of preparation of the American élite in comparison with their British student counterparts. A graduate of Harvard or Yale will usually compare well with those from Oxford or Cambridge. A Phi Beta Kappa graduate of a large state university will write his algorithms with the best of the computer scientists from the University of Reading. The top graduate in business administration from a regional state college will hold his/her own well with a polytechnic graduate in tourism. And certainly in terms of research dimensions, the top American graduate schools need fear no comparisons with any other systems.

There is, however, another approach to judging quality which requires going beyond a comparison of academic élites. We refer to the concept of 'value-added' (or, as some prefer to call it, talent development). According to this term, an institution which admits persons of lower academic achievement but helps them to gain significantly in knowledge and skills may be helping society as much as an élite institution which caters only to the well prepared.

If this broader definition of quality is permitted, then it becomes important for the educational system to become articulated, so that persons of talent discovered at one level will be able to transfer to other institutions and complete the full journey to talent development.

Even taking into consideration the qualifications discussed above, most conference participants and most authors of papers tended to agree that the British were probably more successful in protecting quality.

Relevant trends facing both countries

Although there are obvious differences in the histories and most significant characteristics of the two systems of higher education, three trends facing both countries are very salient for their policy choices relating to access and quality.

Increasing diversity

In both countries, there is increasing ethnic diversity. This diversity will substantially affect both countries. In some ways this trend will be more traumatic for Britain than the United States, because the USA has almost three decades of recent experience with the politics of diversity (with two centuries of historical experience before), though it may be no nearer to accommodating the new diversity than is Britain. Because the British higher education system is so élite, it has scarcely begun to mirror the increased diversity of the country, with its immigration of non-whites from former colonies and the prospect of new immigration from its last colony, Hong Kong. Although Britain has a problem of poverty among many of its new immigrants, the fact is that significant numbers of Britain's immigrants come from among the most educated citizens of their former colonies and do meet the standards set by higher education. Therefore, greater diversity in higher education will likely characterize the next decade and the next century, although it will happen faster – and probably without any great debate about compromising standards – if there is explicit policy attention to recruitment among the immigrant communities that parallels the explicit recruitment abroad now undertaken by British universities. And this latter phenomenon of recruitment abroad by British universities and polytechnics will lead to even greater diversity in the country as a whole if these students either stay after graduation or immigrate in their later lives.

In the United States, the increasing diversity builds on the foundation of accommodating diversity over centuries, although this history does not seem to have made the accommodation any easier. The future is *now* in some parts of the country – especially in California – with large Afro-American, Hispanic and Asian populations. By the year 2000, there will likely be no single ethnic majority group in California. Twenty years later, the same may be true in Texas, Florida and New York. The major challenge facing American campuses posed by the growth of minority populations is to respond to this growth while maintaining standards. Political reality will demand that most institutions of higher education accept growing numbers of each minority group in a manner reflecting their proportion of the population as a whole. The most serious problem will continue to be helping the Afro-American population participate in higher education on an equal footing with majority populations as well as the new minorities.

One challenge that has evolved over the past decade in the United States is the recruitment of women into higher education. Now more than 52% of all students are women. The major unfinished business for women is increasing the number of women in the natural sciences and also increasing the number of women faculty and administrators. In Britain, too, the number of women students has increased more than has their representation in responsible posts either in or outside education.

With both societies becoming more diverse, higher education will also become more diverse. The task will be to maintain standards while keeping the rate of diversification of students and staff in universities and colleges near enough to the rate of diversification of the surrounding societies so that minorities do not experience themselves as being excluded from access.

International competition

As the cold war comes to an end, the impact of global economic competition will begin to have the most direct impact on the life of universities and colleges in both countries. The need to produce both goods and services of the highest quality at the lowest cost in order to maintain standards of living will put great pressure on education. We are being asked to improve the quality of graduates from kindergarten through to graduate school. The pressure that we have begun to see in both countries in the 1980s will reach new levels in the 1990s.

In the United States and Britain, the Japanese have become providers of goods and services, often at the expense of domestic providers. This has produced immense pressure to produce better products and services and has focused upon the educational quality of those who have graduated from our institutions.

In the United States, the Presidents and the Governors have established a number of educational goals for the year 2000. Interestingly enough few have to do with higher education. One should not conclude that this reflects satisfaction with universities and colleges. Instead, it indicates that the politicians do not view the campus as a likely site for dramatic contributions to the improvement of quality of human resources. Correctly they look to the schools.

In both the United States and Britain, educational investment is not going into higher education. The cut-backs of the 1980s in Britain and the antagonism of the Reagan Administration to higher education in the USA have seen a reallocation of political interest and investment at the margin to elementary and secondary education. If one does not count investment in research from the Defense Department and in the health sciences, neither of which contribute much to the actual education of students, the increase in expenditures in higher education has been modest, while the increase in expenditure for elementary and secondary education has been substantial.

The sensitivity to international competition has brought new political attention to universities and colleges that has not brought new resources with it. It has brought new regulations. Many American states have developed monitoring systems to assess quality and to import external examinations to assess students in publicly financed institutions. 'Junior-rising exams' in states such as Florida place hurdles in the way of promotion of students to upper division courses. In Britain there has been much discussion of quality, but the emphasis has been on controlling the institutions rather than the individual students, because the examination mechanisms are already in place.

This concern about international competition is also affecting investment in research. Big science is winning over little science, applied science over pure science. Indeed investment in technology wins over science, and science and technology over all other forms of research. This trend is likely to improve the quality of research in the preferred areas of activity but is unlikely to contribute to the quality of education or to contribute to access to higher education. These trends will be reinforced by the international competition.

Resource constraints

The impact of financial limitations and outright cuts on British higher education has been the most dramatic legacy of the 1980s to the 1990s. The record in the United States has been more complex. In the 1980s there were many states with little real growth in investment in higher education. There were some states with cut-backs of crisis proportions comparable to the British experience – Louisiana and Oklahoma are dramatic examples. Other states prospered in the 1980s and now are facing serious shortfalls in the early 1990s – particularly the north-eastern states of New Jersey, New York, Connecticut and Massachusetts.

The realities of the larger economies in Britain and the United States suggest that even if there is continuing prosperity in the 1990s, the demands of budget deficits and other social priorities are unlikely to allow for much generosity for higher education. In the United States, campuses will continue to rely on tuition increases for whatever growth they expect to see in their budgets, and this reliance will place new limits on access for many students. The attempts to reallocate costs to students through loans in Britain is likely to lead to the reduction of numbers of students from lower socio-economic classes, just as it has in the 1980s in the United States.

The political economy of higher education in the United States is unlikely to move from its current 'emphasis on quality', as Hansen and Stampen have described the current cycle of the history of public investment in higher education. Although there is talk of expansion in British higher education, it is unlikely to include increases in investment per student and not likely to increase access to unserved students from lower socio-economic classes.

The trend of continuing financial constraint will make the choices concerning quality and access more difficult as well as more necessary. With real resources growing modestly and demands growing at a fast rate, the claims for marginal resources will be made by all constituencies. The challenge of forging agreement about the decision rules for allocating scarce resources will be the major task for those who wish to honour both access and quality as they confront the future.

The politics of choice

With the trends of diversity, international competition and financial constraints requiring hard choices, there will be competing political pressures as the choices about resource allocation and future policies are made. The minorities will demand greater support for access. The pressures of international competition will elevate quality as a criterion for all judgements. The natural conservatism of all social institutions – both political and educational – will translate financial constraints into justifications for the status quo, which serves neither quality nor access well.

If we wish to assist our higher educational systems to serve better *both* goals of access and quality, we will need to pose the choices in the political systems in the larger community and on campus more clearly. For the most part, policy choices are taken in different spheres to serve either quality or access, without assessing the implications of one choice for another. The politics of one sector of decision making often cut against consideration of one value or the other. Let us illustrate this reality with two examples – student aid and the use of external examinations to improve quality.

In the arena of debates about student aid in the United States and in the United Kingdom, the conversation focuses solely on the implications for access. The movement from grants to loans in the United States has been decried because of its impact on reducing access. The discussion of a possible British loan programme has focused mainly on the disincentives for participation in higher education. The implication of grants or loans for the quality of education is seldom discussed. Professor Chester Finn has recently suggested that grants and loans only be made to academically superior students as a way to connect aid financing to quality of performance. Of course, such a move could negatively affect the access of students from lower socio-economic groups to higher education. However, one could limit aid to these groups but only award the aid to those among them who do well academically. The fact is that this analysis is seldom made. Both quality and access need to be on the table when one is considering student aid policies.

Several American states have established external assessment systems using standardized tests as mechanisms for establishing standards for under-graduates and for teachers leaving training. Many of these tests are now being challenged because large numbers of Afro-Americans are failing them, particularly in the American South. The impact on access of these tests is now an important part of the debate. The results suggest that any attempt to improve quality through examinations will have a negative impact on certain minorities. This then poses a serious question about what sort of quality the tests are assessing and whether there are other means of improving quality. Once again, the problem is less finding the answer, more posing the questions.

If we wish policy decisions to reflect consideration of the impact of choices on quality and access, we will have to organize ourselves on campus and in the larger society to pose these questions. There are often constituencies on one side or the other, but seldom do these constituencies present the questions about quality and access as questions about trade-offs between two competing and valuable goals. Where the constituencies for quality dominate, we need to raise questions about access. Where the constituencies for access dominate, we need to raise questions about quality.

Conclusion

Both Britain and the United States are pluralistic democracies and have much to learn from each other. Our conversations in this book about quality and access show that our two countries have different strengths but similar problems. We have learned to learn from each other. We now need to learn how to use each other's experience to help each country confront its most pressing challenge. The British can use the Americans' experience to learn more about strategies to increase access. The Americans can use the British experience to learn more about how to create and maintain standards of quality. But neither can mimic the other.

Index

The Society for Research into Higher Education

The Society exists both to encourage and co-ordinate research and development into all aspects of Higher Education; including academic, organizational and policy issues; and also to provide a forum of debate, verbal and printed.

The Society's income derives from subscriptions, book sales, conference fees, and grants. It receives no subsidies and is wholly independent. Its corporate members are institutions of higher education, research institutions and professional, industrial, and governmental bodies. Its individual members include teachers and researchers, administrators and students. Members are found in all parts of the world and the Society regards its international work as amongst its most important activities.

The Society is opposed to discrimination in higher education on grounds of belief, race, etc.

The Society discusses and comments on policy, organizes conferences, and encourages research. It is studying means of preserving archives of higher education. Under the imprint SRHE & OPEN UNIVERSITY PRESS it is a specialist publisher of research, having some 30 titles in print. The Editorial Board of the Society's Imprint seeks authoritative research or study in the field. It offers competitive royalties; a highly recognizable format in both hard- and paper-back; and the world-wide reputation of the Open University Press. The Society also publishes *Studies in Higher Education* (three times a year), which is mainly concerned with academic issues; *Higher Education Quarterly* (formerly *Universities Quarterly*), mainly concerned with policy issues; *Abstracts* (three times a year); an *International Newsletter* (twice a year) and *SRHE News* (four times a year).

The Society's Committees, Study Groups and Branches are run by members (with help from a small secretariat at Guildford). The Groups at present include a Teacher Education Study Group, a Staff Development Group, a Continuing Education Group, a Women in Higher Education Group and an Excellence in Teaching Group. The Groups may have their own organization, subscriptions, or publications; (e.g. the *Staff Development Newsletter*). A further *Questions of Quality* Group has organised a series of Anglo-American seminars in the USA and the UK.

The Society's annual conferences are held jointly; 'Access & Institutional Change' (1989, with the Polytechnic of North London). In 1990, the topic will be 'Industry and Higher Education' (with the University of Surrey). In 1991, the topic will be 'Research and Higher Education', with the University of Leicester: in 1992, it will be 'Learning & Teaching' (with Nottingham Polytechnic) In 1993, the topic will be 'Governments,

Higher Education and Accountability'. Other conferences have considered 'HE After the Election' (1987), and 'After the Reform Act' (July 1988).

Members receive free of charge the Society's *Abstracts*, annual conference Proceedings, (or 'Precedings'), *SRHE News* and *International Newsletter*. They may buy SRHE & Open University Press books at 35% discount, and *Higher Education Quarterly* on special terms. Corporate members also receive the Society's journal *Studies in Higher Education* free; (individuals on special terms). Members may also obtain certain other journals at a discount, including the NFER *Register of Educational Research*. There is a substantial discount to members, and to staff of corporate members, on annual and some other conference fees. The discounts can exceed the subscription.

Annual Subscriptions
August 1990–July 1991

Individual members		£ 43.00
Students & retired members		£ 12.00
Hardship		£ 20.00
Corporate members		
less than 1000 students		£155.00
1000–3000 students		£195.00
more than 3000 students		£290.00
Non-teaching bodies	up to	£295.00

Further information: SRHE at the University, Guildford GU2 5XH, UK. Tel: (0483) 39003 Fax: (0483) 300803
Catalogue: SRHE & Open University Press, Celtic Court, 22 Ballmoor, Buckingham MK18 1XW, Tel: (0280) 823388